Improving the Odds

Improving the Odds

A Basis for Long-Term Change

Rodney Larson

ROWMAN & LITTLEFIELD EDUCATION

A division of

ROWMAN & LITTLEFIELD PUBLISHERS, INC.
Lanham • New York • Toronto • Plymouth, UK

ROWMAN & LITTLEFIELD PUBLISHERS, INC.

Published by Rowman & Littlefield Education
A division of Rowman & Littlefield Publishers, Inc.
A wholly owned subsidary of The Rowman & Littlefield Publishing Group, Inc.
4501 Forbes Boulevard, Suite 200, Lanham, Maryland 20706
http://www.rowmaneducation.com

Estover Road
Plymouth PL6 7PY
United Kingdom

British Library Cataloguing in Publication Information Available

Library of Congress Cataloging-in-Publication Data

Larson, Rodney.
  Improving the odds, raising the class: American education / By Rodney Larson.
    p. cm.
  Includes bibliographical references.
  ISBN 978-1-60709-094-6 (cloth : alk. paper) -- ISBN 978-1-60709-096-0 (electronic)
  1. School improvement programs--United States. I. Title.
  LB2822.82.L37 2009
  371.2'070973--dc22
                                    2009031914

Printed in the United States of America

∞™ The paper used in this publication meets the minimum requirements of American
National Standard for Information Sciences—Permanence of Paper for Printed Library
Materials, ANSI/NISO Z39.48-1992.

Contents

Chapter 1

Introduction–Factories, Statistics, Einstein, and Dice

Today, only one-third of our students graduate from high school ready for college, work, and citizenship. The other two-thirds, most of them low-income and minority students, are tracked into courses that won't ever get them ready for college or prepare them for a family-wage job–no matter how well the students learn or the teachers teach.

. . . This isn't an accident or a flaw in the system; it is the system.

—William Gates III, 2005

When Bill Gates gave a speech in 2005 about the problems with American education, the words didn't paint a flattering picture. The fact that Gates took aim at American public education wasn't surprising since it is a large inviting target. Teachers become accustomed to attacks on education. From politicians to talk show hosts, everyone seems to enjoy picking up a stick and taking a good whack at the institution. What was unique about Gates' speech was its focus: he didn't target teachers or any of the usual focal points of criticism. Rather, he said the problem was the *system* of education itself.

Though Gates' speech primarily targeted the problems of low income urban students, the remarks ended up hitting a larger target: the school system itself. When it comes to high schools in America, Gates (2005) was particularly critical with his remarks:

America's high schools are obsolete. . . . By obsolete, I mean that our high schools–even when they're working exactly as designed–cannot teach our kids what they need to know (p. 2).

The Microsoft founder essentially said that the last process in the system of education (high school) cannot work in its current state.

1

The problems of public education were unwittingly admitted by a California Department of Education Web site where an Edsource (2005) article touted *Fifteen California High Schools that Beat the Odds* (p. 1). The words bring Gates' message clearly into focus.

The article highlights a study showing fifteen socioeconomically disadvantaged schools that *beat the odds* by promoting more students from one grade to the next than other *similar* schools. As a teacher, parent, and taxpayer of California, it wasn't the 15 schools that had *beaten the odds* that captured my attention, it was the hundreds of others that had not. It seems ironic that the Department of Education in California had a report on their Web site that discussed education in terms used for gambling in Las Vegas.

The state should celebrate schools that beat long odds to become winners. However, this implies that the expectation for part of the system is failure. Everyone knows the odds are stacked against a person who chooses to gamble in a casino, and that there are more losers than winners. In Las Vegas or Atlantic City, the expectation of failure is acceptable because they are games, but for an education system to advertise that failure is the norm is unacceptable. Adults take chances and live with the consequences. Schools, however, are a different matter. For kids that grow up in poverty, school is the primary pathway to a better life; it is their chance at a decent future.

As California's education system discussed schools that "beat the odds," it merely confirms Gates' contention that the United State's public education system is failing in its mission to educate the youth of America. Citing many statistics, Gates was particularly critical of education in socio-economically disadvantaged schools, but in the final analysis Gates (2005) concluded that the problem with education is *the system* (p. 2).

Although Gates' view of education is shared by many Americans, most do not want wholesale changes in the education system. In a report published by Hart and Teeter (2004), only 14 percent of Americans reported that schools were working well or pretty well, and 38 percent of those surveyed said that they believed changes were in order for America's schools (p. 2). The majority (52 percent) of respondents, however, did not want major changes in the current structure of the school system (p. 2). Whether Gates' call was for a complete overhaul of the education system, or, mere improvements for the existing system, one thing is certain: improvements to the education system would be desirable.

The question is, "How does one go about doing it?"

There was one preconception used in this study. It is the idea that the most important element in teaching is the point where information is transferred from an instructor to a student. Anything that improves that process can improve education; most everything else does not. If you ask most teachers, there seems to be a lot of "everything else" in the American education system. The primary question that this book will try to address is: how do we instill long-term continuous improvement in the school system? How can we create a system that improves delivery of the lesson in the classroom?

Imagine being given the job of trying to *fix* the public education system in the United States. It's obviously a daunting challenge. It involves predicting the needs of the future as opposed to current fads, and deciding what an American should know. Once student needs have been determined, one would be faced with implementing improvements into the entire public education system. How does one start such a process? Before changing a process, one needs to understand how the current process operates.

The current status of American education is discussed in chapters two and three, and it questions whether the current system is capable of delivering the best instruction. Many would say that the answer is *no*. From a historical perspective, the public education system in the United States has not fallen. There are places where public education is doing a great job. More students are graduating from high school and attending college than ever before. What has changed is an employment market that has a strict bias against less-educated people. For most students, failure in school is now largely correlated with failure in life.

Statistics show that school performance is highly correlated with demographic factors that are beyond the control of public schools. The problem with looking at statistics is that they look at failure and success after the fact. People start offering solutions about what works based on conjecture rather than concrete evidence. The best way to use statistics is to determine the best way to go forward, not as measures of the past. The school system is not proactive in studying how to teach and improve the education process. Thus, parties outside the education system try to make changes and thereby showcase a dazzling display of bias and misjudgment.

The people most responsible for altering the education system are politicians. Whether it is the local level (school board) or state, or federal, politicians believe they have the answers so they try to "fix" the problem. Often their beliefs have little to do with education and a great deal to do with political ideology. One such issue is the idea that introducing a "free market" system in education will lead to improvement. The idea is that teachers and administrators freed by free market flexibility will create schools that work. The *free market* invention is termed a charter school.

The charter schools have not performed as well as *regular* schools thus far. Like existing public schools, some have done very well, but overall, the performance of charter schools has not increased relative to regular public schools.

There is also a movement that has come up with standards-based education and testing. It means that students will be taught the standards outlined in the curriculum. Teachers were teaching subject areas before; now, specific parts of the curriculum are pointed out as "important." This has resulted in rewriting curriculum standards across states, districts, and at the school level. Rewriting standards is a nice way to change the education system, but has anything really been altered where the product is delivered to students? In other words, has the product being delivered to the students improved?

Teachers' unions are another group that affects education legislation. The purpose of teacher unions is to offer advice as they try to protect teachers' rights in the workplace. They've built up a formidable lobbying machine from money collected from union dues. While teachers pay languishes at the bottom of the professional rungs, teachers unions work to protect teachers' *rights*. While unions project a liberal agenda, *free market* advocates promote a conservative agenda. The education system has become a turf war.

As chapters two and three point out, people have lots of ideas about solving the problems of the education system. From fundamentalist religious groups, conservative and liberal politicos, and the intellectual academics, all share their opinions and commentary into education soup while they lobby for their respective positions.

The special interest groups approach legislators about putting forward ideas like intelligent design, prayer in schools, school choice, vouchers, academic freedom, and student rights, and they result in acronyms that no one can remember. Legislators serving everyone's interests will propose laws that micromanage the education process. As the school system tries to engage the interests of every group, does the school factory get off-track in its primary mission? The answer is yes. With so many voices offering suggestions, whose opinion do we listen to?

Given the success rate of most school reform efforts, perhaps none of them.

Everyone is well-meaning in their efforts and aims. They all believe they're right. However, legislation doesn't tailor an education system to those using it. The question is, "How do we improve the basic product of the public education system to meet our current needs?"

Why not come up with an entirely new approach to the education system? Why not begin by focusing on how material is delivered? Why not cut out excess bureaucracy by eliminating education positions that aren't directly involved with teaching?

Although the enactment of No Child Left Behind (NCLB) has not been popular, chapter three discusses how NCLB's largest affect will be to open the gateway for a national education system. Though the United States

Constitution implies that education is a *local* issue and the responsibility of states to decide, recent legislation has clearly shown the federal government is within its bounds to promote an education agenda. This could lead to a new large layer of bureaucracy in the education system.

On the other hand, if the education system is restructured correctly, state and local bureaucracies could be decreased and more money could flow to the classroom by decreasing *middle managers* who don't work with students. It will be one way that increased federal power can represent an opportunity for the education system rather than a curse. If it is reformed properly, an education system can be structured that will permit more resources to reach students. One would have to restructure the education system to remove redundant agencies that waste educational resources.

Perhaps there is currently an opportunity to improve the education system. What is needed is information that allows one to move forward.

Everyone knows that to improve a *system,* one must either come up with a new system or improve the processes that comprise the existing one. In a classroom setting, the *process* is the lesson. How do we improve the lessons that are being delivered to the child in the classroom on a day-to-day basis? How can the education system best help administrators and teachers put a high quality product into place?

If there is one role that the Federal Department of Education can effectively serve, it is to coordinate research on teaching and learning practices. The goal here is to find actual lessons that work with actual skill levels. It isn't as if one has to reinvent the wheel to find superior methods that work. Classrooms are already in place, and brilliant lessons are presented every single day all over the country. We need the education system to find, measure, document, and record what is done. Then, one would need a systematic way to study or distribute the best methods for education. It will take a lot of reorganization and work to accomplish.

First, we should start by defining the type of system we have: factories.

SCHOOLS AS FACTORIES

At the risk of offending my colleagues who teach and the parents who send their children to schools, it is difficult to deny that most American schools are based on the factory model. As kids are moved from class to class and through the grade levels, they are expected to be formed to specifications. The specifications for altering students are termed *curriculum* in schools. Classrooms are workstations and teachers are conduits to transfer knowledge to students. It may sound offensive, but a student is a *product* of the education system. One may be reluctant to view an educational setting as a factory, but schools were patterned after factories and that's how they operate.

In a factory, products are moved along a production line, and they are improved at each station as they become a finished product. The student, likewise, follows a prescribed path through the education system, and is supposed to learn certain skills as he or she is prepared for life.

If one were running a school like a factory, you would want each work area (classroom) to have the best materials possible to prepare and teach a lesson. You would insure that the best methods were used to present the materials, and you would also try to insure that students in the classrooms are capable of learning. At the present time, this doesn't happen in the school system. Students and teachers succeed in spite of the education system, not because of it. The best current predictors of success in school, parental income and education levels, show that schools do not readily create pathways for future success for those who are disadvantaged.

To improve public education, one needs a way to examine the education system, and looking at schools as factories provides one with a way to examine the process of teaching. A factory model is utilized for two reasons. First, the schools were created in a mass production model, and they haven't diverted from that model; and second, methods to improve factory performance are available if they're applied correctly. There is a natural hesitancy to view schools as factories because most people equate factories as places where there is mindless repetition and a lack of creativity.

Perhaps an alternate way to view the factories is as places where raw materials (abilities) are efficiently molded into finished products. Isn't that what schools do? Although no one wants to think of kids as factory products, defining the school as a factory allows one to examine the teaching process as an operation that can be improved. Defining the education system as a factory process will allow researchers to use a variety of methods that improve results while reducing costs.

The parallel between teaching and a factory is found in the systematic organization of the schools, and the aim is to produce a finished product. When a factory spends a large amount of time and effort learning how to create a difficult part, the methods used to create that part are used again. They are used until someone produces a better method of producing the part. Information can be shared about the actual operations that produce a product, and over time there is continuous improvement in the manufacturing process.

The same approach should apply to the education process as well. Lessons are merely operations that are given by the teacher to the student. Shouldn't we study what lessons work best, and insure that teachers use them? Why shouldn't the operation(s) of learning take the same approach as a factory? Some teachers may argue that they *know* what works because of experience. Teachers come up with lessons and delivery style that they think *works* for their classroom, and they're often brilliant, but are they the *best* methods?

Why the education system hasn't adopted a systematic approach toward improving the product of education is a mystery. The school system generally has left the method of teaching to the person teaching the class. A teacher who walks into a classroom for the first time doesn't have a blueprint showing the best way to teach a class. In spite of the fact that teachers have taught these same lessons for years, no has bothered to compile the best methods and techniques that work.

Nothing in schools has been optimized; not a thing. No factory that wanted to work well would operate like the school system. Teachers perform well in spite of the system rather than because of it. Beyond providing a classroom and books to teach with, the system of education doesn't do very much to improve the product. Teaching is a profession that is learned on the job.

The reason that experienced teachers are often better is because they figure out for themselves what works in a classroom. A new teacher walking into a classroom doesn't know the amount of homework that one should assign, how best to present a particular lesson, or how often one should reinforce what has been taught. The teacher must figure out a system that seems to work, all the while plowing ahead with the next lesson.

Can you imagine a factory in the United States that would allow its workers to figure it out how to do the job? One of the reasons that factories are more effective is because they create better techniques over time that lead to greater productivity. A factory worker employs the best techniques for the job because it's the most efficient way to operate. A school system should try to do the same thing.

Great teaching involves developing metaphors that give life to information and make it *real* to a student. It isn't easy to come up with great ideas to present to a class. The best lessons invoke the students' imaginations and provoke questions in young minds. The student will see things differently as a result of the experience. Not only is each teacher responsible for finding these methods, but also for guessing how much homework should be assigned. Wouldn't it make sense to capture and share the best teaching methods?

In a factory, details of each process are studied, and when methods to improve the system are discovered, they are incorporated into the process, thereby improving the production and efficiency of the entire production system. In education, each teacher comes up with his or her own methods for teaching by trial and error. This isn't meant to denigrate the efforts of teachers. The fact is, teachers have kept the system going in spite of the lack of support they receive, not because of it. This is an area where the system of education isn't helping.

In a factory, after deciding what should be made, one of the first orders of business is to determine how long each step in the manufacturing process takes. That way, adequate resources and time can be devoted to each step so that processes are done correctly.

In schools, the curriculum that determines what will be taught is often decided at the state level. School districts in a state must determine how best to employ resources to teach the curriculum. Is there an inherent problem with this system? What happens when schools are asked to teach more?

When curricula are expanded and sent to the schools, have the school days been altered to insure that enough time for teaching is available? Have we optimized our school (factories) to meet the demands of our curriculum? The answer is no. As usual, it is up to the teacher to adjust to meet the demands of the system.

A comparison of classrooms to factories is not meant to demean the role of the teacher. The focus here is not the teacher, but the system of education. No factory expects the worker to invent procedures each day, yet that is what teachers are expected to do. Factories have the sense to optimize their operations. Can the same be said for schools?

As the system of education mandates that schools take on more burdens, it does not adjust the school day. Time is an essential element of any factory process. One must schedule procedures based on the time they take to complete. At the middle and high school levels, most classes are scheduled in equal time allotments. Whether the class is difficult or easy, the schools schedule it for the same time during the day. An example is the addition of algebra to several states' graduation requirements.

As states add algebra as a graduation requirement, students who would normally forego a class like algebra are suddenly expected to take and pass the class. In a factory, one would look at the algebra class as a difficult operation and would allocate more time for its completion. A second factor to consider would be the shape of the raw materials (students) entering into the process. Students with less mathematical knowledge will require more study time to be successful. Thus, the school system creates a system with built-in failure. The system should be responsible for determining how to set up students for success, not failure.

There are many factors that could be optimized in schools. Have schools found the best way to insure that this knowledge or curriculum is learned?

Are there proper materials and study materials to support the curriculum and to develop lessons? Are textbooks written for the needs of students or the desires of people who approve K-12 curriculum? Are the annual examinations used to evaluate schools really helping the students? How can one best use the data we're collecting to improve the schools? When one thinks about it, devoid of information, teaching is like performing brain surgery with a spade.

Okay, that's a stretch. Perhaps what this shows is that teachers are conscientious, have done a good job, but if the system that is supposed to support them actually did so, system-wide improvements would be possible.

ROMEO AND JULIET IN THE FACTORY

Since K-12 education is one of the largest expenditures that state and local governments make, an examination of the efficiency of the system would also make sense. Though literature classes have taught Shakespeare in the United States for many years, has anyone shown the absolute best method(s) for teaching *Romeo and Juliet?* Moreover, can one describe the best homework to give (reinforcement), and the best method of testing for content and retention?

Though Shakespeare's play has been presented hundreds of thousands of times in classrooms, no one has yet determined the "best" way to teach the class to get the main points across. If you were running a factory and you hadn't figured out the best way to make a product, you'd be out of business.

On the other hand, both the state and local levels develop guidelines for what *Romeo and Juliet* should cover in an English class, but no best method has been developed to *cover* the material. Throughout the United States, there is great duplication of effort and cost coming up with standards and guidelines for curriculum and operations. With respect to curriculum, does algebra or *Julius Caesar* need to have different curriculum guidelines in Montana than in Florida?

Students and teachers read the same text and learn the same content, so why should 50 states and 14,000 school districts all develop their own curriculum? In a factory, this would be like making changes in the process without getting improvement. In other words, it's wasteful. Worse, since the education system doesn't capture what works and without a memory, it is a system that will not improve.

There's another instance where education fails as a factory. Can you imagine a company like Intel finding a new way to build a product, but not sharing the methods with another site? In the public education system, the best teaching methods may never make it out to the next classroom, much less into the school system.

The development of curriculum and lessons in our country should be done in a way that allows teachers to have access to high quality instructional materials that have been proven to work through testing. If a teacher finds his or herself confronted with a novel learning situation in a classroom (e.g., an immigrant from Macedonia with limited English skills), perhaps if the need was warranted, the teacher could find materials that would be accessible to the student. The problem is that even if most teachers were able to find such materials, the teacher would probably be precluded from using the materials due to: (a) copyright issues, or (b) using an unapproved text in a district.

The long-term solution is to create facilities for curriculum development that develop and test curriculum and lessons to see what works best. How can a system incorporate methods that work best unless those methods are first studied and then shared? One must develop a comprehensive procedure that tests what works best in the classroom. Each part of the curriculum delivery process should be examined, broken down, and analyzed to see what works, and then this information needs to be communicated to teachers.

Though there isn't currently a systematic way to collect and disseminate information to the nations' schools, it makes sense to create a central depository. Such a system, if developed would create lessons for the K-12 system that are freely available on the Internet to anyone at any time. A child having trouble with a particular lesson could go on-line to see the same idea covered by a *master lesson.*

There may be argument that a federal depository of lessons calls for nationalizing the public school system, but with NCLB, the gateway to nationalizing the schools is open. Whether or not a national curriculum is adopted, the savings from eliminating non-site educational administrators could be substantial to the education system.

If one agrees that some school functions can be centralized, the resulting school system would still need to find a way to improve the school system. Chapter four looks at management methods developed by Dr. Edward Deming that simultaneously improve both productivity and quality. Using statistical methods, companies have been able to break down and understand manufacturing and operating processes to improve their ability to serve customers.

Deming's techniques were first adopted in post-war Japan to help it escape from a reputation of producing low-quality products to become an industrial and technological leader in the 1970s and 1980s. Though learning isn't necessarily a factory process, the processes Deming created can be utilized to analyze the processes of teaching to improve the learning process. The transmission of information is a real process whether it occurs online, in the classroom, or by any means. The lesson that information is transferred to students is based on minute details, and only by knowing what needs to occur in a lesson will education be transformed and improved.

One of the primary tenets of Deming's methods is developing a system that makes progress towards a constant goal. Schools, however, are burdened because in a state capitol somewhere, someone is in the process of writing a law that decides the best way to teach and what should be taught. Though it is the legislator's job to try to adjust the system to meet the needs of their constituents, education, like any system, needs to move toward consistent goals. Education needs to find a coherent way to view proposed change in the education system.

Chapter five puts forward a proposal to examine the education process in terms of entropy or degree of disorder. Why? As more disorder enters an education institution or system, it will create the higher likelihood of failure. Anything that adds to the entropy of a classroom or school that isn't a part of the instruction process will be detrimental to learning. This includes limits for students that are unprepared for class (low prerequisite skills) and items as simple as dress codes. In essence, it provides a focus to bring constancy of purpose (lowering entropy in the system) to the process of education.

One of the reasons that schools in higher income areas do better is that there is less disparity (entropy) among students in classrooms in higher achieving schools. Methods to remove that disparity will improve each class's instruction. The education system needs order so that it can succeed; this is particularly true among low income students. Part of the order should be achieved by careful studies that create curriculum that works the best and making standards for curriculum universal.

This is one of several texts that have suggested using Deming's methods to improve school performance in schools. However, previous books have limited the focus to school sites (Schmoker & Wilson, 1993, p. 22) or districts (Kattman & Johnson, 2002, p. 114). Previous books about implementing quality systems in education have generally focused on the actions of school and district administrators. One problem with employing quality programs at the classroom level is the lack of data. With a few teachers teaching a subject, getting meaningful data from a classroom will be difficult.

Within a school, measuring the effect of one curriculum versus another could be varied by teaching style, composition of students in the classroom, or a variety of other factors. Unless one teaching system is obviously superior to another, it would be difficult to understand the factors that make one system superior to another. The same argument could be made at the district level as well. Not only would classroom variation make data difficult to interpret, there would also be differences in schools to contend with. A large-scale, well-planned study would yield data that could be used everywhere by everyone. Though a well-planned system to develop results for schools could harvest results, schools often take measurements that mean nothing.

The education system has been urged to try to employ business processes in education such as Total Quality Management (TQM). Yet, without information on which to act, these efforts can be futile or counter-productive. An example comes from our local school district, Riverside Unified School District (RUSD), where the district wanted management (principals) to *assess* what was occurring in each classroom of their school.

In order to check classroom quality and to determine whether the lesson was being taught properly, RUSD decided to have the principal of each school walk around from classroom to classroom with a portable data entry device called a palm pilot. In weekly five-minute observations, the site principal is supposed to observe and collect a large amount of information in the classroom to determine whether the teacher is effective. One of the things they look for is whether the teacher has written the California's English Language Arts Content Standard on the chalkboard [PE1]. For example, an English teacher teaching a specific lesson is supposed to write the following standard on the board:

1.1 Identify and use the literal and figurative meanings of words and understand word derivations (English Language Arts, 1997, p. 56).

The principal or vice-principal will observe the classrooms and will note whether students are engaged in a learning process. They will look at the classroom walls to see if original student work is up. They will do it every single week. Why? It's an attempt to adopt methods used in the business world. But there's a huge problem. None of the factors measured actually measure the lesson or the learning that occurs.

One positive factor that comes from the principal's visits to classrooms is that blatantly incompetent teachers can be identified. Removal of an incompetent teacher is another matter. If gross teaching incompetence were occurring during the visits, perhaps the oversight by a principal represents a way to correct the situation. It makes one ask how visits actually help to ascertain teaching quality and then improve it? Considering the amount of time the classroom visits take and the amount of constructive feedback that one could receive, one might conclude that this method of classroom visit is a waste of time.

The palm pilot evaluation program might not be a bad idea if the principal could use the observations to provide information that could improve the teaching process. If the administrator had the resources available, he or she would be able to refer specific teaching methods that have proven effective. Such a program of observation would have merit. How to employ the use of teacher observations is the type of program that could be examined under "real conditions" to find how it can best serve the needs of administrators, teachers, and students. Methods need to be tested under controlled environments using different school to study the methods. If education is going to adopt business practices, it must also adopt the discipline to study the instructional processes so that teaching is optimized under *real* conditions.

The reason businesses improved their efficiency is because they improved efficiency step-by-step. Business people improve efficiency by looking at processes that are relevant. They find things about business processes that can be improved, they offer alternatives, and they conduct studies to find the best way to do things. To do this effectively, they must test situations under "normal" settings. Merely recording what happens in a factory isn't improvement. Monitoring an action without meaningful intervention of a process will not bring a positive change.

Let's assume that improvement of the education process in the United States is possible. Is there agreement that the most important aspect of an education occurs in a classroom during the transfer of information from the environment (classroom) to the student's brain? If this is true, then we have a simplified way to look at the education process. The approach to improving education starts with finding and then implementing the best ways to transfer information. All functions of a school system should be geared toward maximizing student learning in the classroom.

The idea behind writing this book is to offer a systematic way to approach the process of improving public (and private) education systems that is sustainable. The idea is to find proven ways to improve education so that more schools and kids can "beat the odds." The ideas for this book are derived from physics, manufacturing, and common sense, and contain five main ideas for improvement.

1. First, the public education system is currently based on the model of a factory that could improve its use of resources.
2. Second, schools (factories) and classrooms (workstations) must control the level of entropy (disorder) so that teaching and learning can occur. Our factories must have a sense of purpose and uniformity to be effective.

3. Third, methods such as statistical quality control and/or statistical process control needs to be implemented to create "national lessons" based upon acceptable curriculum. These lessons can be created across multiple platforms (books, on-line instruction, video games, computer simulations, and movies) so that it can accommodate multiple learners across the country. This curriculum will be made available to all learners in all places at all times.

4. Fourth, the advantages of the system should be made available to everyone. Under this plan, there will no school or neighborhood put at a disadvantage with respect to availability of lessons (unfortunately, the same cannot be said for school supplies).

5. Fifth, we must rid ourselves of redundancy in the system and achieve cost savings to the system and streamline its purpose.

One might argue that this plan relates to factories and statistics and nothing about children in it. However, every plan here is guided by results from kids and strives to utilize economies of scale to optimize efficiency of the classroom. The idea here is to find a workable framework to address the problems described by Gates and others who seek improvement of the education system. As a teacher, it is easy to see the idea of a factory when students are moved through the education process. Essentially, the classroom is like a factory, and you're trying to impart a change in the student's knowledge or behavior based on your subject area.

Imparting change to students (learning) by improving behaviors or skills is the purpose for schools. If you examine celebrated teachers whose lives have been documented in film such as Rafe Esquith (5th grade, *Hobarth Shakespearians*), Jaime Escalante (high school, *Stand and Deliver*), or Erin Gruwell (high school, *Freedom Writers*) who've created their own education systems, it is because they defined systems for success in spite of the odds. They created the system for success at the level of the lesson, and that is what the education system should do as well.

Rather than hoping that everyone becomes a *super teacher* as Escalante, Gruwell, and Esquith obviously are (or were), teachers should be able to easily acquire and utilize research and lessons that the system has tested for effectiveness in a normal classroom setting. As Bill Gates implied, it is the system of education that must improve.

It was the statistical study of the process of factories that improved the output and quality of factories. The reason to examine schools as factories is to see whether the system can be set up so that each part of the education process can be studied and continuously improved. What should occur is that the education system should provide a better education that is more cost effective. As a parent, the idea of someone's kids having to "beat the odds" to get a good education is unacceptable.

To say that the United States *must* improve its school systems is ridiculous. Businesses can continue to import foreign talent, and the country can continue to maintain economic leadership in the world by importing intellectual talent. Improving public education, however, is what we *should* be doing. The overall plan is vast, but doing nothing or staying on the same course may result in economic segregation in the United States that could destroy the social fabric of the country.

When Bill Gates said that the *education system* couldn't do the job for which it was intended, the response should be to offer solutions to improve education. A comprehensive system for improving education is provided here that focuses on classroom improvement through the use of Deming's management model and reducing disorder (entropy) in the school system that interferes with learning.

Chapter 2

Is There a Problem in Education?

Prior to changing the public K-12 education system, the first thing that should be done is to identify the problem. The primary reason to change any system is to make it work better. In other words, if one is to improve the odds of success in schools, it is important to understand what's being changed. Changing a system for the wrong reasons can make things worse. The next two chapters examine school systems and the entities that affect schools.

To analyze school systems, some of John Dewey's ideas were analyzed to provide perspective to school change. It was surprising to find the insight that the educational philosopher brought to the "modern" education system. Dewey's ideas suggested that the interplay between the teacher and the student is akin to "game theory," a mathematical model used to predict how two parties will react in a situation. Though Dewey's writings predate game theory, he recognized that changes are based on the exchange of information between teacher and learner.

Several sections analyze current education data to determine whether change in education is necessary. Data from the State of California's (2004) public schools was examined to determine where public education is failing. The quantitative data from California's Department of Education clearly shows a trend of predictable data in the system of education. When the data is examined, one understands why California would laud the efforts of fifteen low-income schools that "beat the odds." Schools in low income areas usually don't beat the odds, and when failure occurs, the usual place to look is the actions of the teacher.

As the most visible part of the education system, teachers are often targets of reform movements. Though a teacher can have a tremendous effect on students' lives, he or she is merely a part of a large system. Students are molded before they come to a teacher and are changed until they exit the school system. Thus, a teacher cannot control many aspects of the system they teach in.

While teaching in a classroom depends largely on the skill of the teacher, improvements in teaching alone are not sufficient to improve the education system. This chapter shows that the education system provides little support to the teacher. The current success of education systems is more dependent on parental factors and family income than what is done by educators. Thus, the education system has not found a way to adequately address inequities in the social system.

Historically, education's fate has been left to local jurisdiction. The United States Constitution doesn't mention education, and it has always been consigned to be a *local* issue left to be dealt with by the community. Federalism has been a central feature of the American government, but legislation has moved toward more federal control of the education system. If the government takes on a leadership role, it will need to find a comprehensive way to improve the education system.

It may be time to consider a single system of education to help eliminate bureaucracy and provide common standards based on real data. The legislative framework for this system is already in place.

Prior to examining the current system of education, it seemed that some time should be devoted to examining the foundations of education. There has been no greater influence on American educational theory than John Dewey. Though it is impossible to examine Dewey's vast influence on education, it is possible to examine some of this perspective of American education. Some of his insights turn out to be very illuminating.

2.A. DEWEY, GAMES, PINTOS, AND LOST OPPORTUNITY

When the principles of education are discussed, John Dewey is often quoted. His work as an educational philosopher has had great influence in the field of American education. After receiving a doctorate in 1884 from Johns Hopkins University, he had a long and distinguished career in academia while publishing a prodigious amount of material. His writings about education philosophy make Dewey one of the best known educators in American history.

Dewey's (1916) writings are full of meaning, and a thorough reading of them provides useful insight about his educational philosophy:

It is the very nature of life to strive to continue in being. Since this continuance can be secured only by constant renewals, life is a self-renewing process. What nutrition and reproduction are to physiological life, education is to social life. This education consists primarily in transmission through communication (p. 13).

Dewey's phrase about the relationship of education to social life or society shows his belief in the important role that education has in forming society. The last sentence states that the important element of transmitting values and knowledge from one generation to the next is communication.

Dewey continued with a description of communication in the education process:

Communication is a process of sharing experience till it becomes a common possession. It modifies the disposition of both the parties who partake in it (p. 14).

With great insight, Dewey discusses *modifying the disposition of both the parties*—an idea that was central to the development of a famous mathematic theory.

Dewey's quote essentially describes *game theory* in which the actions of one party are countered by the actions of another. Goldman (2002) wrote the screenplay for the movie *A Beautiful Mind,* describing the life of John Nash as he provided a mathematical basis to discuss actions of economic systems. Several other people in math and economics have utilized game theory to measure the give-and-take that occurs in everything from negotiations to risk assessment. Before taking on the relationship between game theory and education, it is best to give a good example of how the predictive power of game theory can be used to change behaviors.

With game theory one can predict outcomes of an interaction between two parties. In the classroom, students and teachers interact. The teacher will alter his or her game plan based on the abilities of the students and vice versa. The two parties interact with each other. A teacher with a low-skilled class will alter the lessons to maximize the impact on the students in the class. Should a teacher with a low-skilled class teach the same material in the same way as a high-skilled class? Is it even possible given the constraints of the current system? Is there anything the system could do to change the interaction?

For the most part, kids learn to read, write, and perform mathematical operations the same everywhere. The same concepts have been taught for years, but there's no *best* method for teaching a lesson. A well run factory would optimize the lessons for the operators so that as much work (teaching) could be done as possible. In fact, one of the most powerful ways to use information in a system is to predict where failure occurs, and then prevent it.

The predictive powers of game were used when Ford Motors tried to weigh the cost of rear gas tanks in a model called the *Pinto* versus the cost of lawsuits. There was a cost-benefit model prepared by Ford in an inner-office memorandum (Sept. 18, 1973) showing that for $11 per vehicle, the cost of settling lawsuits with victims of burned Pintos would be less than installing the safety feature(s). The savings were estimated to be $88 million for Ford. With Christmas coming up, and year end bonuses to be paid, who wants to spend money on safety?

As Pinto gas tanks ignited during rear-end collisions, the cost of lawsuits and damage to its reputation outweighed the profits saved from an $11 per vehicle modification. The court's punitive actions changed the company's policies.

In the case of Ford, court settlements resulted in changes of behavior by the company. What game theory tries to measure are the factors that affect performance. The reason that Dewey mentioned interactions in education is because teaching involves many factors that work during the interaction between teacher and learner. There are certain inputs that will improve student participation in the education game and therefore the amount learned. It is important to understand the inputs to the education process in order to modify the process.

In retrospect, Dewey's words were prophetic. He said education "modified the disposition of both parties. . . ." However, Ford Motors, to its credit, knew that the reward from the $11 cost per Pinto gas tank would result in over $80 million in savings. Someone made a conscious decision (albeit foolish in retrospect) to save money at the expense of lives. With the Ford Pinto, the outside influences that affected education were profits. The company decided to cater to its shareholders (bosses) rather than the stakeholders (drivers) and paid a price.

One might say that Ford made a huge mistake with the Pinto, but one might also applaud the company for knowing the costs and risks of building a car the way they did. Can someone honestly say that the inputs and costs of the education system are known with any certainty?

Who are the stakeholders and who is served by the school system in the United States? If one wanted to use a tool like game theory to model how changes into the system would affect outcomes, could it be done? There are many stakeholders that need to understand how new inputs into the education system will affect outcomes.

Examples of stakeholders are education administrators at the federal, state, and local levels that have expectations about school performance. There are also teachers backed by powerful unions. There are also politicians that must vote on funding for public education, and at the local level there are citizens who are asked to vote on higher taxes to support the education effort. At the school site are administrators: principal, vice-principal, and counselors who all need to understand the best way to channel limited resources toward students to maximize results.

At the focus of those limited resources is the most important stakeholder in education: the student. The student unwittingly puts his or her faith in the system. It is the student that must live with the education system's success or failures. There is no other product that the education system prepares other than the student. The ability of the student to excel in our society and culture determines the success or failure of education.

All of the stakeholders mentioned affect the education process. All of them need data to make decisions. Levin and Belfield (2007), from the Center for Benefit-Cost studies at Teachers College, Columbia University, conducted a study to show the effectiveness of education spending in Minnesota. They showed the benefits to taxpayers, such as increased graduation rates (p. 2), that could be gained from additional spending in education. They were able to determine that certain activities and programs gave "benefits to the taxpayer" at higher rates (p. 3). They used their study to estimate the extra benefits that would accrue to the state by preventing drop-outs. Cost-benefit analyses such as these would be a great benefit to the education system.

These studies are good, but they don't prevent a problem from happening. It is a good way to justify putting funds into education, but effectively applying them to do the most good is the theme of this book. The current system of education seems incapable of using data in a strategic manner to improve student performance.

The school is a very complex place and the need for information about where to spend money to maximize education is crucial. Individual schools are not places that are set up to perform effective studies of what works. However, using school sites across the United States, the government would be in a position to find what works well and what doesn't.

2.A.1. Trends in Education

Reports of failure in the public school system are not uncommon, and in many cases, student failure rates can be predicted with a large degree of accuracy. For the school system to improve, it is necessary to know the best methods and resources needed to intervene to prevent failure. If one can predict when and where failure occurs in a school system, then it follows that one must develop practices that allow schools to intervene to prevent failure from occurring. It is a tragedy when a person in a Ford Pinto bursts into flames following a rear-end collision. It is also a tragedy when a student ruins a chance for a decent life from the failure to attain a good education.

When charts compare earning potentials for college graduates against those who fail to graduate from high school, the data shows that dropouts are largely condemned to lives of poverty. Does an education system that asks students to defy the odds succeed any better than Ford did when they knowingly put cars on the road that can explode on impact? Like the Pinto, the education system's affect on an individual can last a lifetime.

Though not versed in the intricacies of game theory, most of us understand that education is one of the primary ways a country has to modify its population. For most, education is the surest way for an individual to gain access to better jobs and higher pay. Many people, like Bill Gates, believe that the education system is failing in its mission. For many Americans, especially those who live in low income urban areas, education is failing. Though the education system has continued to school American students for a longer period, the costs of the effort have far outpaced inflation. The following graph shows that gains from producing a more educated electorate have also been associated with rising education costs as shown in Figure 2.1 (Johnson, 2007, p. 22).

Figure 2.1 shows that the cost of educating American students has increased faster than inflation. The higher costs of running education systems can be attributed to a myriad of reasons, but when Americans question public education spending, the question that needs to be asked is: *is society getting a good return for its dollar?*

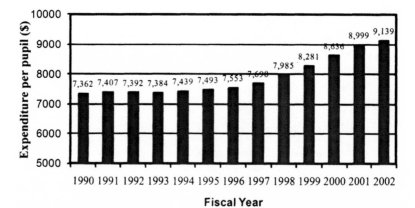

Figure 2.1.

The return that society derives from public education could be determined by techniques such as game theory. If sufficient data is collected, one can create models that predict whether spending more on interventions in public education will lead to a net increase in productivity for the United States. It is clear that benefits accrue to those who pursue higher levels of education. Wages rise in relation to the amount of educational attainment (Earnings and Education, 2006, Figure 1). *Educational Attainment* (1998) shows that there are many costs to the country when students drop out of school. Students who drop out of school are more likely to be unemployed (p. 4), live shorter lives (Meara, Richards, & Cutler, 2008, p. 1), and are more likely to be incarcerated (Harlow, 2003, p. 3).

Data can be used to predict the social and monetary value of spending resources to educating people. Students that drop out of school are more likely to reject societal values and become a burden on society. A report by Warren, Horowitz, and Riordan (2008) showed that at the beginning of 2008, 2.3 million American adults are currently being held in jail (p. 5).

The costs associated with incarcerating over 1 percent of the nation's population are quite large. It cost $49 billion in 2007 to cover prison costs (p. 11). In 2005, it cost $23,876 (p. 11) to incarcerate someone for a year, which is far greater than K-12 per student public education costs. It would be interesting to do a cost-benefit analysis to determine if more education funding would serve as a viable alternative to building more prisons. In some ways, the data showing the relationship between incarceration and

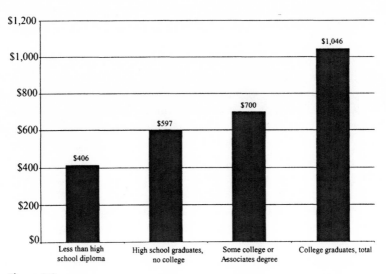

Figure 2.2.

education indicate that America's prison system may be analogous to a fleet of burning Pintos. It would be useful to develop a cost effective way to lower drop-outs while improving educational quality. The problem is that people are already upset about the high cost of educating American children.

2.A.2. The Educational Divide

It shouldn't surprise one that Dewey (1916) had some insights about how the cost of education would increase along with the complexity of society. He also warned about the problems of a schism or divide in the educational process.

> As societies become more complex in structure and resources, the need of formal or intentional teaching and learning increases. As formal teaching and training grow in extent, there is the danger of creating an undesirable split between the experience gained in more direct associations and what is acquired in school. This danger was never greater than at the present time, on account of the rapid growth in the last few centuries of knowledge and technical modes of skill (p. 14).

How this statement applies to the United States in 2008 makes it more profound than it was in Dewey's time. It is likely that Dewey is describing the differences between vocational training and academic schools. Perhaps Dewey saw that the "direct associations" were the home life and that of school. The undesirable split could be the schism that students experience when they are from backgrounds that do not support a future based on education. Essentially, the *split* that Dewey predicted is found in performance by students in the public school system and subsequent college matriculation rates. The difference is that in 1914 when Dewey wrote about the *chasm,* learning in an apprenticeship or getting a job in a factory would provide a means for a decent living. That is clearly not the case now.

This phenomenon, termed *The Educational Divide,* is discussed in a short article by Weicker and Kahlenburg (2002), who state that we are heading toward a country that contains two versions of America: one for the rich and one for the poor. The article points out that the education of middle class students attending schools with high poverty levels is also compromised (p. 1). The story of American education is not only about the education system, but about a society that experienced rapid change. Education statistics tell a story of an education system that has continually improved educational attainment, but not fast enough to satisfy the needs of the rapidly changing society it serves.

Since Dewey philosophized about education, there has been a significant change in the American employment picture. When Dewey published his articles, a high school dropout could work in a factory or find work that provided a decent living. The landscape has changed, and now a lack of education can create barriers to opportunity that can follow a person for life.

The truth is, the public education system in the United States is servicing more people than ever before in the country's history. As the *Digest of Education's Statistics* (2007) shows in Figure 2.3, the number of people who've completed high school has continued to rise while the number who have dropped out prior to obtaining a fifth-grade education has fallen. The graph shows that the number of people earning bachelor degrees or higher (graduate degrees) continues to increase, but the figure is still less than 30 percent of the population for people 25 or older. With a technology-based economy, a college education provides the best opportunity for economic success.

The results indicate that a "serious split" is occurring in the school agenda. There is more pressure on legislators and school administrators to direct students toward college and universities, and the poor are being "left behind." Education has become not only a gateway, but also a barrier toward achieving success in the United States.

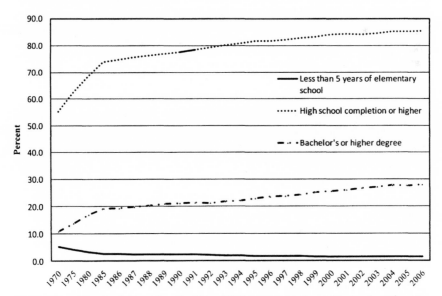

Figure 2.3. *Digest of Education Statistics 2006* (2007). National Center for Education Statistics, July 2007.

Schools are serving more students that ever before, but the education system is not aligned with America's economic needs. A college education is becoming a necessary step toward middle class life.

One of the truths that the education system must confront is that many students will not have the skills or desire to attend college. As a service industry, public education needs to understand and embrace this point of view. While a college education is a desirable goal, it should not be the sole goal of the education system. This issue also concerns the types of employment that are available in the United States. If we don't develop and maintain a base of middle-income jobs that don't require higher education, the country risks having a majority of its people live in poverty. That being said, we shouldn't blame the education system for things that are beyond its control. The job is to train people to become good citizens who will make informed decisions about the democratic process.

If problems in education are not addressed, the United States will become a country of working poor who serve the wealthier elements of society. For all the freedom in the United States, most high paying jobs are available only to people who are educated and have an avenue to travel toward a decent lifestyle.

For all the people who suggest that education isn't doing a good job, the data suggest that more people are being educated for longer times than ever before in American history. Public education may not be living up to Bill Gates' expectations, but the decline of the American education process has been over-reported. When Gates' (2005) said that high schools were "designed to meets the needs of another age" (p. 2), he assumes that schools did meet the needs previously. Schools have always varied in quality and some students were not well served by the system. A K-12 education has always been a generic process, but whether it's good enough is a question that should be asked.

Given the education system we have, teachers and administrators have been working hard to move kids through the system. The truth is that the world around us is changing so fast that education isn't keeping up. In the words of Shimon Peres (2004), a Nobel Laureate:

> The global economy is changing. Wealth is no longer coming from the land. It is coming from the human mind. Human imagination and creativity are the sources of a country's future wealth and prosperity. It does not matter how much land and natural resources we own. It only matters what we can imagine and create. It does not matter what we know. It only matters what we will learn (p. A-19).

Though primarily referencing emerging economies, Peres' statement fits the United States as well. Our country's ability to maintain its position cannot get bogged down in ideological fights. "What we will learn" (Peres, 2004, p. 2) refers to the capacity to evolve to the world's changing demands. We need a system that can teach effectively and adapt to new information relatively quickly. Would that be the American public education system?

Public education is like a large ship at sea that is rudderless, without power, being pushed one way or another as the wind blows. Rather than providing a rudder and engine (in the classroom), many who wish to change education go up to the command center and spin the wheel.

The teachers are in the engine room (classroom) trying to conduct classes[PE1]. The visitors (politicians) to the ship's command center call down to the classes and say; "While you're fixing the engine and rudder, could you give me a report on how well I navigated the ship?"

"Sure. I'll bring up the report with some water," a teacher replies. It's leaking down here; we're taking on water. There's lots of it."

"Oh, let me spin the wheel again and see if we can navigate the ship to a place with less water." Then the politician politely asks, "I'll bet you could use some computers, eh?"

"No, but if you could give us some buckets, it might help," the teacher responds.

The politician doesn't hear since he/she is already giving a press conference about how the computers are going to help education.

The politician might provide computers, or toughen academic standards, but it all amounts to window dressing. It doesn't change what's happening in the classroom.

The changes that education needs are not cosmetic or based on lobbying groups' needs to promote new products. One should not expect imagination and resources to flow down from our elected leaders to the classroom to help. The odds for improving the education process for America's K-12 students will not come from pieces of legislation that tinker with the education process. It's important to understand the inputs that will bring the desired outcomes from education. The truth is, we don't have the system that can do it.

2.B. ARE PUBLIC SCHOOLS THAT BAD? IF SO, THEN WHY?

When the State of California boasts about schools that *beat the odds,* one could view it as an admission that for some, the positive affects of education may be a long shot. Americans know that education will have low levels of success among certain populations. For people who want to reform education, the expectation of failure is accompanied by numerous calls for change. Often the proposed changes have more to do with political ideology than changing classroom performance.

Schools have historically been battlegrounds for public opinions and disputes. With the end of the Civil War, slavery was outlawed in the United States, but the public schools proved to be the battleground to end segregation. Segregation in the schools was ended by the Supreme Court when Brown v. Board of Education (1954) overturned Plessey v. Ferguson (1896) to make segregation in schools illegal; nevertheless, the battle ended up at school sites. The schools are still battlegrounds for issues such as separation of church and state and the issue of school prayer. The latest and largest battle being fought for schools is the desire to show that the free market is superior to any form of government control.

The American education system currently hosts a battle between free market advocates and labor unions. On one side is a group that favors vouchers and charter schools to enable more choice in the education process. They contend that more choices will always serve the consumer better. Another powerful element in the battle is the teacher's unions who try to promote teacher's rights and generally oppose increases in work demands on their constituents. Here the idea is not to find either side right or wrong, but to recognize that in wars there are unintended casualties.

As people fight for entrenched ideas, sometimes the ultimate goal of better education is lost. That has happened in American education. One example is the issue of private versus public school performance.

It is a generally accepted axiom in America that private schools do a better job educating America's students than public schools. Mendez (2005) reported that a public agenda poll conducted in 1999 asked whether public or private education provided a better education. The results showed that private schools were perceived as the better option by 52 percent of respondents, with 19 percent believing public schools were superior (p. 1).

It was a surprise, then, when Lubienski and Lubienski (2005) released a paper that disputed private school superiority. The study was based on the examination of results for public and private school performance using the National Assessment of Educational Progress (NAEP) for fourth- and eighth-grade students. It showed that when the data was adjusted for economic factors in the schools, upon examining scores in mathematics the public schools actually outperformed the private schools (p. 1).

A report released the following year (Braun et al., 2006) concluded that although private schools had higher test scores than public schools, when adjusted for demographic factors the results show the following:

Based on adjusted school means, the average for public schools was significantly higher than the average for private schools for grade 4 mathematics, while the average for private schools was significantly higher than the average for public schools for grade 8 reading. The average differences in adjusted school means for both grade 4 reading and grade 8 mathematics were not significantly different from zero (p. iv).

The data suggest that the private schools do no better than public schools when they're given similar student populations to teach. What is being suggested by these studies is that whether the school is public or private is not as important as demographic factors. This data clearly runs contrary to current prejudices against public schools, and the authors concluded that it might be time to re-examine the concept that the private sector is better than the public sector in educating American youth.

Another idea championed by the free market advocates is that *innovative* public charter schools would perform better than *normal* public school counterparts. Charter schools were a central part of the NCLB package passed by Congress to let free market innovation improve the schools. The charter school is an alternative school that uses public funding, but has more freedom than the *regular* public school. The idea is that a school, freed from the dictatorial control of the public school system, will flourish as innovative techniques flow from the classes.

The results have not supported this free market concept. A Rand Corporation report by Zimmer et al. (2004) that examined student performance in charter schools stated that examining standardized test results from both elementary and secondary schools (Academic Performance Index, API) in California in the years ending 2000–2002 showed that:

the average growth rate for charter schools in each of the three years was not significantly different from that of other schools with similar changes in demographics (p. 43).

A new federal study that examined the effectiveness of charter schools showed that:

After adjusting for student characteristics, charter school mean scores in reading and mathematics were lower, on average, than those for public non-charter schools. The size of these differences was smaller in reading than in mathematics (Braun et al., 2005, p. vi).

Unfortunately, the charter schools seem to have stumbled in the realities of the market they entered. Free-market forces haven't proven to be as effective as advocates hoped. This is probably because the inherent problems faced in similar situations in private and public schools extend to the charter school.

The policy decision for charter schools is not based on better educational or teaching techniques. The primary reason for supporting the formation of charter schools is the belief that the *laissez faire* structure of these schools would lead to better achievement. The reasoning was that school personnel would be freed from the rigid guidelines and structure of public schools, and therefore be able to do a better job. Unfortunately, the evidence hasn't supported this contention.

Does this mean you can just go down to the local public school and happily enroll your child? No, what it means is that if you live in Pacific Palisades or other high income areas where the demographics predict that the schools will have high test scores, you can probably use the public school system. It is both tragic and ironic that wealthier people, who generally have access to the best private schools, also have access to the best public schools.

To illustrate the point, one can look at the public schools in high income areas. An examination of a CNN/Money (2008) story that provided the top incomes by zip code in the United States shows that Kenilworth, Illinois has 82.9 percent of its households earning more than $100,000 per annum (para. 3). Test results from GreatSchools.Net (2006) for the 3rd, 5th, and 8th grade show students that meet or exceed standards (Table 2.1). From the results, one can see that Kenilworth parents can be fairly confident in their elementary school's ability to educate their children.

The results for schools from the wealthiest zip code could be compared to lowest income in the United States. The problem with this is that people are very eager to find out and publish information about the richest zip codes in the country, but poverty isn't given as much attention although it is quite common.

The National Center for Children in Poverty (2008) states that 18 percent of kids in the United States grow up in poverty, and 40 percent of children

Table 2.1.   Results of School in Most Affluent Zip Code in the United States (GreatSchools.Net, 1996, p. 1)

	% Meeting or Exceeding Standards (2004–'05)	
School/Grade Test Results	*Reading/(State)*	*Math/(State)*
Kenilworth, IL (3rd)	96%/(67%)	100%/79%
" " (5th)	97%/(63%)	100%/73%
" " (8th)	97%/(73%)	85%/54%

Source: Greatschools.net. Test data. It is the Joseph Sears school (K-8) with 580 students. <http://www.greatschools.net/cgi-bin/il/district_profile/582/>

qualify as low income (*Quickfacts*–Web site). David Berliner (2006), a researcher at Arizona State University, stated that:

> A "good" zip code can make a bigger difference than good parenting. Take two students in the same school with identical family backgrounds—the first lives among wealthy neighbors and the other among poor. The difference in their scores can be as much as the gap between the 10th and 90th percentile!
>
> But move that child from the 'hood to the 'burbs, and watch his scores soar. . . ." (p. 1).

What is interesting is that education is normally seen as the means to attain a higher income. The entire point of education is to enable people to better themselves. If the capacity to get a good education is decided by wealth, then one must conclude that the education system fails large segments of the communities being served.

At present, the best advice to anyone trying to choose schools for their children is to become rich and move to an affluent neighborhood. If you don't live in an affluent neighborhood, you can check to see what schools in your local area have the best scores. If you happen to live near the poverty level, you're probably more concerned with getting by from day-to-day than school choice. Due to demographic factors, it's likely that you live in the vicinity of a poor school, and because you have few resources, taking and retrieving your student across town to the better school is financially impossible.

The best predictor of whether a student or school will succeed or fail is not race, but parental income and education levels. (erase sentence). Even within a district with similar policies, it is the characteristics of parents that determine school success.

To show the effect of parental income, the student achievement scores of two of the highest income areas in the country were examined. According to Webster and Bishaw (2006), in California the Median Household Income (MHI) for 2005 was $53,629 (p. 3). Two of the areas with the highest MHI's in California in 2006 were Pleasanton, $101,022, and Newport Beach, $97,428 (p. 6). When examining district Academic Performance Index results from the 2006 year in Pleasanton and Newport Beach school districts, it showed that even though both districts have healthy MHI's, the areas were vastly different with respect to their K-12 populations.

Information taken from California's Department of Education (2007) shows that Pleasanton's school district included over 11,000 students. Of their total population, nearly one thousand were *English Learners*, a group that learns English as their second language. In 2006, the base Academic

Chapter 2

Performance Index (API) score for the district was 880 out of a possible 1000; an excellent score.

In Pleasanton, only four percent of the students are involved in reduced or free lunch programs. Pleasanton is an area where 80 percent of the parents have a college degree and 40 percent have graduate degrees. The English Learner population, though large, primarily consists of families who have come to the United States for employment in the high technology sector in Silicon Valley. Thus, the English Learner API of 862 seems to reflect the family proclivity and ability to support the education process (Table 2.2; API scores).

Whereas Pleasanton's schools seem to have a more homogeneous population, Newport Mesa School District is more the case of *Haves* and *Have Nots*. In Newport Mesa, 40 percent of students participate in the reduced or free lunch program. Forty-seven percent of parents have college degrees, and 20 percent have graduate degrees (Table 2.2). In Newport Mesa, 20 percent of students have parents who didn't graduate from high school, whereas in Pleasanton only 1 percent of parents didn't graduate from high school. Thus,

Table 2.2.   Achievement Scores from Pleasanton and Newport Mesa (California)

Pleasanton API Scores		
Subgroups	Number of Pupils in 2006	API
African American (not of Hispanic origin)	232	774
Asian	2,283	952
Filipino	258	886
Hispanic or Latino	845	777
White (not of Hispanic origin)	7,158	876
Socioeconomically Disadvantaged	414	715
English Learners	997	862
Students with Disabilities	1,120	697
Newport Mesa		
African American (not of Hispanic origin)	187	700
Asian	721	878
Filipino	136	837
Hispanic or Latino	6,264	674
Pacific Islander	121	746
White (not of Hispanic origin)	8446	846
Socioeconomically Disadvantaged	6694	680
English Learners	4,968	646
Students with Disabilities	1,683	626

Soruce: API scores from 2006, taken from California Department of Education, *Dataquest.* http://dq.cde.ca.gov/dataquest/

Newport Mesa shows a wide variation in demographic factors within a district even though sites share similar curriculum standards, teacher pay, and instructional materials.

In Newport Mesa, some of the parents have spent a lot of money for close access to the Pacific Ocean and the right to have schools that are segregated by income. Though only separated by a few miles geographically, Corona Del Mar High and Costa Mesa High are very different places. According to California Department of Education (2006a) figures, the Corona Del Mar (API: 866) students are 86 percent White, 8 percent Asian, 87 percent of parents are college graduates, and only 3 percent of students qualify for free lunches. At Costa Mesa High (API: 709), the population is 51 percent Hispanic and 33 percent White, with 28 percent of parents graduating from college. Fifty-three percent of Costa Mesa High's students qualify for free lunch.

This shows that within a school district, where education policies are roughly equal, demographic factors can drastically alter school performance. If a parent at Costa Mesa wants to send his or her child to higher scoring Corona Del Mar, the free market advocates would argue it is the right of parents and students to do so. Under NCLB, if schools do not meet achievement goals, the students of *underperforming schools* are allowed the option to choose other schools within a district.

Does this "free market" solution really change anything? Although the Newport Mesa District doesn't have *poor* schools, under NCLB, Costa Mesa high school still faces a fairly high probability of not meeting NCLB performance targets. If Costa Mesa's students start going to Corona Del Mar, would the students from Costa Mesa get a better education? A second question relates to the rights (if any) of parents who have chosen high income areas because of the "good" local school. Do they have any rights in this scenario? What about the kids who cannot change schools due to a lack of transportation or discomfort in the new school?

In Newport Mesa School District, a parent might have the opportunity to send their kids to a high performing high school. In schools in East Los Angeles or Compton, a parent sending a child to an underperforming school may not have much choice.

Compton is a low-income school district that has historically been associated as having a large African-American population, but as more Hispanics have moved into the area, the areas ethnicity has become predominately Latino. Unlike Pleasanton where 80 percent of student's parents hold college degrees, in Compton Unified, 37 percent of households reported that neither parent graduated from high school. Only 11 percent of area households had parents that were college graduates. The district has 100 percent participation

Table 2.3. Compton Unified Achievement Scores (2006).

Subgroups	Number of Pupils in 2006	API
African American (not of Hispanic origin)	5,518	580
Hispanic or Latino	15,392	614
Pacific Islander	197	633
Socioeconomically Disadvantaged	21,291	602
English Learners	13,412	607
Students with Disabilities	1,168	452

Source: Dataquest, API scores from 2006, taken from California Department of Education, http://dq.cde.ca .gov/dataquest/

in free lunch programs, and 54 percent of students were identified as English Learners (Ibid, Table 2.3).

The poor test results from school districts like Compton are often cited by many as evidence of the failure of the education system in the United States. With a high percentage of socioeconomically disadvantaged students, the odds are against the student. People look at the results of Compton Unified and say that the education system needs to be reformed. Some free market reformers argue that schools must be run more like a business. This argument pretends that the market approach will improve education because it will better serve the consumer or *customer.*

The problem with the argument is that students in neighborhood schools aren't shopping around. They are showing up, and the education system that is supposed to serve them is failing. As Bill Gates said, "It is the system."

Free market advocates like to believe that having better choices will result in a better product for the market. There is no denying the benefits of a free market system as a way to develop and distribute goods and materials. What is left unsaid is that freedom to pursue customers will not necessarily serve everyone equally. Nordstrom is a high-end fashion retailer that is found in locations throughout Southern California. Checking their locations shows that the closest Nordstroms to Compton is 10 miles away in the Cerritos Mall. Nordstroms' stores are located in wealthier areas of the city. They can forego areas like Compton with lower incomes and let Compton's residents come to them. As a business practice, it makes perfect sense.

This may be defensible for a high-end fashion store, but what about for schools? For schools, it isn't a question of economics, but of morality. The students in Compton and other low income areas deserve a better shot at the American dream.

Education is by definition a method of teaching issues of right and wrong. By its very nature, education is a moral enterprise.

Those who favor free market reforms need to recognize that the free market is not a moral divining rod. The free market measures people's wants and needs and puts a price on them. It has proven to be a great medium for the distribution of goods and services, but it tends to favor those who pay the most, and not based on need. Some of the tools that have made the free market effective in delivery of products can be applied to education. However, we must find a system that allows students in any setting to get a good education.

One factor that should have more of a free market attitude is transparency of education funding. Each public school should be able to show how funds are utilized. Taxpayers feel that education is important; however, they do not want to throw money into a system they feel is ineffective or wasteful. Americans know that having educated people is good for democracy and good for the labor pool, but are unwilling to put money toward programs that aren't effective. If the costs and benefits of educational interventions could be broken out, the taxpayer would have a better sense of what they're getting for their money.

The government must play both a regulatory and free market role. Besides trying to deliver a service to all customers, the government is also responsible for insuring that the education product being delivered is actually good for the customer.

On the other hand, choice doesn't necessarily mean the product is what a student needs. A purely free market system in education is a mistake. That is where standards come into place. Given the choice, most kids will take a course of action that provides immediate gratification rather than work toward long term rewards. Most students will take high grades in easier classes over lower grades in hard classes if given the choice. Unless there are sufficient environmental factors to motivate students, many will take short-term success over a rigorous education that is difficult and may lead to failure. Freedom of choice is good, but it should not come at the expense of a good education.

The chapter began by asking whether public education is as bad as perceived. The answer is both *yes* and *no*. Where there are parents with more relative wealth and education, schools tend to work well. Perhaps the bottom line is that one's political ideology should not form the basis of how education systems should be run. Parents of children entering a school don't care if the ideas for improving education are Republican, Democratic, or Green. With regard to children, the one thing that all parents want is the best school system possible. As citizens of the United States who firmly wish the continued success of our country, we all know that innovation and education will be keys to that success.

Perhaps it is wise to take a closer look at some of what might be impediments to improving the education system.

2.C. FIGHT IN THE HALLS

Since the United States can arguably be called the flagship for free enterprise in the world, there are some who look to capitalism as the solution to all problems. So, it isn't surprising that some have called for free market capitalism to solve the K-12 education woes. Through many have embraced Adam Smith's laissez faire free market economic system as the path toward educational improvement, there is a flaw in the argument. The question that must be asked is, "What if there isn't really a demand for your product?"

As anyone who's attended school knows, a large part of the job of an educator involves coercion. Students may not want to study Shakespeare or algebra, but they do so because of a promise of a better life in the future. Much of what is done in education is based on a currency called future promises. As in politics, future promises are the currency of education, and the degree to which students (or voters) buy into a system is based on their experiences.

As we look at the laws of supply and demand, the demand for education is entirely based on perceived future requirements. Once a student stops believing in the currency of future promises there is little chance of getting them back as a customer. When presented in these terms, it makes sense that students whose parents are wealthy or who've attended college have higher graduation rates and do better in school. The tie between education and future success has been established.

There is another element that feeds into supply and demand in the education picture. Education is a competitive enterprise and students often worry about failure. As we examine the inputs into the education process, the feedback from the education process is sometimes negative. Students who experience failure in school are less likely to believe in education as a path to future prosperity.

Wealthier kids with highly educated parents see the direct positive effects of education as evidenced by lifestyle and wealth. Therefore, they value education. Lower income kids with less educated parents have the opposite experience in life. They are less likely to know role models that can validate the education experience. Therefore, there is little direct value to the currency of future promises. Unless the issue of maintaining student interest in education (demand) is addressed, any other issues are moot.

As far as supply is concerned, free market advocates believe in using a *research based* program. What follows are policy recommendations that have been developed by the Pacific Research Institute. In a report, Izumi and Cox (2003) state that to improve California's education system it should:

- Use empirically proven research-based curricula.
- State schools must use empirically proven research-based teaching methods.
- Comprehensive use of the state academic standards as goals for student learning, guideposts for teaching, and tools for teacher professional development.
- Reform the state's school accountability system by requiring all low performing schools to be subject to the system's accountability measures.
- Implement a school-choice accountability option like the one being used successfully in Florida.
- Adopt value-added testing to measure the longitudinal performance of individual students.
- Reform education finance by block granting categorical funds and ensure wise use of funds by local districts through the school-choice accountability option.
- Implement differential pay for teachers based on shortage areas and consider merit pay for high performance.
- Reform the teacher collective bargaining process by streamlining or repealing those aspects that prevent the delivery of high-quality education services (p. 11).

Is there anything inherently wrong with these recommendations? Let's return to the idea that these policies primarily target failing schools. That's why it has "low performing schools" and "school choice" as items being recommended for adoption. Is there anything in these suggestions that is going to help students believe in the education system? In fact, is anything here directly targeted at the student (demand) in this market based system? As usual, the main target of the change is the school and the teachers (supply), though the brunt of the problem is targeting issues that deal with demand.

The ideas proposed by the Pacific Research Institute's (PRI's) Report Card are not bad. In later chapters, the issue of *empirically based* lessons will be discussed. This simply means that the methods have been proven through research. There isn't anything wrong with asking schools to deliver a better product, and this book will examine methods to improve classroom instruction while cutting costs. However, the PRI ideas devote more money and emphasis toward administrators, while the key to any academic success is in the classroom. Though there are plenty of discussions about tough standards, benchmarks, and accountability, what matters is what occurs in the classroom.

The new teacher going to his or her classroom for the first time will have books (hopefully), desks, a room, and kids. There will be curriculum standards to guide the teacher, but at present, no one is going to discuss the use of empirically based teaching methods. Where is all the research-based training supposed to come from? The only certainty for the teacher is that there is a population of kids in the class who may or may not be ready to accept the material.

One of the research-based techniques was shown to personnel in the local school district. The technique stressed to teachers was the proper use of *graphic organizers* to introducing a new topic to students that will integrate their prior knowledge of the subject. When thinking of the process, the graphic organizer is just another word for *set* that is a term that gets students ready to learn and orients them to the material.

As an example of a graphic organizer, when teaching a lesson about *natural rights* for social studies, it is nice to invite students to see what they know about peoples' rights during various periods of time. A timeline is drawn out and the post-enlightenment period is shown to be rather small. The student is asked to think of previous eras when kings, emperors, pharaohs ruled. An invitation is tendered to students to tell what would happen if a commoner were to cross a king or pharaoh in some manner. Generally, the student gets the idea that any offense to the old rulers could be fatal and at least harmful to one's health. The same offense is presented to the current president of the United States, and the student will correctly surmise that the commander in chief can't order a secret agent to kill the offending party.

Students understand at that point that the natural rights of man are both rather new ideas in terms of history. Whether the teacher creates a graphic organizer that shows how enlightenment thinkers altered political thought, teachers have always put lessons into context. That's what good teachers do. From Plato and Socrates to today, teaching methods haven't changed all that much. Whether it's called a graphic organizer or another term, teachers think of ways to engage students as a natural part of the learning process.

How is this applied in the real world? Let's suppose that a paid consulting group was invited in to provide guidance to a school system. The consulting group has been invited to the district because it failed to meet No Child Left Behind requirements for improvement for two small groups in the district (English learners and special education). The consultants came and studied the entire district and then made recommendations. One of them is that the district should use graphic organizers.

Meetings are arranged to tell *all* the teachers of a 42,000 student district that graphic organizers must be used. Many other meetings are held at the district level and reports are written to show that the district has followed the consultant's recommendation. Must one ask if this sort of intervention is going to have a positive effect on the education system?

When looking at education, it is important to recall that teachers and administrators are only one part of the equation. It should be noted that all the changes suggested by PRI were aimed at the "supply" of education. They ignore the "demand" element. As discussed here, students must also get future promises in return.

What is needed is a way to improve the product that is supplied to the classroom, while simultaneously improving student demand. This can only be done if more resources reach the student so that meaningful interactions can be established. The only way this will be done is to cut non-essential administrative waste from the education system so that more resources can be devoted directly to the student.

2.D. ECONOMIC SEGREGATION IN CALIFORNIA'S SCHOOLS

If one considers the United States as an on-going experiment in democracy that has lasted over two hundred years, one would conclude that democracy and capitalism seem to work well. The country has been blessed by an economic expansion that has lasted through most of its history. The borders of the country have physically expanded, and enterprising people looking for a new life and opportunity have added their energy to a vibrant economy.

Democracy, innovation, and expanding economies are complementary forces that go together quite well, and the United States' citizens have generally experienced personal freedom and a good lifestyle. The model of success in the United States has always favored those with initiative that allows them to prosper in business. Over the years, the economy has become increasingly based on technology (computers, biotech), and the ability to obtain jobs in technology is based on education.

For most people, the capacity to enjoy a high standard of living in the United States has become highly correlated with a person's level of education. People with higher levels of education will earn more money, better job opportunities, and arguably, better lives. One could argue that education is a key to both the continued expansion of the economy as well as success of the democratic process. Education has been viewed as a tool to attain a better life in the United States, however, an analysis of state test reports show that certain demographic groups may not have the same opportunity to experience "the good life" if education is the gateway to success.

A philosophical question that should be asked is whether it's time to make a national commitment to public education. With 50 states and over 14,000 school districts struggling with educational issues, what is the most efficient way to serve all 14,000 school systems? Perhaps it would pay to examine the issue of education from the standpoint of a single system.

Would a business owner who owned thousands of factories that built the same product hire people to figure out how to do virtually the same operation in every location? The most efficient way to study what works would be to study various methods under actual circumstances, choose the best methods, and then share them with all the factories. That is how economies of scale work for a large enterprise.

As taxpayers, we all are paying for the services of people to reinvent the wheel at each education office. When you consider that these same redundancies are repeated at the state level, the enormity of the waste confronts a person. What is amazing is that all this rewriting of curriculum and toughening of the standards is done without any change to the factories. If 20 new items were added to the algebra curriculum, a factory would schedule for extra time to do the operations. That doesn't happen in schools.

In fact, the current system works on toughening up the standards, while taking more time to test students. It is one of the dumbest factory systems on earth.

Ironically, the education system doesn't even have a system in place to learn from itself. This represents a structural problem in the education system. Resources could be redeployed to directly serve students if each district wasn't pretending to reinvent the wheel.

The current focus of the educational system is based on trying to meet standardized test results. One would think that testing would be something in which schools would excel, but it isn't the case. The goal of testing should be: (1) to measure student performance; (2) measure learning; and (3) improve instruction. For years, schools have given end of year tests to every student, but how does this yearly testing help the student? Though it's a centerpiece of No Child Left Behind, and designed to measure student performance, is it really effective in helping schools perform? On one hand, the state tests will show how well a student is doing relative to others, but does it help the student improve performance? Personal experience would suggest that it doesn't.

Last year, at year's end my daughter took tests appropriate for a second grader. The test results were mailed to parents about a week before the start of school. According to the district office, the results are mailed home prior to being received by the district. Thus, as a parent, I'm not sure how meaningful test scores are when the staff of a school has little opportunity to use them. What good are test results if the school doesn't have them when the next year starts?

If a teacher doesn't have the state's test data before school starts, how can instructional practices be analyzed and improved for the following year? Student performance has been measured, but can one tell how much has been learned or tell how to improve instruction? Thus, the testing system is flawed. There are consequences for the school in terms of test scores, but do the results have meaningful impact on actual instruction? What good are the standardized tests if they can't be used to improve student performance?

The truth is that the results are primarily used to evaluate schools. The data from the California public school system supports the premise that there are certain factors that one can use to predict school performance. By examining graphical results from California schools (Figs. 2.4–2.9), one can clearly see trends, but is this historical information of any use?

The following graphs are derived from Academic Performance Index (API) data obtained from the California Department of Education (CDE), (2006b). They provide a rough sketch of the problems facing both the educator and the statistician. In the following diagram showing how API scores change with parental education, one can see that school performance for students with more highly educated parents tend to have better scores.

The only thing that one can learn from the data is that in general, a higher level of parental education tends to lead to better scores. In the survey for this graph, students were asked to describe the highest education of their parent (guardian). The categories were: non-high-school graduate (1); high school graduate (2); some college (3); college graduate (4); and post-graduate (5). Of course, this data shows trends that indicate a problem, without addressing a solution. Perhaps it says that the status of the students' current life has to be taken into account when planning an education program.

As an example of how the data is computed, Bill Gates' family would have rated a "5" because Melinda Gates graduated with an MBA from Duke. Bill would have been a "3" because he dropped out of college to do something with computers. However, he may also have scored a "5" since the Harvard Gazette (2007) reported that Gates "earned" honorary doctorates from Harvard (para.18) and Tsingua Universities (Kirkpatrick, 2007, para. 2). In any case, statisticians break down the data into manageable bits. So, we might look solely at the percentage of non-high school graduates and see how schools fare when the parents didn't complete high school. The results (CDE, 2006) show that as the percentage of non-high school graduates increases, scores in schools fall (Figure 2.4 and 2.5).

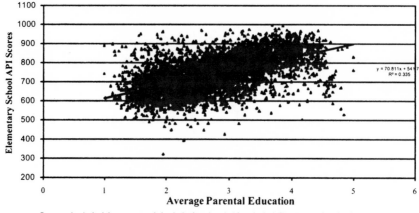

For parent education level, the average parental education level was determined for each school. The values were determined for the most educated person in a student's household. The values were: 5 - graduate education; 4 - college graduate; 3 - some college; 2 - high school graduate; and 1 - did not complete high school.

Figure 2.4. Average education of parents versus API scores of California's Elementary Schools

It's a nice graph, but what one is looking at is a snapshot of history. If one looks up schools that beat the odds, it doesn't mean that one will be able to reproduce those results at other schools. Generally, the stories of high achieving schools or classrooms are tied to the "great man" theory (2008) attributed to Thomas Carlyle, who stated that "The history of the world is but the history of great men."

The idea that people, teachers, and principals can overcome their surroundings to accomplish great things is a central idea in teaching. These rough statistics allow one to pick out the extraordinary. One can pick out the outlying point where a school defies the odds and has surprising scores. Great men and women generally have characteristics that aren't part of a system. They're great because they rise above the system. That doesn't mean that their systems are applicable to other places, but it does show success is possible. It means that someone can thrive in spite of the current system.

As for low-scoring schools, there are usually plenty of factors that can explain why students do not perform well: low income, high-crime rate, too many liquor stores, not enough religion, poor teachers, ineffective administration, low-parental involvement, and on and on. Statistics like the ones shown here are interesting and can be used by proponents or opponents of education systems, but they do nothing for the process of learning.

Some liberal proponents of education systems will say that more money needs to be put into low-income areas. They may be right, but where and

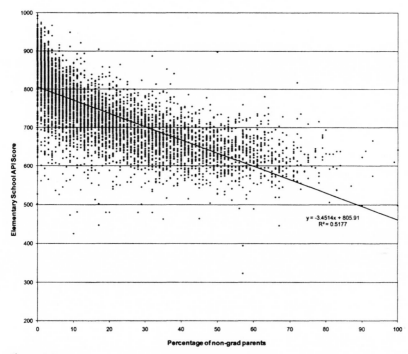

Figure 2.5.

how? Those who oppose putting more resources into education can point to the schools that succeed in spite of their circumstances and say, "Look, it can be done. They're doing it." But how?

Education statistics back the assertion made by Bill Gates and others that public education is failing to adequately teach students that are economically oppressed. Thus, their chance of escaping poverty is lost. It is entirely conceivable that the United States is creating an economic minority that is destined to fail. If one examines the arguments made in *Brown v. Topeka Board of Education*, and applies it to the poor (economic minority), the words of the opinions in Brown are still relevant today:

It is at the elementary or primary education level that children along with their acquisition of facts and figures, integrate and formulate basic ideas and attitudes about the society in which they live. When these early attitudes are born and fashioned within a segregated educational framework, students of both the majority and minority groups are not only limited in a full and complete interchange of ideas and responses, but are confronted and influenced by value judgments, sanctioned by their society which establishes qualitative distinctions on the basis of race. Education cannot be separated from the social environment in which the child lives. He cannot attend separate schools and learn the meaning of equality.

Segregated education, particularly at the elementary level, where the emotional aspects of learning are inextricably tied up with the learning process itself, must and does have a definite and deleterious effect upon the Negro [economically disadvantaged] child. It is particularly true that when segregation exists at the elementary level it is hard to distinguish between fact and fiction-the fiction in this instance, being an arbitrary classification on the basis of race.

It wouldn't be difficult for one to make the jump showing that we now have classification of students based on economic factors.

While examining education statistics from California, it is clear that there is a problem based on economic status. They show a clear trend that discriminates against lower-income students with less-educated parents. Why is this?

It is clearly apparent that a systematic way to approach classroom and school improvement is needed. The element that is common to low performing schools is that they have higher levels of entropy or "disorder" in the school or classroom. By disorder, it doesn't mean students that are out of control. It refers to students who are not on the same page academically when they come into the classroom. When looking at API (2005) results for middle schools in California, the results of schools were graphed to show the affects of poverty (percent free lunch), percentage of low-proficiency English speakers (English learners), and parental-education level. Of the three graphs, all demonstrated negative (degreasing) relationships between academic performance of the school and higher percentages of low-income (free lunch; Figure 2.6), limited-English speakers (Figure 2.7), or parental education (Figure 2.8).

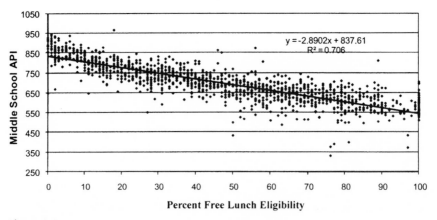

$y = -2.8902x + 837.61$
$R^2 = 0.706$

Percent Free Lunch Eligibility

Figure 2.6.

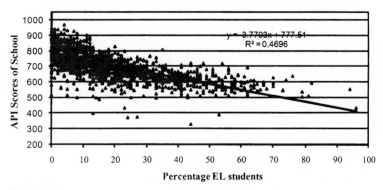

Figure 2.7.

The data suggest that schools in poor neighborhoods with large numbers of non-native students and parents with low levels of education will do poorly.

Unfortunately, a reasonably intelligent person looking at this data would say, "Who doesn't know this?" In fact, if most people were asked to write a relationship between expected achievement of schools versus statistics such as household income, parental education level, or ability to speak English, they would draw a line predicting the same results that are shown here. Bill Gates wasn't telling anyone anything new when he described the state of America's schools. It's a known fact. Just ask a real estate agent. They sell people properties for higher prices when there are good schools in the neighborhood.

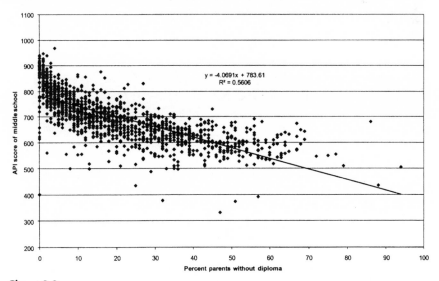

Figure 2.8.

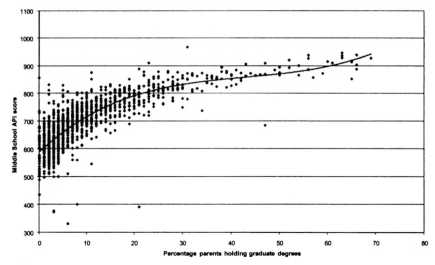

Figure 2.9.

There are two things that one should note from these statistics. One is that these graphs showing school performance are of limited value in the overall improvement of the school systems. They form one of the cornerstones of No Child Left Behind (NCLB) for it tells parents where the "bad" schools are. The truth is, one can predict with high accuracy where the bad schools are without using these graphs. So, on one hand, NCLB's plan to give everyone data is good, but it really doesn't mean very much. What's needed in a way to fix schools.

What No Child Left Behind requires is that each school measure each demographic group (white, black, Hispanic, etc.) and show improvement for each group each year. In the federal guideline by Spelling (2005) that helps states implement NCLB, the progress that each school is supposed to make is called Adequate Yearly Progress (AYP).

> Because each state is unique, no two state accountability plans are identical. States have designed unique approaches to meeting NCLB accountability requirements that fit their own context.
>
> States may continue to use school labels, scores, and other accountability elements (including existing state interventions and rewards) that educators, parents and the public already understand. Some states, such as California and Louisiana, use state accountability systems that pre-date NCLB as additional academic indicators. Other states, such as Texas and Virginia, give schools two separate ratings - a state rating and an NCLB rating. In a few states, like Ohio and North Carolina, meeting AYP is a condition for schools achieving the highest state rating (p. 7).

The foregoing is from a document that discusses guidelines for compliance for the NCLB program. It discusses the guidelines for AYP. One of the goals of the education system is to find data that can be interpreted and is meaningful. It is obvious from this that each state uses its own system of evaluation. Why is this? Why shouldn't someone have a firm grasp of what the scores mean? The Scholastic Aptitude Test (SAT) and ACT, formerly American College Testing, are both nationalized tests that people understand across the nation. Why can't the states come up with a testing method that can be analyzed throughout the United States?

There is a misconception that people in the Education Department have about testing. In Spelling's (2005) preamble to the "No Child Left Behind: Roadmap for Implementation," he states that "The best management tool we have for improving schools is student achievement data" (p. 2).

Let's consider this statement. At the end of the year, one measures student scores for the entire year. The scores in specific courses can be analyzed and compared among different schools. Does this data tell anyone how to do their job better? More importantly, does it do anything for the kids being educated? Can someone look at the data, walk into a particular school, and tell a teacher in Room 43 what they should be doing to improve student performance?

Does this data being collected tell anyone how to create and prepare a better lesson? Can a principal view test data from his school and meet with individual teachers with suggestions for improvement. Does this data even identify where a specific method succeeded versus a failing method? This data is collected at the end of the year, and a teacher may or may not see the results before the new school year starts. How is a teacher supposed to use this data? The truth is, the data shows good schools, bad schools, and mediocre schools, but does very little to improve schools. How is the *process* of education improved?

In a factory, to improve the product and productivity, you improve the process. Every day people across the country are teaching similar lessons. Some are good, and some not as good, but most teach the same facts. There may be variations on curriculum standards, but for the most part teachers find their own method to teach.

Even if teachers had developed the best lessons, our school factories haven't shared the technique across town, or even to people within his or her school. American education is a system that doesn't even learn from itself. With every new teacher, they must go through the rigors of class control, finding the lessons that work best, and with every class taught the process must be repeated.

Why can't the system of education develop lessons at a national level that use the best software, production teams, and create curriculums for multiple learning styles? Why isn't there a national laboratory that studies the best way to teach students, and then uses the best and brightest minds to create lessons that can be delivered across the United States? The best management tool in a factory is statistical quality control (SQC) or statistical process control (SPC), and factories have used the techniques to make mammoth-sized leaps in both quality and cost controls. If the federal government has a real role in education, it is in the development of quality lessons that meet the needs of students.

2.E. IMPLICATIONS OF THE DATA

One conclusion that can be reached from looking at data from public schools is that Bill Gates was right. The public school system isn't teaching a large percentage of the population it's entrusted to educate. It is failing to educate everyone to a "high level." The data for the previous section shows that students in areas that are socioeconomically distressed (poverty) will likely go to a school that is inferior, and the students will have less of a chance to advance in life due to the lack of an educational opportunity. This is the same point that Gates made in his speech regarding the education system in the United States.

Though Gates' remarks didn't surprise many, what was surprising is when Braun, Jenkins, and Grigg (2006) showed that when adjusted for economic factors, private schools tend to do no better than public schools. This was surprising since it's a generally accepted idea that private schools are superior to public schools. However, the data support the notion that parental income and education are the best predictors of student success. Thus, if a student is born into a rich family, they will have a greater chance of achieving academic success. Conversely, a student born into a poor family is unlikely to find a pathway to success through school (p. 1).

When adjusted for socioeconomic factors, there was little difference between student performance in public and private schools. This shouldn't be surprising because both public and private schools are operated in the same way. For the most part, the foregoing data shows that school effectiveness is largely dependent on two factors: (1) family income and (2) parental education level. These are factors that the student cannot change. The one thing that the system can do is insure that the delivery of information is presented in the most effective manner.

One question that goes to the root of Bill Gate's displeasure with the school system is: why does the education system fail lower income students more than higher income students? There are many reasons that are given.

Mark Frenette (2007), a Canadian researcher, examined the relationship between family income and college attendance. He wanted to know why higher income kids are 250 percent more likely to attend college. The study attempted to tease out factors leading to lower school test scores and concluded that parental influences and high school quality attributed to 84 percent of the problem with lower test scores; only 12 percent was attributable to lower income (p. 23). This results imply that being poor doesn't necessarily condemn one to poor academic performance.

Obviously, parental involvement is a very difficult thing to measure. However, while working in alternative education, meeting with parents and observing their parental and social skills, one often sees a high correlation with student performance.

There are a thousand different reasons that are given for lower performance in low-income households, and there are a thousand ways that are proposed to help the situation. As educators, there is little that can be done to address poverty; however, one factor that can be examined is the quality of a school's operation.

As an educator, one becomes aware of several things that determine school quality. The first thing controlling school quality is the quality of the teacher in the classroom. A second factor is the amount of support a classroom teacher receives. As the year begins, for the most part, a classroom teacher is given a room key, a set of books, and students to teach.

There are department chairs that can help plan lessons and school district guidelines for what to teach, but for the most part the teacher works in an isolated environment. Some schools also have mentoring programs for new teachers in which veteran teachers help provide guidance to the new teacher. That being said, the teacher has to figure out what works best to deliver material. There are suggestions for how material could be presented in teacher editions of textbooks, but a teacher must also take into account the level of the students. It's a tricky business.

There is uniformity in a factory, and the students walking into a classroom have a purpose. The curriculum describes the knowledge that is supposed to be imparted to the students; that's the change that's occurring on the factory floor. If you were a factory owner, you'd want to insure that the best operation was performed to transform your raw materials into a finished product. Would you allow your employees to go out onto the factory floor and figure out the best way to do things? No factory hoping to stay in business would allow its employees so much leeway in choosing how to do their jobs.

Can one assume that there is actually a statistically correct way to approach a lesson? Wouldn't it be best to make sure that teachers have the best methods and materials to support the teaching of each lesson, and also to insure that a proper amount of time is spent on each teaching operation? If such information exists, we aren't aware of it. Our school factories have not optimized any of these areas, and thus Bill Gates writes that the system is "broken." It isn't necessarily true that the system is broken; let's just say that the schools haven't been optimized to be productive.

This isn't where we blame teachers, and this isn't where we blame the schools. This is where you applaud the teachers for coming up with innovative ways to transfer information. Teachers must optimize their lessons on the fly; that's part of teaching. However, the education system should provide better access to methods and an infrastructure that takes the guesswork out of teaching.

In fact, there is a structural problem with the education system. The education system is run as a factory, yet methods to improve the factory system have not been applied to schools. When examining this, one of the reasons became evident: the education system needs to optimize operations at the school.

2.F. IF ONLY THE TEACHER WOULD DO THE JOB RIGHT

There is no doubt that teachers take the brunt of criticism from perceived failures in schools. One of the center pieces of NCLB was to create laws to make us all "highly qualified" to be in the classroom. The fact that one has to propose such legislation tells me how teachers are perceived: they're unqualified. As in any profession, we all know that there are both great teachers and some that are an embarrassment to the profession.

As with any profession, teaching is occupied by people of different levels of competence, and like any profession, it always will be. Even at an excellent school, there will be excellent and mediocre teachers. Teacher quality can make a large difference in the education a child receives. People in the education profession tend to be more sensitive to teacher quality than the general public. If there's one thing a teacher doesn't want their own child to have, it's a poor teacher.

Teachers with kids are more likely to schedule a meeting with the principal of their child's school. On the day of the appointment, the parties exchange pleasantries, sit down, and the teacher/parent will say "My little Dewdrop is the brightest star on the planet and must get the best teacher you can offer." The teacher will say this because in the current system, most teachers know that the key to a good education is the teacher.

The principal, if scientifically trained, will point out that it is impossible to have a "star" on a planet for it would burn up everything around it. The parent with a sense of humor would say, "Like my savings account, time, patience, and any other aspect of life."

"I see your point," the principal replies. She or he would look down at the teaching roster, ask what grade your Dewdrop will attempt, and then tell you that "We'll put Dewdrop with Ms. Williams. She's one of our best teachers." The parent will thank the principal and leave.

At that point, you've left things up to the hands of providence and Ms. Williams. Then you must pray that Ms. Williams doesn't get seriously sick, undergo a mental breakdown, take maternity leave, or allow dependents to collect on her life insurance policy. In that case, you could end with a substitute, and it's likely that little Dewdrop will go straight into the academic waste bin.

When parents go to their school asking for the best teacher, they understand that the teacher is the primary engine of the education process. As a teacher, I assure you that this shouldn't be the case. There should be quality or a high probability of quality in every classroom. The system of education should find a method to help ingrain that quality into the education process. My question is: why doesn't the system find a way to deemphasize the teacher and make the process of delivering the material more important? Every lesson has a best way to deliver and reinforce the material; the methods just need to be discovered.

The school system could also determine the amount of time needed for the lessons a teacher is assigned to teach. Given a proper lesson to teach and a method(s) that works, the role of the teacher will be de-emphasized. As a parent, when you walk into your child's school, what they learn, and not the teacher, should be the focus of education. The system shouldn't depend on teachers; it should depend on an excellent system that has the tools to teach. That means having the right curriculum, for the right student, at the right time. The reason that schools in high income, educated neighborhoods do better is that the students fit the curriculum. This is an important point to understand about the factory system. The more kids that fit the curriculum, the better the school will do.

A discussion of the factory system will be done in more detail, but think of the factory that needs to do 12 separate steps to complete a widget. The first step has to be finished before the second step, the second step before the third, and so on. Now, what if you put the widget that has only finished the fifth step into the tenth operation? Let's say that the tenth operation is to put wheels on a car. The eighth operation might have been to put on the axle that the wheels are attached to. What would the factory worker at the tenth workstation (wheel attachment) do when he sees all the cars coming without axles?

The worker would find nowhere to place the wheel. What if many cars came to his station incomplete? Some have completed four, five, six, or seven operations, and all are clearly in the wrong place. If you're in a factory, you would have to slow down, try to fix the problems that have been sent to you, and the production level would drop.

If you apply the logic of the factory example to the classroom, you find that teachers are often faced with very difficult work conditions. Suppose you're an English teacher in an urban classroom. It's likely you'll walk into your 10th-grade classroom to teach *Julius Caesar* and over half of your students will read below the 8th-grade level. Are students who are poor readers ready to take on Shakespeare's play? The truth is, the teacher, like any factory worker, will have to slow down to accommodate the students who are unprepared, or plow ahead and teach the material to get through curriculum mandated by the state.

The strategy to slow down the delivery of the material will bore the students who are advanced and need to be challenged, and the strategy to move quickly through the material will confuse slower students, thereby increasing the rate of failure. All teachers face this situation on a daily basis. In low-income schools, the majority of students will have low skills, and the teacher will either slow down or "dumb down" the curriculum. The same situation applies to the teacher assigned to teach algebra to students who don't know multiplication tables and long division.

Our current education system operates like the factory from hell. In a normal factory, one would take the rejected parts and rework them and salvage them. Schools use a variety of solutions to address poor students. Some proactive schools will make students attend after school class sessions when they are failing classes. In such cases, the students will sit in a study hall and study the material from their class. If this is done, then the students can avoid failing their classes.

In many cases, however, students will go through the class and receive a failing grade without significant intervention. A student simply sits in the class and receives a failing grade at the end of the quarter or semester. If the grade at the semester is a fail, the student must take the class again; the student is essentially reworked by the system. Thus, a student may sit in a required class several times without passing.

Our schools, unlike the factory, cannot merely try to rework the failing student and then throw him or her to the wayside; or can we? A report by Bridgeland, DiIulio, and Morison (2006) prepared for the Bill and Melinda Gates Foundation stated, "One-third of all public high school students–and nearly one-half of all Blacks, Hispanics, and Native Americans fail to graduate from public high school with their class." Nearly half of the students (47 percent) in the study said that one of the reasons they dropped out was because school wasn't challenging, and 33 percent of the drop-outs said that failing in school was a factor in their decision to drop out (p. 3).

What you observe in these two statements is the problem of a dysfunctional factory. In the first case, students weren't challenged and dropped out because the teachers were teaching to lower-level students, thus losing the interest of better students. Let's assume that the teachers in many classes were doing their best to accommodate low-level learners. Some students are bored.

The second situation, dropping out due to failing grades, occurs when a teacher sticks to the state-mandated curriculum that doesn't accommodate slower students. Therefore, you end up with students dropping out because they've been overwhelmed. These students fail because the teacher is teaching to the standards.

The first line of defense between your child and ignorance is the parent or extended family. The next line is the teacher, and the teacher (or teachers) that create the experience in the classroom due to personal initiative. As we've said, a teacher going into a classroom for the first time is armed with books, knowledge, and little else. In the case where a teacher faces 150 students a day, the incentive to create intervention programs to target slow students is not high. In spite of large numbers of failures, there isn't actually a set method for dealing with students needing extra help.

The problem is that no one has actually worked out the best ways to teach and reinforce lessons in the schools.

When a teacher goes into a classroom, there hasn't been a statistical evaluation of the best way to present the material, reinforce ideas, optimize homework,, proper remediation, feedback, and evaluation or testing. If one perceives the teacher as the hero and villain in the education story, it's because they are. While teachers and school administrators keep the education system afloat, teachers are tinkering with their lessons to try to find the best method to transfer information to their students. Teachers are innovative, but the system should provide more help to find optimal ways to teach.

If the system doesn't build better processes into education, it'll always be looking to beat the odds.

2.G. DELIVERY AND ECONOMIES OF SCALE

If you've been to school, then you've probably experienced sitting in a classroom with other students at workstations called desks, while a teacher provided you with information. The teacher lectures, students take notes, and every so often the teacher gives the students an examination to see whether they've learned anything. When one thinks of schools, it is generally a classroom full of kids being taught by a teacher.

People may look fondly or with dismay at their classroom education experience. Some will say that it did the job; others will say that it didn't. That really isn't the issue at this point in history. The point is that the education system will have a difficult time sustaining itself due to economics. The current educational system is pricing itself out of existence. It doesn't matter what politicians, union leaders, and everyone who has ever been in school say about the subject, the convergence of higher teacher salaries without higher efficiency in the education system spells doom for the system.

The reason that education costs so much is that teachers are getting higher wages, but the productivity per teacher has remained relatively constant. Measured against other workers, there has not been an increase in productivity. From historical data in the United States, it was concluded that real output increased at the rate of 1.6 percent per year. To put this in terms of what it means to a classroom teacher, look at Table 2.4. The increase in productivity for people in the United States from prior to the Civil War to the year 2000 was 1.6 percent per year. Thus, due to advances in technology, better techniques, and better education (perhaps) the overall average output of people increased. Farmers grew more crops, factory workers built more widgets, and due to increased productivity, the country held a competitive edge. If we apply the same rationale to teaching, to match the countries productivity, a person who taught 25 full time students in 1840 would have to teach 297 in the year 2000.

Most school administrators would welcome changes that allow a teacher to have over 100 full-time students assigned to them; think how easy it would be to create the school budget for the next year. Fortunately, such practices are not condoned. Besides being educationally unsound, the teachers' unions have set up limits on class size to prevent wide-spread walkouts by both teachers and students. Hussar (2005) examined class-size ratios for pupil-teacher ratio in the elementary and secondary schools over time and found that it decreased from 16.7 to 15.9 students per teacher from 1989 to 2002. They projected that the class size ratio will continue to decrease to 14.6 students

Table 2.4. Theoretical Students Per Class when Measured against Historical Measures for Worker Output.

Year measured	1840	1860	1880	1900	1920	1940	1960	1980	2000
Students per class	10	15	19	23	29	37	60	85	119
Students per class	25	38	48	58	73	93	149	213	297
Students per class	34	51	65	79	99	126	203	289	404
Output per Worker	4950	7490	9448	11477	14430	18328	29514	42083	58791

Source: Students per class is modeled using historical output per worker ratios derived from Baier et al. (2004).

per teacher by the year 2014 (p. 27). Therefore, it appears that economies of scale do not appear favorable to the current system of public education.

What is the nation looking at with regard to salary expenditures for the nations' 1.47 million teachers? According to the U.S. Department of Labor (2005), mean annual wage for the teachers is $46,990 per annum (p. 1); therefore, $68.9 billion goes toward teacher salaries alone. The expenditure on teachers' salaries may seem large, but the figure doesn't include money for retirement and benefits. The real cost to taxpayers is over $100 billion and this figure will continue to increase. This is for an education system that fails many that it is intended to serve, is a costly, and seems unable to promote social advancement on a routine basis. Unless a different course of action is taken by American education, the economic segregation currently experienced in the United States will become greater. The current system of education will continue to incur higher costs, enjoy no economies of scale, and be doomed to failure. If one considers that the goal of education is to enable people to increase their station in life, then results among the poor are already failures. Unless a different path is chosen, the economic segregation currently experienced in the United States will become more intense.

When George W. Bush came into office, he initiated legislation called No Child Left Behind that attempts to create avenues to increase educational performance and accountability. As a parent and teacher of a school-age child, the data do not look good. The administrators of a school district have the responsibility to channel resources to where they will do the most good. But the data in this case is three to four years old. What good is it? How can concerned parents and teachers find out how well their districts are using finances?

Perhaps individual schools and districts need to have both economic and scholastic measures to determine the effectiveness of administration and to increase accountability. The reason that school budgeting doesn't tell us as much as it's supposed to is because it hasn't been designed to give operating guidance for education; it is designed to meet government accounting standards. If an operating budget of a system cannot be used by people to make decisions, it has failed. Perhaps it's all a moot point since we're measuring an examining a system that is failing in its current form and will continue to do so unless the entire education system is adjusted to meet the needs of society.

The truth is that education in its current form will fail due to two massive problems: (1) education system, and (2) economies of scale. The system referred to is the factory model of education that is currently in place and has been for years. The economies of scale will further burden the system unless it is imbued with new ideas and technology and then adapted to meet the needs of kids. Unless the system is overhauled in a manner that places some economies of scale into the public education system, the traditional school will continue to face economic and societal pressures that will overwhelm it.

There is one aspect of K–12 education that Americans don't want to change. They do not want the federal government taking control of their children's education. People have a strong attachment to federalism and the local controls that are given for items like education. Since control of education is given to individual states, and then to local communities, federal control of education will be met with resistance. If you follow the idea that optimizing lessons and the education system will lead to better instruction, one might ask how the federal government can be involved at all. How can the current Department of Education improve the learning environment across America?

2.H. LAW: IF YOU TAKE THEIR MONEY, YOU WILL DO AS THEY SAY

When one thinks of economies of scale, it refers to getting more product from a larger system than a smaller one due to an ability to maximize resources. This means that as an entity grows larger it can produce a product at less cost. To put the question to the education system, one should ask, "If we were to examine the education system as one, rather than 14,000 separate entities, would there be cost savings?" That is the question. Can the federal government play a role in helping to reduce, rather than increasing costs of teaching American students?

Many will say, "We don't want the federal government taking over the schools." Yet, with No Child Left Behind (NCLB), the federal government is dictating local decisions. Rather than adding to the paperwork that already burdens schools, perhaps it would be wise to examine whether the Department of Education should change its role in education. What if it changed its mission so that its primary role was to find and develop the best ways to teach lessons?

What if the Department of Education opened test centers that would find and document how to best teach each subject? Rather than handing out grants to educators wouldn't it be preferable to try different types of education methods under actual conditions to find out what work best? Not only would this tend to tell educators what works, but it would also tell us what does not. It could tell us how much time should be devoted to each lesson, and perhaps give us information about the best ways to run schools. After the best lessons have been developed, what if the curriculum and materials for those lessons were made available (in multiple languages if necessary)?

What if that material was then made freely available to everyone in the United States (teacher, parent, students)? Given the fact that the best lessons are made available, the states could then choose the methods (lessons) that work the best and adopt them.

Realizing that such a process could take years—well, so what? If you created a system that continuously improved teaching methods and materials using Edward Deming's methods (Chapter 4), the local districts could discover the ways to structure their resources to maximize learning (by lowering entropy). The truth is that nationalization of the school systems can occur. With No Child Left Behind the door has been opened for a national curriculum.

In this document, the argument has been to change the system of education by creating support systems that help the students learn. This means cutting out politicians, school boards, and administrators who want to implement the latest and greatest ideas of "education reform" or, conversely, want to make education the way it "used to be." The bottom line is to give teachers and students the best methods possible to ensure that education is optimized to teach students.

For most people, having a central authority in charge of education is a terrible idea. The autonomy of having local people to complain to and about is an important part of our founding father's vision of democracy. We fought a war against the British to keep from having taxation without representation.

The ideas of federalism are still strong in the American psyche, and many feel that local control, no matter how bad, is preferable to control by a central authority. Let's be clear about what is being proposed here. The idea is to use a central authority to perfect learning materials and methods and then provide those materials to every student in the country. This doesn't mean that every place in the country will learn exactly the same thing, but it does ensure that each student will received lessons based on methods that work.

Would there be a problem if the federal government provided high quality lessons and materials to districts and allowed them to implement their use? Would the taxpayer have a problem paying for a system if it benefited the entire system of education? The reason that this question is important is because recent laws have laid the groundwork for federal control of schools. Perhaps it is best to dictate how that control should be implemented?

The structure of that control can be positive if it's done correctly. Perhaps instead of looking at the changing laws as a problem for schools, the federal government can find and evaluate systems that work better. If we look at the factory analogy that has been presented previously, we know that the goal of a factory is to create the best product possible, using the best technology, at the least cost. Can the federal government find a way to give each classroom (teacher and child) the best education materials and methods to teach each subject to a student? Frankly, if they're going to "manage" education through legislation, that's their job.

The point of good management is to remove risk through the use of methods to improve a process. In schools, this means improving the quality of the lessons and materials that a student receives. There are times when the local educational agencies (state and district) do not do a good job of evaluating materials such as textbooks. An example of this is the Algebra II book used in our school district. It teaches somewhat advanced methods of math for the secondary student, but uses explanations that have gaps when presenting the material. Independent testing centers could examine both methods and materials in actual classroom settings before the districts adopt them.

The one who suffers most by having a subpar text is the student. It is the student who will have to overcome the book's inadequacies, and, ultimately, their scores will suffer when they take a college-entrance examination. The book was chosen by committees (in California at both the state and local levels). The teacher and student are stuck with it. The text wasn't "road tested" to see if it actually worked. It may have been that one of the authors of the book did such a great job on the Algebra I and geometry books that the district assumed the new book was also good. The fact that it isn't is unacceptable to the consumer, but the student (and teacher) take what they're given.

One of the functions of the federal government in education should be to create lesson depositories that can help anyone with their homework at any time. These lessons should be made available to anyone with online access and should compensate for a variety of learning styles. Videos could be made that show a relationship between real objects and the creation of formulas that represent them. Perhaps a small historical video could be developed that relates the historical development of both the math and its uses in history. All of these things could be done in high quality presentations because they would be used not only by millions of kids per year, but could also be used for many years.

This sort of reasoning can be applied to every part of the curriculum. For instance, in a government class, why not have Supreme Court justices give some background on the history and the workings of America's highest court in a video? Better yet, there could be interactive programs where students could prepare to become voters by voting on certain aspects of government. School is supposed to be a practical learning place where mistakes are made, so why not let kids in government class have to vote on some current issues each year. Their assignment would be to defend their vote.

The federal government could supply an excellent curriculum that could be provided at no external costs to the schools, whether they were private or public, and to home-schooled students as well. It could have rating systems "on-line" and comments from students and teachers who've used the products. Isn't that what one does when he or she shops for a product? The idea is to provide the best educational materials to as many students as possible, and to insure that no student gets an inferior curriculum.

The potential drawbacks to such a system would be that everyone would be learning the exact same thing, and some might feel it wouldn't be *healthy* for the country. People would argue that there would be too much homogeneity in the United States' educational process. It also might be argued that there could be too much federal interference in local matters. The idea of a national curriculum has been discussed before. In fact, with the new century that brought Goals 2000 and then No Child Left Behind into being, and both have helped usher the wishes of the federal government into the American education process.

The NCLC Task Force (2005) stated the goal of federal intervention in the education systems of the United States is:

> to close or dramatically narrow the differences in achievement among American students that cross lines of skin color, ethnicity, immigrant status and wealth. The success of American democracy and our economic future depend on a society in which everyone is educated to their full potential (page 1).

In 1994, when Goals 2000's (1998) was signed into law, it described its aims toward curriculum as: "Goals 2000 supports State efforts to develop clear and rigorous standards for what every child should know and be able to do." The difference between Goals 2000 (1994) and NCLB (2002) is that the latter law had more power to dictate state action though a spending clause.

A "spending clause" as found in Article I, Section 8 of the Constitution is described by McColl (2005) as a contract in which the state is paid for meeting the specifications of a federal law. This allows Congress to mandate a state's behavior even when no constitutional authority is present (para. 7). Thus, a state's behavior in matters such as national tests or national curriculum could be tied contractual performance for meeting federal standards (para. 7). The idea for funding under the clause, like the subsequent funding for No Child Left Behind, creates a situation in which schools receive funding from the federal government for meeting certain requirements. In NCLB, the federal government creates a situation where it can use funding to impose it's will on state educational processes, and it makes it likely that a national curriculum could be implemented.

In 1987, the Supreme Court created a spending clause in *South Dakota v. Dole* (1987) that opened the door toward federal intervention in state matters through monetary measures. In the case, the court held that withholding "a small percentage" of federal highway funds was "mild encouragement" (p. 211). With NCLB, the door is opened toward federal intervention into state education policy since federal funding is tied to specific performance by educational entities. Thus, through the use of the Commerce Clause, Congress could enforce federal education measures such as a national curriculum through the enforcement of federal funding.

There are many who believe that measures by the federal government to strong-arm states through the withholding of funds crosses a line not supported by the Constitution. An article by Bork and Troy (2002) argues that the original purpose of the Commerce Clause was to "to vest the federal government with the ability to protect commerce between the States from the discriminatory interference of self-interested States" (p. 853). The original intent of the law was to prevent individual states from treating each other as foreign powers and wasn't intended to open the gates to federal power over state transactions. Conservative views (from the standpoint of the Constitution) claim that the framer's intent in the Commerce Clause was not to cover federal control of education.

One might also recall that the original framers of the Constitution thought that a slave was only counted as three-fifths of a person in the original constitution. The question does not relate to the framer's intent, but to what would be in the best interests of the nation.

The inequity in the American system of education is a problem that needs to be addressed and perhaps the Commerce Clause is the correct means to redress the matter. The Court used the Commerce Clause to intervene in the case involving Ollie's BBQ (*Katzenbach v. McClung,* 1964), a family-owned establishment that had been in business since 1927 that specialized in barbequed meats and homemade pies. The restaurant brought the suit to challenge the constitutional validity of the Civil Rights Act of 1964, since the establishment had violated the law by refusing to allow Blacks to use its common dining area. The establishment did sell "take-out" food to Blacks from a window, but did not allow them to use the property's dining facilities area.

In *Katzenbach v. McClung* (1964), the Court held that the case had "close ties to interstate commerce" because it served "food that came from out of the state." The Court determined that the seating policy did not have to directly impact commerce since the restaurant received food that moved in interstate commerce and found that in Article 1, Section 8, that Congress had the right "[T]o regulate Commerce with foreign Nations, and among the several States and with the Indian Tribes." Congressional power also extends "[T]o make all Laws which shall be necessary and proper for carrying into Execution the foregoing powers and all other powers vested by this Constitution. . . ."

In *Katzenburg v. McClung* (1964), the Court found that by restraining minorities from using the restaurant's facilities, interstate commerce would be affected, since Black patrons would not travel as much, thus reducing the flow of food from out-of-state since more food would be ordered if the minority population could frequent the restaurant as well. Blacks would be less likely to travel if restaurants did not serve them, and thus would order less food. Thus, racial discrimination in restaurants would affect interstate commerce by reducing the amount of commerce (para. 9). Bork and Troy (2002) concluded that the Commerce Clause grants Congress great powers to remove barriers to commerce (p. 853). With the strong relationship between educational quality and income, the Commerce Clause could be used by Congress to remove barriers in education.

In decisions that may decide whether the federal government can dictate state educational policy, the answer seems to be "yes" if there is a monetary incentive that comes with compliance (*South Dakota v. Dole*). In *Katzenburg* (1964), the control of state performance was tied to a broad interpretation of the Commerce Clause and enlarged the powers delivered to the federal government. The point where the controversy currently sits is described by *United States v. Lopez* (1995), a case that examined whether Congress could regulate state and local rights when federal funding was absent.

In a 5-4 decision, the Court examined whether the Commerce Clause gives Congress the ability to regulate all domestic issues without spending federal funds. The case examined whether the federal Gun-Free Zone Act of 1990, which prohibited all persons from knowingly carrying a gun within 1,000 feet of a school zone, was covered under the Constitution. The Court held that the issue was not covered under the Commerce Clause since the definition of "commerce" relates to the traffic of goods between states and in the case where a single individual's actions are concerned, it exceeded the bounds of the Commerce Clause.

It is not intended to say that these words comprehend that commerce, which is completely internal, which is carried on between man and man in a State, or between different parts of the same State, and which does not extend to or affect other States. Such a power would be inconvenient, and is certainly unnecessary.

The Court did acknowledge that an act such as having a gun on campus could affect interstate commerce, and they accepted the premise of the government's three arguments that stated:

The Government argues that possession of a firearm in a school zone may result in violent crime and that violent crime can be expected to affect the functioning of the national economy in two ways. First, the costs of violent crime are substantial, and, through the mechanism of insurance, those costs are spread throughout the population. See *United States* v. *Evans,* 928 F. 2d 858, 862 (CA9 1991). Second, violent crime reduces the willingness of individuals to travel to areas within the country that are perceived to be unsafe. Cf. *Heart of Atlanta Motel,* 379 U. S., at 253. The Government also argues that the presence of guns in schools poses a substantial threat to the educational process by threatening the learning environment. A handicapped educational process, in turn, will result in a less productive citizenry. That, in turn, would have an adverse effect on the Nation's economic well being. As a result, the Government argues that Congress could rationally have concluded that §922(q) substantially affects interstate commerce.

What is of interest here is that the Court did acknowledge that "a threat to the learning environment" could be considered as having an affect on interstate commerce, but because the scope of the incident is local and covered by laws covered within the state itself, the act of having a gun on campus didn't violate interstate commerce, and therefore the Commerce Clause is not a vehicle that gives unlimited powers to the federal government. Yet, given the current climate with respect to educational policy and rulings on the Commerce Clause, could a national curriculum be implemented by Congress? The answer isn't certain.

The idea of having a national curriculum is appealing because it could help streamline the educational process in the United States. Rather than having each state and school organization go through the effort of coming up with standards, a national standard for what to teach could be established, multiple levels of curriculum could be developed that would help students no matter what their preferred mode of learning is, and no place would be without an excellent curriculum. Under the case of *Katzenbach* (Ollie's BBQ), the court seems to be favorable to the idea of a national curriculum under the guise of the Commerce Clause. In *Katzenbach,* they construed that the needs of affected Blacks were not being met at the local level, thus the Court created power through the Commerce Clause.

If the Court saw, as Bill Gates says, that schools are failing many that they are intended to serve, then the Court will uphold Congressional passage of school reform that creates equity and improves the economic status of affected students. The Commerce Clause, then, could be used to justify passage of national curriculum legislation.

In essence, then, the issues pertaining to education in the United States are up for interpretation. It is clear that where states take money from the federal government there is an implicit agreement to follow federal dictates. It would also be advantageous for school systems to have a properly designed system of tests that will allow one to assess school systems across the country. What is the point of having separate assessment systems in each state? In *The Case for a National Testing System,* Davey (1992) brings up many advantages for having a national testing system in the United States. A national assessment system would allow districts and schools to be evaluated on an equal basis. She argues that the current measure of comparison between different locations are the Scholastic Aptitude Test (SAT) and American College Test (ACT). This measures only the college-bound populations of a district and doesn't profile the entire class (p. 1). Davey is right. We need a way that reduces the number of government-mandated assessments so that Americans have a clear way to evaluate schools.

Since the government (Congress) can pass laws that can change the entire educational system, perhaps it would be best to find methods that will help the system of education improve and simultaneously cut costs. Since Americans perceive public education as being in serious trouble, there will be changes. The next chapter will point out some of the perceived problems of the public education system.

Chapter 3

Pedestals, Problems, and Perception in Education

Govern a great nation the way you'd cook a small fish. Don't overdo it.

—Tzu, 570 B.C., p. 365

The quotation from Lao Tzu describes a system of limited government that appeals to many Americans. Many teachers working in K-12 education wonder if the education is the overcooked fish in Tzu's metaphor. In many places, there is growing regulation of the school site. As more oversight is imposed on schools, teachers spend more time catering to administrative functions that aren't conducive to positive change in the classroom. It isn't difficult to guess how most teacher's feel about the situation.

Job satisfaction among American teachers was the subject of a National Educational Agency (2007) survey. The results of the survey suggest that many of the country's 3.5 million teachers are not brimming with professional contentment. The survey was taken to determine what factors prompted people to leave the teaching profession for other occupations. One might suspect that low salaries would be the chief complaint among teachers since compensation for teachers is relatively low, and an NEA report shows that in 40 states, salaries failed to keep pace with inflation (p. 1).

For most teachers, however, the primary complaint about teaching isn't the money. When a survey conducted by The Center for the Future of Teaching and Learning (2007) looked at California teachers who leave low- and high-poverty schools, the reason cited most often was bureaucratic impediments and the second was the lack of district support. The third issue mentioned by people leaving the profession was low morale among teachers (p. 1). All of these issues seem to indicate that teachers perceive themselves to be facing the educational world without adequate support.

If there is low morale in teaching, it might be due to the fact that teachers bear the brunt of any problems in the educational system. There is a general feeling that teachers are ultimately responsible for the success and ills of the educational system. When people were surveyed by the Public Education Network (2003) about how they wanted education to change, the number one answer (27 percent) was *improve teacher quality* (p. 14).

Farkas, Johnson, and Foleno (2000) asked college students about the drawbacks of teaching, and the first two issues cited by respondents were related to personal safety (89 percent; p. 14), 78 percent cited low pay (p. 9), and a third issue that 76 percent of respondents agreed upon was that "Teachers today are often made the scapegoats for all the problems facing education"(p. 14). Thus, a college students' view of teaching was of a job that was under-compensated, dangerous, and that teachers are unfairly blamed for many societal ills.

If college students who've recently attended schools understand that teachers are scapegoats, they also understand the obstacles that teachers must deal with. Like many people, college students think that classroom issues (discipline) are foremost on teachers' minds, but the majority of teachers are more concerned about administrative processes of schools. They are also concerned with being the scapegoat for perceptions of underperformance by American students. The educator today is aware of a "top-down" management style that doesn't take teachers' opinions very seriously.

Many people are aware of the political influences on the schools, and it seems strange that legislators have gained so much influence in the education system. Though filled with good intentions, many legislative efforts have been detrimental to the educational process. Things that sound "good" when stated among other politicians don't work that well when translated into the school environment. Thus, a politician who promotes legislation for schools can do more harm than good. One such measure has been No Child Left Behind (NCLB).

Since it was introduced in 2002, NCLB has had a huge impact on the way schools operate. Like any test, it asks students to be evaluated in the subjects in their classes for the year. One of the burdens created by NCLB was the requirement for at least 95 percent of students in each minority "subgroup" to be tested in order for a school to pass. NCLB also requires improvement for students in each subgroup (blacks, whites, Asians, special education), and the idea is that all subgroups will be served by the educational process. Each subgroup needs to improve on the previous year's mark for a school to pass.

Not surprisingly, Rameriz (2007) reported that that 8 percent of all federally funded schools were failing NCLB standards. As pointed out in chapter two, it is easy to predict school district failure with demographic factors. True to form, most of the schools occur in "Low income, ethnic minority districts in California, Illinois, Michigan, New York, and Pennsylvania" (Rameriz, 2007, para. 2). This creates a situation where efforts at schools are directed to test improvement (program improvement).

The reason that NCLB doesn't work is that it creates more reporting requirements, but hasn't changed the product (lesson) being delivered in the classroom. Any evaluation of student performance should have the aim of improving student performance and using the data to improve the system itself. What can be gained from a test that students don't have to take seriously?

Suppose that your job evaluation was based on how seriously school kids decided to take a test. The students take tests that have no meaning to them; they have no personal incentive to do well and no detriment(s) from doing poorly. Yet, the tests are used as the yardsticks to measure school improvement. If politicians wanted to make the tests more relevant, they could. They could tie test scores into future events such as being eligible to get a license. They could link test scores to tax deductions for parents. A child that doesn't show improvement from the previous year wouldn't be considered a write-off for tax purposes, but politicians won't do that. It's much easier to focus on teachers.

Schools are forced by a political system to plan curriculum around tests that students take without any incentives (other than moral suasion). When the students do not show the requisite achievement levels, the ability of teachers is called into question.

There is a *popular* assumption that one of the problems with teachers is that many of them are unqualified and that the material is too difficult to teach. There are lots of articles that discuss the problem of someone teaching "outside" their field for a high school class. It was a major concern addressed by No Child Left Behind, but in 2000 when the fervor for NCLB was near a peak, the U.S. Department of Education statistics showed the following (Staffing Survey; U.S. Dept. of Ed., 2004; Table 3.1).

The issue of non-credentialed teachers received a lot of attention in NCLB. One of the cornerstones of the program was to make sure that every teacher in every class was a *subject specialist.* The implication is that having a degree or minor in a subject is necessary to teach a specific subject. Although it is good to have a degree in a particular area (math, science, English, history), once teaching skills have been developed, teachers can provide instruction in a new area.

Everyone knows of people who are effective while learning a new job. If low-skilled teachers were the problem, then one would expect that lower

Table 3.1.   OUT-OF-FIELD TEACHERS: Percentage of Public High School Students Taught Selected Subjects by Teachers without Certification or a Major in the Field They Teach, by Minority Concentration and School Poverty: 1999–2000

	Math	*Science*	*English*	*Social Studies*
Low minority	7	5	5	6
High minority	15	10	10	9
Low poverty	7	5	4	5
High poverty	14	16	12	8

Source: (U.S. Depart. of Education, 2000).
Note: Major refers to a teacher's primary fields of study for a bachelor's, master's, doctorate, first-professional, or education specialist degree. Major field can be an academic or education major. "High-minority" refers to schools in which 75 percent or more of their enrollments are minority students; "low-minority" refers to schools with a minority enrollment of less than 10 percent. "High-poverty" refers to a school in which 75 percent or more of students are eligible to participate in the federal free or reduced-price lunch program, a common proxy measure of poverty; "low-poverty" refers to schools in which less than 10 percent of students are eligible to participate in this program. See supplemental note 1 for more information on poverty.

scores in low income schools would correlate to teacher credentialing. It is certainly desirable for all teachers to be certified in the areas they teach, but lacking the proper credentials doesn't mean that a class will be poorly taught. The implication is that teachers' lack of knowledge is a large problem in the education system. The data really (U.S. Dept. of Ed., Table 24–1; 24–3, 2004) shows a 3 percent (social studies) to 11 percent (science) differential between credentialed and non-credentialed teachers in high versus low-poverty schools. The differences in test scores are much greater.

Knowledge of a subject is important for teachers; however, it is implied that having teachers with more knowledge will somehow fix the problems of the education system. The truth is that in most cases, effective teaching and learning is due to many factors. The reason that teacher improvement is singled out to improve schools is that it's perceived to be an easy fix. It's a way for an outsider to address the "problems" of the schools without addressing the system as a whole. When anyone thinks of education, the first symbol of the educational system is the teacher, and it is the generally the teacher who forms the connection between the school and parents.

A concerned parent placing their kid into a class at the beginning of the year understands the value of having a good teacher. Who can blame parents for wanting the best for their kids? What a teacher does in the classroom is a major determinate of student success. A teacher should have a certain level of competence to teach a class; however, a great algebra teacher may not be able to teach calculus and may not be certified to teach math. By the same token, a teacher who has passed a competency test in his or her field may be a poor teacher.

In most businesses, an administrator would be able to make personnel decisions based on performance or abilities. It is the local administrator's job to apply the best personnel to the task at hand. As previously mentioned, it is necessary to understand the problems of education to solve them. NCLB did not.

What will fix the problems of education? The answer isn't likely to come from piecemeal efforts of legislators. The last chapter showed that federal laws can dictate the actions of America's schools. Perhaps it's a good time to examine the current structure of education to look for ways to improve it. This chapter will examine the basis of law that dictate the intent of legislation, and examine the redundancy in the educational system. This chapter will show that the presence of multiple parties in the educational process is wasteful, and restructuring should be done to prevent waste and to ultimately improve the system.

This chapter was headed by a Chinese quotation that warned against excessive interference by government. The current chapter will show the various groups that meddle in the educational process. Their attempts to "fix" education actually waste resources and time that would be better spent on kids. As a teacher, one can see the game playing out between those in power, with little substantive change in the classroom.

The normal scapegoats of the educational bureaucracy are teachers and site administrators who are increasingly burdened by demands from the system that is supposed to help them. The following will examine the current structure of American education and the parties who oversee the process. The odds are, one could come up with a better system.

3.A. POWER FROM LAW?

The concept of public education is generally accepted as a necessary part of the country's political and social process. An education system is designed to create an educated electorate that will allow people to participate in a democracy. The framers of the Constitution (1791) make no mention of education, though the Tenth Amendment states:

> The powers not delegated to the United States by the constitution, nor prohibited by it to the States, are reserved to the States respectively, or to the people (Article 10).

This would imply that the states, if they decide to take on the burden, are responsible for setting up a proper educational system. There isn't direct reference to education in the Constitution (1791), and therefore government's prescribed role in education is to "promote the general Welfare" (Preamble) of the country. In a country founded on democracy, America has embraced the idea that educating its' citizens does serve to promote the general welfare of the country.

Aside from general welfare, the only mention of schools is Article X that describes powers left to the states. The amendment to the Constitution that reconfirms federalism and this leave the issue of education to state and local governments.

At the state level, most lawmakers have allowed for local control of schools, and at the local level, laws permit the creation of bureaucracies to administer the schools. Each one of the local schools districts creates its own laws, elects its own officials, and promotes its own interests. As a state that educates 10 percent of American children, California offers a good example of the bureaucracy that can channel resources away from the classroom. The state's Constitution and educational code will be briefly examined to show the good intent of lawmakers. Education legislation in California (and many other states) shows that too much of anything isn't always a good idea.

3.B. ORGANIZATION AND CHAIN OF COMMAND

The nation's most populous state has historically taken the issue of education seriously, and California's lawmakers have had success in its effort to create a superior public educational system. The state has created a higher education system that includes the University of California and California State University systems that are supported by a system of community colleges. There is also an expansive kindergarten through 12th-grade public-education system that was once one of the best school systems in the country. After property tax reform was passed by voters in 1978, the funding for schools has diminished, and California's school systems have suffered when measured against national standards.

An examination of American educational laws showed that California has more detail in its Education Code than most of the other states. Rather than creating a framework, the Assembly and Senate bodies in California have started to write laws that even cover curricular details in some subject areas.

One of the problems with this process is that *over-regulation* can be counterproductive. As businesses often point out, there is a cost associated in dealing with excessive regulation, and the same can be said in public education. When the burden of following the law interferes with the education process, it diminishes the process of education.

Like all states, California's state constitution covers the education of its citizenry (California Constitution, Art. IX). The intent of the Education Code, found in Article IX of the California Constitution, states:

SECTION 1. A general diffusion of knowledge and intelligence being essential to the preservation of the rights and liberties of the people, the Legislature shall encourage by all suitable means the promotion of intellectual, scientific, moral, and agricultural improvement. (California Constitution, Article IX).

It is interesting that California's Constitution recognizes the relationship between education (knowledge and intelligence) and democracy (rights and liberties), and two of the objectives promoted (scientific and agricultural) relate to the commercial success of individuals. It probably goes without saying that "agricultural improvement" has lost its impetus as one of the focal points of public education in spite of the large agribusiness presence in California.

The law does imply that the state intended the schools to promote vocational education in addition to promoting the ideals of a democracy. Since the property tax initiative (Prop 13) that cut educational funding, the state has gone away from promoting vocational classes in favor of a college preparatory curriculum.

The structure of California's education system is further discussed in Article IX, Section 9 of the Constitution:

The Legislature shall have power, by general law, to provide for the incorporation and organization of school districts, high school districts, and community college districts, of every kind and class, and may classify such districts.

The Legislature may authorize the governing boards of all school districts to initiate and carry on any programs, activities, or to otherwise act in any manner which is not in conflict with the laws and purposes for which school districts are established.

The SBE, by statute, is the governing and policy-determining body of the California Department of Education (CDE). Statute also assigns the SBE a variety of other responsibilities . . . (California Constitution).

Cunningham (2007) stated that California's constitution lays the groundwork for the formation of the State Board of Education and the California Department of Education. The control is vested with the governor, Assembly, and Senate that all influence the laws and the budget of the state's public schools. The school system is headed by the state superintendent who is aided by a State Board of Education, as well as the Department of Education. There is also a county superintendent of schools to head the 58 county school programs (p. 18). Within the counties are six types of school districts: 561 elementary school districts, 88 high school districts, 329 unified school districts, six districts for the California Youth Authority, three districts for state special schools, and nine state Board of Education charter schools (p. 8).

Oversight of both the California Department of Education and the State Board of Education is the State Superintendent for Public Instruction; the only elected non-partisan constitutional officer in California's government. The duties are summarized as follows:

> The Superintendent is the executive officer and secretary of the California State Board of Education and the director of the California Department of Education (CDE). The CDE administers California's public education system at the state level (p. 10).

The governor's budget for California (2007/08) shows 17 positions supported by the education secretary's office that total 2.2 billion in budgeted expenditures. The state's Department of Education employs over 2,500 people at a cost of over $38 million per annum (Gov. Budget, 2007). The K through 12 education budget in California takes up 31 percent of the total state budget ($45.4 billion) and is supplemented by over $21 billion in federal funds to cost in excess of $66 billion in 2007–08. That works out to about $10,500 in expenditures per student.

The governor's budget (2007–08) report describing expenditure per student in California showed that the state expended $10,649 per pupil in 2005–06. It amount was projected to be $11,541 per student for the 2007–08 school year (Governor's Budget, 2007–08). The reported expense per student for 2005–06 at the local (district) level was $7,521 per student. Even adjusted for inflation, more than a 20 percent discrepancy exists between funds available for education and funds getting to kids. One might be inclined to ask, "Where is the money going?"

In California, one could surmise that the funds are being used to build all the schools needed to cover recent population increases, but that isn't true since the majority of building funds come from issuing bonds (Facilities, 2007, para. 3). Thus, one can conclude that over 20 percent of the money is being siphoned off to sources that don't get to schools.

When this issue of "lost funds" is discussed, one argument suggested is that the funding for schools goes to administrative expenses. The money that reaches schools pays for the administrative expense of the district's administrators. The *real* administrators who work at schools with kids are thus already considered part of the local K-12 funding. What is the purpose of all of the administrative personnel who aren't working with kids?

As in many states, California's school districts take revenues from taxpayers and then redistributes them to schools. It takes a large bureaucracy to determine how funds should be distributed. However, if over 20 percent of monies spent for K-12 education are spent on off-site administration, is it a good system? One would wonder why there is a "middle man" that exists between funding and the schools that need it.

The question that one might ask in the current education system is, "Are there too many leaders?" Legal requirements for public schools begin with the federal government as evidenced by No Child Left Behind (NCLB). The government has the capacity to create laws that form the framework for states to follow, and the obvious role should be the Department of Education. The U.S. Department of Education has 4,500 employees and a $71 billion dollar budget that is dedicated to:

- establishing policies on federal financial aid for education and distributing as well as monitoring those funds
- collecting data on America's schools and disseminating research
- focusing national attention on key educational issues
- prohibiting discrimination and ensuring equal access to education

Federal data show that elementary and secondary education expenses were $584 billion for the 2006–07 fiscal year (Dept. of Education, 2007, p. 1). Federal expenditures comprise only 8.9 percent of the total (Appendix. 3), but schools systems must comply with Federal regulations to obtain funding (Table 3.2).

As discussed previously, the U.S. Constitution gives local governments the authority to set up systems for the general welfare of its citizens. With regard to education, each state can dictate how educational organizations can be set up and how they are funded. Thus, the state creates the primary level of bureaucracy, but must kowtow to the federal government's wishes if it wants the funding. A good part of each state's education bureaucracy is devoted to applying for and satisfying the requirements for the federal government's program.

Table 3.2.   Total Expenditures for Elementary and Secondary Education in U.S.

| | *(Dollars in Billions)* | | | |
| | 2005–2006 | | 2006–2007 | |
Source of Funds	*Dollars*	*Percent (%)*	*Dollars*	*Percent (%)*
Federal	$50	8.9	$52.0	8.9
State	241.0	43.2	253.0	43.4
Local	213.0	38.1	223.3	38.2
All Other	55.0	9.8	57.0	9.8

Source: United States Dept. of Education (2007). "Total Expenditures for Elementary and Secondary Education in the U.S., Fiscal Year 2007 Budget Summary."

The $50 billion in federal monies distributed for the 2005–06 school year was apportioned to 48 million students—a little over $1,000 per student. This is money that is collected by the federal government and then returned to the states. How much of the money is going to people whose job it is to apply for the money, redistribute it, and then account for it? This is an increasingly important issue since lawmakers increasingly tie funds to outlays, thereby creating more oversight.

Since the budgetary structure of the California Department of Education is taking over 20 percent of the education budget, 20 percent of the funds are being siphoned off before the money ever returns to the schools. Every person processing funds or making sure that districts comply with federal regulations is a person that costs taxpayers money and takes money from schools. And consider that the levels of bureaucracy and waste are repeated to some extent at the state and local (district) levels. This is a situation that has been created by legislators and, unfortunately, they're the ones who have to fix it.

3.C. THE NUTS AND STRIPPED BOLTS OF STATE LEGISLATION

Most of the funding for education is collected at the state and local levels. Would it surprise anyone to find that legislators try to influence the education system by channeling funds to meet objectives they support? With a prescribed percentage of California's K-14 budget slated for education by "The Classroom Instruction and Accountability Act" (1988), and with two large university systems to support, 50 percent of California's budget is devoted to education. With so much of California's funding devoted to education, it's easy to understand why legislators have turned their attention to the state's education code.

The purpose of California's lawmakers is to ensure that the present and future needs of the state are met. Each law that is passed should be based on need and will create a mandate for action. An example is found in a law that targets underachieving schools that need extra help. The following California law, "Instructional Materials," fits the requirement. Was it necessary to write the following law §52055.6 into the California Education Code with regard to funding schools?

> 52055.600. (a) The High Priority Schools Grant Program is hereby established. Participation in this program is voluntary. (b) From funds made available

for purposes of this article, the Superintendent shall allocate a total of four hundred dollars ($400) per pupil to schools meeting eligibility requirements pursuant to Section 52055.605, for implementation of a school action plan approved pursuant to this article, in accordance with all of the following: (1) In the first year of participation, a total of fifty thousand dollars ($50,000) for planning purposes. (2) In each subsequent year of participation, a total of four hundred dollars ($400) per pupil, or a total of twenty-five thousand dollars ($25,000), whichever amount is greater (Classroom Instuction Act, 1988).

Frankly, here is a situation where a program is set up so that underperforming schools can be addressed. Does it apply to all underperforming schools? No, it just applies to the ones who make the effort to apply for the money. If you have an administrator who doesn't know about the program or decides not to apply, it means that each student in the program will lose $400 per student of additional resources. These are schools that scored in the bottom of the state standardized tests. If the schools are slated for improvement, why is there a need to apply for funds?

In their accountability for the High Accountability Grant Program, in order to get funds, the school must submit a "school action plan." Here is another point where one has to be baffled by the logic of the situation. In essence, one is asking the school that has failed to submit an idea for the best way to spend the money.

Shouldn't the "authority" in this case be the state Department of Education? Since the school isn't performing well, so shouldn't the state mandate the school to use specific methods to improve the results? Should the Department of Education ask for a plan in exchange for money, or should the state be dictating a course of action? If you were running a business and you knew how to make things better, you'd prescribe a solution. What does this tell you about the state of education?

In this instance, the legislature of California has approved a law for low-performing schools. They've created an application process, and this means that the law has increased the administrative expenses of the government. Rather than telling the failing school what they must do to receive funding, the school prepares a proposal to apply for the funds. A school that fails to apply for the funds will not receive funding, thereby depriving its students of an educational opportunity.

Do the legislators really understand what they're doing to the system? Apparently they do. The pending legislation in California has a Web site (http://www.leginfo.ca.gov) that allows one to search for proposed legislation. Typing "education" into the online search engine produced 907 hits, which means there are 907 pieces of proposed legislation with the word "education" in the title. There were 228 bills with "high school" in the title. Some of the titles included:

AB 128: Violence Mitigation Pilot Programs
AB 173: Pupils: academic support program: dropouts
AB 150: California Financial Literacy Initiative
AB 347: Pupils: high school exit examination: intensive instruction and
    services
AB 466: Pupils: average daily attendance

Of course, there are plenty of other bills (223) to examine. They cover everything from counseling, how to count attendance, professional development for teachers, facilities funding, charter schools, compulsory school attendance, steroid testing, graduation requirements, supplemental instruction, a number of career technical proposals, and proposals regarding special education programs.

The foregoing bills are but a few of the proposals for educational change. This tells one that the legislature is very active in the education process. Each one of these legal proposals will create paperwork for someone in an office to fill out, and the people administering the program will not be teaching. Not only does each law tend to create more administrative expenses, they also insure that funding must be spent the way the legislature dictates. This gives school site administrators less discretion on how to allocate resources to solve problems.

With the passage of each law, there tends to be more paperwork, more administration, and less freedom for schools and districts to act independently. With so many bills proposed, and so many already in the system, the amount of waste in the system is tremendous.

For those residing in other states, it isn't just those crazy Californian legislators writing education law—other states seem to be doing the same thing. An informal search of pending laws (Assembly and Senate Bills) in several states showed a lot of effort directed toward education. Thus, it isn't an isolated phenomenon for legislators to be attempting to direct the course of the educational system (Table 3.3).

The current discussion is not based on demonizing the legislators of any state. Their intentions are good, but what are they actually accomplishing? The intent of the education system is to create a system so that curriculum can be effectively introduced to the student. That occurs in a classroom. To improve education, the primary focus is at the point of attack, and that is where information is delivered to students.

Table 3.3   Education Bills Pending

State	Search Term	Number of Bills Found
Minnesota	"K-12" in text	159 Bills in House; 194 Senate Bills
Arizona	"K-12"; "Education" in text.	118 Bills
Missouri	"K-12" education	286 documents
Vermont	Bills with "Education" in text.	98 documents.
North Carolina	K-12	342 Documents for House
	Education	Senate – 276 Documents
New York	Education	869 Bills

See References Under Legislative Education Search (2007) for sites and dates of inquiries.

It takes effort to write laws and even more to champion them through the legislature. Obviously, people want to improve education, and legislators are trying new ways to help. However, there is a sense that the system is groping in darkness, trying to find a light switch. Until someone finds the switch, politicians in every state are rolling the legislative dice looking for answers. Our nation's students deserve better.

As each state writes law and tinkers with the education process, the federal government also decided to impose its will on the process. The passage of No Child Left Behind (NCLB) added more legislation and more reporting requirements to the state. Most states have complained that the reporting requirements of NCLB are burdensome and about "unfunded mandates." Though the states cannot tell one how much *their* laws cost the education system, they're quite precise about NCLB's costs.

In a study of the costs of implementing NCLB, Mathis (2005) showed that the law adds 0.9 percent to total education spending and leads to an increase of between 2 and 2.5 percent in administrative costs due to the law. The federal government supplied 4.6 billion in new funds to cover the costs. However, the article asserts that NCLB costs $11.3 billion to implement (based on a 2.25 percent estimated increase in costs due to the law). The author of the study claims that creating a "standards based curriculum" throughout the United States would require $140 billion, or an increase to the education budget of 29 percent (p. 1).

When the federal government puts a law into place, the states cry about "unfunded mandates." However, having examined the large number of laws that are being proposed by state legislators, one would have to believe that they would also burden the states in a manner similar to NCLB. Mathis et al. examined NCLB's history after five years and said that the law has 588 mandates for action and the authors suggest that would require $155 billion (27 percent) in additional funding in order to create equal opportunity. Amazingly, the authors state the following:

The largest cost, however, is in the design and implementation of instructional
and support programs to assure that every child passes state standards regardless
of handicap, social circumstances or economic deprivation.

Is the author claiming that prior to NCLB the states weren't designing
and implementing "instructional and support programs to assure that every
child passes state standards. . . ."? One would assume that states were always
interested in children meeting some guideline. NCLB doesn't exactly make
anyone do anything differently in the classroom. It is primarily a management
exercise. History, English, mathematics, and other subjects do not change
very much. A top-down edict like NCLB that details an accountability system
hasn't changed the subjects either.

School districts have to follow the laws of both the federal and the state
government. How much of a school district's time is spent trying to meet the
needs of "upper management" at the state and federal levels? Any teacher
will tell you that the current system spends a significant amount of time
focusing on a "top-down" education system to meet legal requirements
imposed by governments.

To begin this chapter, the status of teacher satisfaction was examined and
the primary complaints were bureaucratic impediments and lack of district
support. Given the structure of the educational system, it isn't surprising that
districts have little time to listen to their teachers. There's also little doubt
that costs associated with meeting stringent legal requirements are a burden
on public schools.

This would represent a perfect time for free market advocates to say that
government is the problem. The problem isn't merely related to the government,
it is a lack of formalized practices. The intervention of random and excessive
legislation into the education system increases both its inefficiency and cost.
The education system needs to be streamlined so that students are served more
effectively. Though the current system is clearly trying to find an answer, the
answers will come from classrooms, not staterooms. Yet, this doesn't necessarily mean that the private sector would work better for schools. Unfortunately,
for the service sector, there isn't a lot of good data on the public versus private
argument, but studies of utility companies do show interesting results.

Kwoka (2002) conducted a study of public and private utilities and found
far lower electricity generating costs for private utilities. The author hypoth-
esized that higher rates for private utilities were due to increased regulatory
requirements (p. 278). Kwoka (2005) also found that public utilities have
advantages in the *retail distribution* of power (p 22).

Though the analysis of power generation and education are very different,
the argument that public schools are less cost efficient could be caused by

standards or legislation that creates higher costs to public schools. Likewise, the public school must serve all populations of students (Griffith, 2008), whereas private schools can refuse to serve certain populations (special education and special needs), which is a factor that can also lead to higher costs to public schools (para. 1).

It's evident that public education could benefit by streamlining the processes to administer schools. The legislature should recognize that the need for education is to optimize the system, but it must first understand that legislation is part of the public education problem.

This is particularly true when the legislature decides to present a bill that creates change at the classroom level. An example is imposing algebra as a high school graduation requirement.

RAISING THE STANDARDS: THE CASE OF ALGEBRA

When examining the debilitating effects of legislation on schools, one can look at the addition of algebra as a graduation requirement in California's schools. The idea was started in 1999 when the Board of Education decided that the California High School Exit Exam would include algebra concepts. In response, former State Senator Poochigian (2008) decided that it would be good for all students to take an algebra class prior to graduating. Therefore, he sponsored legislation calling for an algebra requirement for each child (Poochigian, 2008, para. 8).

To justify the inclusion of an algebra requirement in California's curriculum required an interesting leap of logic. The purpose of the state's exit examination is to see if the sum total of a student's mathematical knowledge is sufficient. It isn't meant to measure knowledge in a particular course. Legislators in California were convinced to approve algebra as a graduation requirement, according to California's Department of Education in "Questions and Answers" (2005–06), because of the algebra requirement on the state exit examination. To graduate, students must pass the California High School Exit Examination (CAHSEE) covering the following materials:

> The mathematics part of the CAHSEE addresses state mathematics content standards through the first part of Algebra. It includes statistics, data analysis and probability, number sense, measurement and geometry, algebra and functions, mathematical reasoning, and Algebra I. Students must demonstrate computational skills and a foundation in arithmetic, including working with decimals, fractions, and percentages. The math part of the exam is composed entirely of multiple-choice questions (Calif. Dept. of Ed., 2005–06, p. 1).

As one may note, the CAHSEE or exit examination covers math content through the first part of algebra, therefore, one of the reasons for placing the *Algebra Requirement* (2001) into the California Education Code was certainly a stretch. The language of the regulation is included so that one can admire the handiwork of California's legislators.

> 51224.5. (a) The adopted course of study for grades 7 to 12, inclusive, shall include algebra as part of the mathematics area of study pursuant to subdivision (f) of Section 51220. (b) Commencing with the 2003-04 school year and each year thereafter, at least one course, or a combination of the two courses, in mathematics required to be completed pursuant to subparagraph (B) of paragraph (1) of subdivision (a) of Section 51225.3 by pupils while in grades 9 to 12, inclusive, prior to receiving a diploma of graduation from high school, shall meet or exceed the rigor of the content standards for Algebra I, as adopted by the State Board of Education pursuant to Section 60605 (Cal. Ed. Code, 51224.5).

This lovely bit of poetry, enacted as California Education Code §51224.5, could be interpreted to say that high school students must take and earn passing scores in a year of instruction in a good algebra course to get a diploma.

Does this fit into California's constitutional requirement? Is an algebra course somehow included as part of the "general diffusion of knowledge" that is "essential to the rights and liberties of the people"? This is indicative of the movement of standards toward those that will meet college entrance requirements. The legislators have deemed that a college education is the best course of action for students, but what about those who don't intend to go on to college? Is the state doing the best job of preparing all students for life?

When the legislative system decides to pass a law that affects the system is there any recognition of what affect it will have on the people served? There is no doubt that algebra teaches some wonderful reasoning skills, but should a rigorous algebra course serve as a barrier to graduation? There are signs at high schools that tell students that those who earn a diploma will earn a graduate $200,000 more over a lifetime than a dropout. If algebra is a barrier to better life for some people, what is the justification for the requirement?

Does a person whose education terminates with high school need algebra to succeed in life? There are many people who face life without a diploma due to the algebra requirement. A law requiring algebra places the school in the position of creating dropouts or non-graduates, or offering a watered down algebra course. Neither option fulfills the school systems' obligation to either the law or the student. The state legislators in many states have implemented an algebra requirement for high school graduation.

Is there any evidence that students that take and complete algebra will be better citizens or better prepared for life? More importantly, if the student doesn't complete a rigorous algebra class, should such a student be designated a "drop out" and face the economic and psychological pressure of lacking a diploma because they lack talent in math?

Legislators have seen factory jobs disappear along with other middle-income jobs that support families without a college education. Since the United States has become a country based on "intellectual capital," the argument for more rigorous education is appealing to state legislators. What legislator wants to be thought of as "soft" on education? It is easy to vote for tougher graduation requirements, and frankly, wouldn't a vote against tougher academic standards make a legislator look "weak" on education. Of course it would.

The problem is that legislators will be voting to produce standards for a world that doesn't exist. Many high school students will never attend a four-year college, much less graduate. Shouldn't the student who doesn't intend to go on to a four-year college gain more from a K-12 education? Don't they deserve training that will allow them to get jobs?

California's high schools have moved toward a college preparatory curriculum at the expense of programs designed to promote vocational skills. It is well and good to create legislation that guides students toward a college education, but the percentage of California's students eligible to attend a four-year public university upon graduation is 33.7 percent. This data, for 2003–04, shows the percentage of high school graduates who have taken the classes necessary for entry to the state university system (University of California or California State University systems). In the 2003–04 year, the schools received an average of $6,887 per student to educate its students.

For thirteen years in the K-12 setting, schools are training students and using a considerable number of resources to do so. If the goal of the schools is for college preparation, is the public school system serving its mission to the general public if it offers little to non-college-bound students?

Recalling that the purpose of public education is to promote the general welfare, it would seem that gearing resources toward the college bound (minority) isn't doing the job. As hard-working, free-market advocates, one can assume that the framers of the United States Constitution weren't preparing people to be on welfare. Education should prepare people for the future. An examination of California's 2004 graduating class included 375,000 high school graduates, 91 percent of which graduated from public schools. Of high school graduates in California, 26,333 enrolled at the University of California (24,196 full time), 38,877 enrolled at the California State University (37,018 full time), and 120,322 enrolled in the California Community Colleges (60,242 full time).

The total population served by California's colleges is 185,532, which means that 49.3 percent of California's 2004 graduates were served by public colleges. The education system channels its resources toward preparing people for college, and the community colleges have picked up the slack for a lot of vocational training. However, for the large population of students who do not pursue college, how will they be trained?

What is the incentive for students who do not want to pursue a college education to attend school? If not given a proper incentive, or a means to gain admission to college, aren't they likely to lose interest in school, become disruptive, and finally, fall from the ranks? When students realize that they are not college-grade material and that education does not offer them a direct means of advancement, they begin to quit. Lacking motivation to continue their education, many become a disruptive (and disinterested) part of the education process, thus increasing the disorder (entropy) of the education system. There should be purpose to the public education for all who attend.

Of course, aligning the purpose of our schools with the needs of society is the role of legislators. If they create a system that meets kids' needs, many of the incentive problems can be solved. Those are problems at the state level, but our education systems are also overseen at the local level. We have county and district systems and people appointed to oversee the processes. Are our local school board members astute enough to oversee the process?

3.D. THE MYTH OF LOCAL EDUCATIONAL CONTROL

The United States was founded on the belief that local control was an important part of the political process. The nation's constitution gives each state the power to create legislative units that will take care of items that are important to the welfare of the people. Each state has laws that allows for local jurisdiction to form a local educational agency and to hold elections for people to represent the beliefs of the district. As an elected body, the local board of education has oversight control over the local school district and can also serve as a sounding board for community concerns.

The role of the school board is to serve as an oversight committee to run a local school system. The board is elected by the community and it hires the manager of the schools (superintendent) and provides an avenue for community involvement to occur. The superintendent has the job of organizing resources and implementing a program to meet the needs of federal, state, and local governments. The superintendent will hire people that will help create an educational environment that promotes learning by making maximal use of resources available.

How many school boards and superintendents are there? A search in the federal Common Core of Data (2005–06) showed that the state of Texas has 1,265 school boards, California has 1131, New York has 813, and Vermont has 360 (search engine/district search). In all, there are over 14,000 school boards across the United States. Each of the school boards is required to implement a set of laws that has been developed at the federal, state, and local level. A superintendent exerts a great deal of time and energy trying to come up with a plan to run a school system given the resources at his or her disposal. The idea behind school boards is that it gives the local citizenry the opportunity to have some control over the education that children receive. Each of the school boards runs a school district, and each district is responsible for coming up with curriculum to run the schools.

The importance of school boards is to allow for community control of schools. As described by the Arkansas School Board Association (2006), a description of the primary roles of a school board in the local school organization includes:

• establishing the organization's goals
• determining major policies and operations
• establishing the general organizational structure
• appraising the performance of the CEO, which in school districts is the superintendent (p. 14)

The primary idea behind a school board is an organization to give local control to the school systems. With NCLB and state policies predominating, one must ask whether a local school board has much real power. If the organization's goals, policies, and structure are already in place, its final role is appraising the CEO or superintendent.

As laws increasingly move authority to the state and federal levels, one must wonder if local part-time board members have the ability or the knowledge necessary to provide the oversight function entrusted to them. Without skills or knowledge, can local control of education be effective?

3.D.1. Instructional Materials (There's Trouble in River City)

In California, the state chooses the learning materials that the school district are allowed to purchase (approved materials), and the use of any materials that do not meet the state Department of Education's (DOE) guidelines will violate the law. In a way, the DOE does districts a favor since it eliminates some of the vendors from consideration. At the district level, the process of picking new textbooks and other instructional materials is left to committees of teachers that choose from the state's choices.

With over 14,000 school districts choosing curriculum, and many eager vendors looking to sell materials, is it any wonder that mistakes will be made on occasion? One of the mistakes that was reported by Laney (2005) involved the Chicago suburb of Wilmette, which evaluated math and reading programs used in the district:

> According to these parents—all educated people, some former teachers, some with graduate degrees from the University of Chicago—the schools in Wilmette District 39 have been testing worse each year since 2000. I checked the Illinois Interactive Report Card site and the graph there shows the Wilmette parents are right. The ISAT Standardized Test Scores show a downward trend each year since 2000. The parents blame the school board for the slump and for the curriculum they have for math and reading.
>
> Math is taught by "The Trailblazers Math Program." Reading is taught predominantly by "Whole Language" rather than by traditional systematic phonics. While "Hooked on Phonics" claims great success in tutoring students on how to read, Wilmette schools don't teach that way (Laney, 2005).

Thus, it seems that the parents believe the curriculum selected for Wilmette was substandard, and the locals were going to exercise their power to get rid of the board.

Here's a situation where the school board approved the new instructional materials, but probably had no knowledge of their efficacy in the classroom. The call for a new board could bring in a new administrator who could then select and buy new learning materials, and the district could then see if results were improved. In the meantime, the students have lost because the schools were playing curriculum roulette.

It is a situation where materials should be evaluated by an independent outside agency, the Department of Education's role in the education process should be to test curriculum, lessons, and materials for effectiveness. We have government agencies looking at the safety of consumer products, the safety of pharmaceutical products (FDA), and the fate of chemicals in the environment (EPA). Why doesn't the Department of Education evaluate curriculum using an independent testing model to determine its relative worth? If it were to set up a laboratory system in the classroom to monitor and show the effectiveness of educational products, perhaps the following scenario could be avoided.

This process of selecting new books occurs when a school organization brings in or invites several publishers to come by and showcase their products. The publisher will respond by sending their best salesman to sell their product to a district. Is there really a yardstick to measure the effectiveness of a product that no one has used? Of course, each publisher will have done "tests" and they will claim that their product can produce prodigies if used correctly. They'll probably even have data that supports their contention. I don't mean to draw parallels, but Meredith Wilson's (1957) musical *The Music Man* is a good example of how academic programs are marketed and chosen. It is also an example where the free-market approach can fail unless there are ways to verify statements made by a publisher's salesman.

In *The Music Man,* a traveling salesman named Harold Hill visits a small Iowa town called River City and sells the locals on the necessity of buying a new, revolutionary music program that will transform their kids into more successful individuals. The same sales pitch used in *The Music Man* is given to school systems all over the United States, and in most cases, the representatives for a company will say that their products are "best." The salesmen will present and give their products to a committee of teachers to evaluate, and the teachers will look at the materials and try to guess whether they will work. The teachers will make a recommendation, parents will have an opportunity to look at the materials (public display period), and finally the district will make a decision to buy or pass on a particular product. Given the fact that the teachers will not have actually used the product they are buying, are their recommendations really valid?

The United States has a system of education that is predicated on having lots of Harold Hills who work for educational publishers selling products to school districts. The question is why? Is it to promote competition? Is the idea to generate innovation in curriculum design? The answer is "No." The purpose of having sales representatives visit school districts is to sell a product. With the budgetary constraints of today's school district, when school districts choose a product, the teachers will use it for several years before having the opportunity to get new materials.

3.D.2. Community Evaluations of Schools and Districts

The voice of the community in school-related matters is the school board. They have the responsibility for hiring managers to oversee the operation of the local school system. The population of a school system is supposed to elect people, but what criteria do they use?

The education of the local population is one of the most expensive and important items that a community undertakes. The function of the school board is to represent the will of the people in the education process. The problem with this approach is that the management function entails both oversight and direction of the operation of a system.

The board of directors of a company is supposed to oversee existing operations and to see whether management is steering the company in the right direction for the future. With regard to schools, the school board is supposed to engage in similar pursuits. The first order of business is to make sure that the school system is being run properly. The second order of business is to insure that the future needs of the district are being met. This entails both an economic and scholastic examination of the district. The financial matters will examine how funds are used to serve the school system. So, in a Jeffersonian democracy that values the voice of the people, the public should have a fair way to assess how well their school system is doing or there will be no way to judge their effectiveness.

People in companies should be elected to their position based on the skills and experience they bring to the position. It should be the same for the school board.

In the United States, most people vote for school boards based on issues that are unrelated to the overall function of the school. People use the public schools as a means to interject issues of race, religion, and ideological causes, but rarely look at the management issue in education. Thus, people do not examine the performance of their schools and school district when they vote, as much as they vote for the ideology supported by a person running for the school board.

Religious ideas have long fought for inclusion in the classroom. One religious-based issue that faces schools has been the teaching of "intelligent design" in the classrooms. Intelligent design is the idea that the world is put together in such a complex matter that it could not occur without forethought. Thus, it accepts the idea that a creator (God) has designed the world. The intelligent design issue, like school prayer, is an issue that resonates with people who want religion taught in the school.

There is ample evidence that the process of evolution is occurring; however, there is no evidence that it is being guided by a supreme being. To be fair, there's no evidence that evolution isn't guided by a supreme being either. However, modern science feels that putting God into the biology curriculum is a bad idea. Should the local school board have the right to impose an unproven or unsound curriculum into a school system? An example of issues that get people interested in school boards was reported by Raffaele (2005) in a debate going on in Kansas:

> We would have no interest this year if not for the intelligent-design issue. It is the overriding concern," said school board president Sheila Harkins (para. 10).
>   The school board has defended the intelligent-design mandate, saying it merely wants students to know about holes in Charles Darwin's theory. In a

recent newspaper campaign ad, the incumbents included the policy in their list of accomplishments over the past three years (para. 11).

The first words from the school board president tell more than the rest of the article. "We would have no interest this year . . . ," Ms. Harkins declared. Perhaps the fact that there is no interest is more important than the issue of intelligent design. Is it true that the people of the community have no interest in how the schools are doing?

The real issue should be how well students are prepared for uncertain futures. How will the student survive in the dog-eat-dog Darwinian world? How fit are the kids for the world they'll enter? The truth is that for most school systems, general test scores are given out to the public, but unless there is a controversial issue, most people in the community do not follow school performance very closely.

What about the performance of school boards with regard to "normal" issues? Tobin (2006) reported that the city of Tampa is faced with many problems with their schools. As such, the people look to the school board to rectify the discrepancies:

It also faces some weighty decisions that could affect the district for another generation. They include:

- How to proceed after 2007, when the district's legal obligation to maintain racial balances in schools expires. Will Pinellas continue to emphasize integration or will it edge toward a system that favors neighborhood schools? A citizens task force is working on the issue and will report to the School Board.
- How to downsize a system faced with chronic budget problems. The district plans to cut nearly $20-million this year to meet expenses and restore depleted reserves.
- How to address the achievement gap between white and black students in the face of two class-action suits that claim the district has not properly educated black kids.
- How to direct and work with superintendent Clayton Wilcox, who has brought major changes to the district since the board hired him in 2004 (Tobin, 2006, p. 1).

Although an issue such as intelligent design tends to grab peoples' attention, the day-to-day issues facing a district are even more daunting. The article points out many of the problems facing public schools including budgetary shortfalls, inequity in education to specific groups, and local control of schools.

As the article states, the Pinellas County School Board, which includes Tampa Bay and St. Petersburg, is dealing with issues of race and inequity in educational opportunity for black students. The issues involved in trying to solve such problems include: logistics, legal, financial, and issues pertaining to the curriculum. When the prospective board members were interviewed, what were their qualifications for the position?

> xxxx seeking her fifth term, is the board's senior member. She said her values are "fairness, equality and respect.
>
> xxxx said she will emphasize her community experience as an active mother in the 1980s, from PTA leadership to district committees that worked on student discipline and maintenance issues. In the 1990s, she called on every school as a representative for an encyclopedia publisher. Between that and substitute teaching, she said, "I've seen this district from one end to the other.
>
> Among the catalysts for xxxx's campaign was the district's 2003 decision to move away from Apple Macintosh computers to Windows-based personal computers. "That made me start thinking about how policy is set, how decisions are made," she said (p. 1).

Given this information, do these people sound like they're ready to oversee a crisis on the Pinaellas County School Board? The Pinaellas County Schools (2005) operates over 140 schools and serves 148,000 pre-school through adult public school students and is the 22nd largest school system in the United States. The 2005–06 budget was over $1.2 billion dollars (p. 1). Honestly, one applauds anyone who runs for public office in the United States, but the function of a school board member is to represent and oversee all functions pertaining to the local school district. This includes budget, planning, curriculum, and policy issues.

If the present system is maintained so that local communities maintain power, the communities need more information about school policies and budgets so that they can make informed decisions. With so many administrative duties on their plate, can school boards be expected to provide oversight to instructional processes as well?

3.D.3. Evaluating the Effectiveness of a District

To examine the quality of education in a school district, one must look at how well students do in the schools and assess how well managers are using available resources (money). As a parent, the best way to see if one school does better than another is through the use of standardized test scores. Is there an overall scorecard to determine how one school does when compared to other schools?

There are comparisons of schools based on test scores, but there isn't a card that tells whether music and art are emphasized in a school. Also, there isn't a comparative grading of facilities that are used to educate students.

For instance, the playground equipment of an elementary school should be evaluated against a standard to show a parent how a school stands up against others. As a parent and taxpayer, you hope that the district you live in does a good job with your tax dollars, but the truth is that the information given to parents in the form of standardized test scores is not enough to make a valid decision about a student's school.

If examining the school district's performance, other than test scores, what does one look at? Do you rely on "word-of-mouth" to investigate a school? One can physically visit a school, but unless all the schools are visited, how can one make a comparison.

If information about schools is difficult to gather, how about district performance? California, a city of roughly 280,000 people. Riverside is a "unified" school district, and this means that the governance of all K-12 education is covered by one agency. How might one determine whether this district is doing a good job? The most obvious factor to examine would be achievement scores from individual schools. This is the basis on which academic performance is based. From the state Web site showing academic statistics, the average Academic Performance Index (API) "base" score for a child in the public schools in California is 709.

As a parent, what does an API score of 709 mean? Does an API score of 709 indicate relative success? For that matter, if a parent is looking to put their kid into a school because of its API score, what can one gather from a school's results?

If you come from out of state, how does the score of a California school compare to schools in Illinois (or any other state)? Does it serve the purposes of education to have a multitude of scoring systems all trying to assess student performance? For those saying "yes," I wonder what the rationale would be.

In the United States we tend to bring the legal process into every possible situation. In many cases there is agreement across state lines. I may not know whether a right turn is legal when I drive into a new state, but I can still read the speed limit signs. Education needs to standardize how it reports data across the United States. There's no reason this shouldn't or couldn't be done and many reasons why it should be. From the standpoint of education, is algebra different when it crosses state boundaries? Does history change? Do scientific laws get altered across state boundaries? The answer to all of these questions is a resounding "no."

If I decided to move to Kidney Stone, Kentucky, and wanted to know how the schools are, as a consumer I should be able to look at a simple chart that tells me how the school compares to others in the nation. What are the chances of a student who goes through the school being either college or prison bound? These are things that consumers and voters need to know.

A second parameter to judge the efficiency of the district is spending per student. In the year 2002–03, the federal government's Department of Education reported financial results from each school district. The database allows one to perform searches that will permit one to compare financial parameters from various districts. Using this tool, there was one disturbing result from the Riverside Unified School District (Public School District Finance Peer Search, 2004).

In the year 2002–03, RUSD spent $36 million on administrative expenses out of a total of $268 million of current educational expenditures and $313 million of total expenditures. The percentage of administrative costs for all surrounding districts (30-mile radius) when measured against total expenditures for the year was 9.99 percent on average. The highest percentage of administrative expense was attributed to RUSD at 11.51 percent. This was 1.5 percent higher than the average administrative expense reported by surrounding districts and means that $3.7 million of the funds were paid toward administrative spending for RUSD over the "average." This leads one to ask, "Is this a significant amount?"

The fact that in 2002-03 RUSD spent 1.5 percent more of its budget on administrative expenses than surrounding districts was a bit troubling. As a per student measure, it means that RUSD was spending $881 per student on administrative expenses, while the average for surrounding districts was $783 per student. This means that nearly $100 of resources for each child in RUSD was being used to support administrators. What does that mean for a mid-sized Riverside school (800 students) the size of Alcott elementary? That $80,000 could have been used to support student services. For the principals at most schools, finding an extra $80,000 in a budget would be a godsend.

At Alcott Elementary, the ability to use these administrative expenses would allow the school to buy 40 computers at $2,000 each. Perhaps it could have represented two field trips for each student at the school, but instead was used for off-site administration. If one applies the 2002–03 figures for RUSD to the high school level, for a school of 2500 it would represent the loss of a quarter-million dollars of funding that was lost to the school site.

This issue was never discussed in the local paper. It was never discussed at all. It was never discussed by members of the school board in the Minutes of their meetings. Yet, it represents quite a bit of money that was being channeled to administrative expenses and away from students. RUSD's management team may have had legitimate reasons for its excessive administrative expense relative to surrounding districts. Even if one assumes that the expenses were justified, they were never reported in the local paper. How can citizens make decisions about how local schools are run without information? The real issue is developing uniform ways to report and evaluate information about districts should give greater transparency to communities about where education funding is being spent. This type of information is needed for voters to evaluate the people running school districts.

It is obvious that districts need to publish their financial results in a way that allows a community access to the information. For communities to remain involved in the education system, the schools should develop standards for reporting information that are useful, universal, and easy to understand. Every school should have figures that delineate the amount spent for various categories. The voters must also know what they're getting for their money.

3.E. VOCATIONAL EDUCATION

Article IX of the California Constitution (1849) describes the intent of the state's education system as a way to promote "intellectual, scientific, moral, and agricultural improvement" (Section 1). Most of us recognize that the "agricultural" improvement is based on the economic needs of California. Thus, the framers of California's Constitution were quite aware of the role that vocational education plays in the economy. The relationship between good workers and a productive economy has always been apparent.

What is less apparent is the value that vocational programs have to K-12 education. Prior to 1978, California schools supported a wide variety of vocational programs. When the state's voters passed a tax reformation law, it dramatically changed the income available for California's K-12 education system. The loss of tax revenue in California due to Proposition 13 (property tax initiative passed by voters) drastically reduced the level of economic support districts receive. Thus, legislators were forced to make changes in the system of education. They chose to eliminate the expensive vocational programs from K-12 programs and began focusing on college preparatory curriculum in the schools.

Over the years, the state has trimmed its budget by limiting the number of vocational programs in its public schools. After years of neglect, Governor Arnold Schwazenegger is supporting the reformation of vocational programs in California's schools (Office of the Governor, 2005, p. 1). The reason that vocational education is brought up is because it is an area that is important to the many students who do not have college aspirations when they attend high school.

The reason that legislators feel good about moving the public education system toward a college preparation curriculum is based on the economics of future earnings. Using Census Bureau data (Table 3.4), it is easy for an educator to show the importance of education. Students are often shown some form of the following chart that shows that people with more education earn more and are unemployed less. Does this mean that the public school system should only try to teach to the university level student?

Table 3.4. Education Level, Unemployment Rates and Median Salaries.

Education Level	Unemployment Rate (2003)	Median Salary (2002)
Less than high school	8.4	22,584
High school graduate	5.5	29,800
Some college, no degree	5.2	35,505
Associate degree	4.0	36,784
Bachelor's	3.3	48,896
Master's	2.9	56,294
Doctorate	2.1	77,216
Professional	1.7	85,921

Source: (U.S. Bureau of Labor Statistics, 2004).
Note: Earnings for year-round full-time workers 25 years and over; unemployment rate for those 25 and over.

Obviously, it would be nice if everyone had a college education, but not everyone is cut out to go to college. If high schools have cut vocational training, who will train the non-college bound student? Equally important is how to motivate non-college bound students in a system that doesn't meet their needs?

Who Is the School System Trying to Serve?

Obviously the nation doesn't have the same demographics as California, but the Golden State has a diverse economy and has extremes of wealth and poverty. An examination of the workforce showed that California employs 14,500,000 people according to the 2005 first quarter results of the state's Department of Labor's Occupational and Wage Data (2005). The average hourly salary was $20.88 per hour and the average worker earned $43,429 per annum. A sampling of the job titles and the number of employees who work at those jobs is presented in Table 3.5.

Table 3.5. Selected Top Service Occupations in California.

Occupation	Number of employees
Office and Administrative Support	2.7 million
Sales and related occupations	1.15 million
Food Prep and Serving	1.04 million
Production Occupations	1.1 million
Construction and Extraction	0.74 million
Installation, Maintenance, and Repair	0.50 million

Source: (Occupational Employment (May 2005) and Wage (2006).

These occupations were chosen as examples because most do not require a college degree. Is it fair to either the employers who hire these individuals or to the students looking for skills to be a part of an educational system that is looking for college graduates? By the same token, if the emphasis of an educational system is to place people in college where they can qualify for higher income (better) jobs, how successful is a system where only one-third are qualified at graduation for a four-year college?

There are people who make a good living working in the occupational definitions described above. They contribute to society.

33080 Each child is a unique person, with unique needs, and the purpose of the educational system of this state is to enable each child to develop all of his or her own potential (California Ed. Code, Sec. 33080).

The California Education code states the issue well. Unless vocational programs are developed, it is unfair to students who will not receive further state assistance in furthering their "own potential."

Unless the educational system is restructured to free monies for vocational programs, the state does a huge disservice to many constituents.

3.F. TEACHING—OBVIOUSLY A PROBLEM?

The primary link between curriculum and the student is the teacher. One of the primary objectives of the school is to transfer "relevant" information that has been chosen by "experts" to students. The teacher is a conduit of information responsible for insuring that the material arrives safely in the mind of the student. When the teacher isn't doing his or her job correctly, the student's education is compromised. Yet, how is one really supposed to insure that the "right" information has reached its target.

For those who haven't thought very much about teaching in a classroom, the idea of preparing a lesson for students is simple, yet difficult. First, the teacher should have the intent to teach a particular lesson. That seems obvious. Second, one must figure out the best way to deliver the lesson. Third, there should be some checking during the lesson to see if the students are actually getting the lesson. Fourth, there is often some sort of homework that helps the student reinforce the lesson learned. Finally, at some point, there is an examination to see if the material has been learned. What you realize as you plan for the day of a teacher is that those lessons aren't so simple after all.

It isn't easy to teach. Not everyone is suited to the job. Sometimes it's difficult to measure what effect a teacher has had on students. Perhaps that's why is so difficult to rid the system of teachers who aren't doing to the job. One of the things that NCLB did was to permit change to occur in underperforming schools, and among the options is the replacement of site administrators or teachers. However, replacing an ineffective teacher is not an easy process.

Since the teaching system hasn't determined what lessons work best, is it surprising that getting rid of bad teachers is nearly impossible? Reeder (2005) cited an 18-year study that was done in Illinois to examine efforts to dismiss tenured teachers. In a state with 876 school districts, only 61 (7 percent) have even attempted to fire a teacher (para. 9). Only 38 of those districts were successful in their attempts to ouster targeted teachers (para. 10). Out of over 95,500 tenured teachers, the state gets rid of seven (7) per year, and only an average of two (2) per year for poor job performance. The remainder were fired for gross misconduct (para. 10). One of the reasons for the low number of firings is because the tenure system (a guaranteed job after 3 or 4 years) makes it difficult to fire incompetent teachers (para 11).

As an article by the Hoover Institute (Schweizer, 1999) reports, "Getting rid of teachers who have committed crimes is difficult. Getting rid of teachers who are simply incompetent is nearly impossible (para. 15)." What administrators at schools try to do is to pass the incompetent teacher to another school—a process that is called the "Dance of the lemons" (para. 12). Thus, the teacher is reassigned, but is still teaching (para. 11). Given the current climate, is the suggestion to get rid of low-quality teachers even viable? For that matter, how willing are teachers to be part of a "reconstitution," where virtually the entire staff of an underperforming school is replaced to meet one of NCLB's corrective actions?

Brady (2003) points out the corrective actions imposed by NCLB on schools that fail to meet the federal criteria. As they begin the process of "improvement," schools start out with school planning, technical assistance, and novel ideas such as tutoring (p. 11). If that doesn't work, the idea is to make the school day longer or change the principal (p. 15). Once the situation is severe, one of the ideas for improving poor performing schools is to replace the curriculum (Brady, p. 17).

This sounds odd since many states and districts have "state approved" curriculum, and textbook manufacturers are already writing their books to meet state needs. When it comes down to it, the teacher will be largely dependent on the textbook that has been approved by the state and the local school authority. The question that needs to be addressed is: how will rewriting the curriculum for the school (or district) help the teacher instruct kids?

One of the options for poor performing schools is to close the school, (p. 16) and to reopen it as a charter school (p. 17). However, the government's own study showed that charter schools, and for that matter private schools, didn't seems to improve school performance when equivalent demographic indicators were used to compare schools. Brady states that the government's solution is to have an outside expert consult with the school, and if all else has failed, one is supposed to turn operation of the school to the state (p. 15).

Most of the solutions provided by NCLB revolve around leaders making great changes. A new principal, curriculum, teachers, ideas will all come out to beat the problem. The common thread among most of the solutions is, "By golly, if you just change a few of those bad teachers, we can get these kids to learn." It's a gambler's mentality. It's short term; it has no memory. It is the idea that if you just play hard, finally you'll turn things around.

What the data overwhelmingly suggest is that Horatio Alger's ideas are still in vogue, even if his books aren't. We all still like the idea of someone overcoming adversity to make it. The problem is, we're not looking for a story of the week; we're trying to create a stable and profitable factory. It doesn't happen by chance.

3.G. THE PROBLEM OF PERCEPTION

The most valuable of all education is the ability to make yourself do the thing you have to do, when it has to be done, whether you like it or not . . . (Huxley, 1907, Reflexion 120).

When gambling, one of the devices used by players is the bluff. In card games (such as poker), it occurs when one or more of the players tries to act as if the cards they hold are better than they actually are. When other card players in a game see a player make a large wager, they must determine whether to challenge the bluff or to fold. The person who bluffs can win the game because the other players feel weak and unable to compete.

As discussed previously, the field of education is an ideological battleground, and the battles are not all about education. When one does not have solid facts with evidence to back one's argument, people are discussing "things unknown." The decisions made to determine how schools are operated are made by politicians in state capitols. Whether it's a right wing "free market" argument arguing for the virtues or competition, or an argument for "equal opportunity" presented from a liberal perspective that says "more is better," most decisions about education are made based on ideology rather than on adequate data.

Isn't it time to start an education system based on actual data? It's time to re-create a system that can save money and simultaneously provide better education. The current educational system is like a large poker game where the players transfer.

The *American Heritage Dictionary* (2000) describes the word "perception" as: "the knowledge gained by perceiving," and "the effect or act of perceiving" (online). It is through perception, not merely guesswork, that educational decisions must be made. To do so, one needs to develop a system that will use information wisely so that the K-12 education system can improve.

Education is perceived as a problem because it costs too much and delivers too little. There is widespread dismay about public education in the United States, and everyone talks about what the education system should do, but there are not any real solutions to the problem. If you perform a search of the Internet using the words, "education, policy, and reform," there are over 28 million hits. One of the first sites is the home of the Education Policy Institute (2008), a Washington based organization that:

> [S]eeks to improve education through research, policy analysis, and the development of responsible alternatives to existing policies and practices.

Another organization is the Progressive Policy Institute (PPI), which promotes the formation of a "progressive agenda" in the United States that includes charter schools. I don't want to poke fun at an organization, but they define their mission as:

> PPI's mission arises from the belief that America is ill-served by an obsolete left-right debate that is out of step with the powerful forces re-shaping our society and economy. The Institute advocates a philosophy that adapts the progressive tradition in American politics to the realities of the Information Age and points to a "third way" beyond the liberal impulse to defend the bureaucratic status quo and the conservative bid to simply dismantle government.

Although I'm not quite sure what all that means, the "Third Way" is a democratic think tank that seeks progressive change based on the information age ("powerful forces").The PPI Web site did have an article by Paul Hill (2006), a professor at the University of Washington, that made sense. Hill makes a great argument in the preamble of his paper:

> These realities demand new educational approaches that allow for various types of schools that have the freedom to innovate to meet students' unique needs. However, our public education system is incapable of such problem solving because it is oriented in precisely the wrong direction. Today, public education policies and administrations are organized to serve the needs of the institutions and the adults that work in them (p. 1).

The current configuration of California's schools is a modified factory system in which students walk themselves from classroom to classroom where they are supposed to learn at each classroom (workstation). The teachers claim that class size and the diversity within the student population will dampen their efforts. Although class size is a major problem, perhaps in the factory system, student diversity represents a larger problem than class size.

> Today's public school system tolerates new ideas only on a small scale and it does so largely to reduce pressures for broader change. The current system is intended to advance individual, community, and national goals, but is, in fact, engineered for stability. That is normally a good thing. We want schools to open on time, teachers to count on having jobs from one day to the next, and parents to feel secure knowing that their children will have a place to go to school.
>
> Stability alone, however, is the wrong goal in a complex, fast-changing, modern economy. Students—disadvantaged students, in particular—need schools that are focused on providing them with the skills they will need to succeed in today's society, schools that are flexible enough to try a variety of teaching methods until they succeed in reaching these goals. The existing structure of public education, and most of today's schools, were not built to serve students with special needs and it does not work for them (p. 1).

Dr. Hill's plan to radically change the school system calls for something called a portfolio management system, in which the school district would alter the way that funds are distributed in the system. Some of the ideas include funding schools individually based on attendance and lowering the barriers for parents to have school choice. The problem is that many of the ideas are similar to NCLB's desire to combine education and the market system. He is right, however, in the idea that students need schools that provide students with skills, and that flexibility in putting the correct curriculum with the right student is necessary.

Although calling for bold new steps to change the current role of principal, teacher, and school board, the actual guts of the school might be similar to what we already have. Dr. Hill is correct in his desire to restructure the funding situation, but it is the system itself that needs to be addressed. His papers have addressed funding, but here he embraces a market approach. In his paper Dr. Hill speaks of programs that have worked, more hours of instruction in poverty schools (p. 7), but his focus primarily is on restructuring so that parent's can control school choice.

The best idea about portfolios was to call "building the capacity of schools and educators to implement a variety of quality instruction models" (p. 7). The idea of improving instruction is good, but the idea of a market-driven education reform is not. There's nothing particularly market-driven about public schools. The pay sucks, working conditions are mediocre, and it isn't prestigious. The one thing that is nice about the job is the kids.

If good research finds ways to help teachers help the kids, most teachers will implement them. That will improve schools. If we keep looking to market forces, we'll be gambling with America's future.

3.G.1. Discussing Solutions

When discussing educational issues, one of the problems is that viewpoints are often biased by pre-conceived views. Even with the best intentions, having pre-conceived notions or prejudices can cloud one's judgment. The problem is that all experiments usually proceed with an outcome in mind. An example of this can be found in a well thought out list of objectives by an organization called the Center for Educational Reform (2008) that states that it would like to invoke change to do the following:

> The Center for Education Reform drives the creation of better educational opportunities for all children by leading parents, policymakers and the media in boldly advocating for school choice, advancing the charter school movement, and challenging the education establishment (About CER, 2008, para 1).

A similar argument is made by The Thomas B. Fordham Institute (2008) that believes that all children deserve a high quality K-12 education at the school of their choice. On their *Who We Are* (2003–2008) page, the Institute states its convictions:

- Parents should have the right to select among a variety of high-quality schools for their children.
- All students, teachers, and schools can meet high standards, with the help of results-oriented accountability systems informed by rigorous assessments.
- Every school should deliver a content-rich curriculum taught by knowledgeable teachers.
- Schools must serve first the educational needs of children, not the interests of institutions or adults. (para. 5).

The four ideas mentioned above could have been directly derived from the federal law we recognize as No Child Left Behind. There are many institutes trying to re-create education, but it must involve getting down in the factory and making things work.

Of course, everyone wants good schools. The point is that the current system of education, using resources in their current manner, is doomed to failure. As Bill Gates (2005) said, "the problem is the system." Yet, by spending so much time arguing about ideology rather than putting forth credible data and studies, we create a place where "ideologies" are placed before children.

It doesn't matter if it's a private, charter, or public school, it seems that it would best to create something that will help any student.

3.G.2. Community Letters and Opinions

One of the good things about the education system is that it is an area that most people understand at some level. People who have been to school have developed opinions about what is good or bad in education. There are many opinions about what makes education effective or what is detrimental. Thus, people present school related opinions about: teachers, schools, school administrators, teacher's unions, student attitudes, funding levels, poor values, curriculum, social promotion, societal inadequacies, and poor parental involvement as factors that need to be addressed to "fix education."

The people that criticize the education system don't criticize in a vacuum. There are many people who criticize the education system. One of the country's largest school districts, Los Angeles Unified School District (LAUSD), came under sharp criticism for the performance of its schools. High dropout rates and low test scores prompted a great deal of public criticism. In fact, the mayor even decided to take power away from the local school board so that he could "fix" education.

The mayor of Los Angeles, Antonio Villaraigosa, to his credit, didn't merely tell everyone how bad the schools were—he personally interceded into the political process to attempt to make them better. As mayor, his office helped promote the California State Assembly Bill (AB 1381) to allow the mayor to take power from the local school board and effectively transfer it into the hands of the mayor (para. 7). The outgoing superintendent of LAUSD, Roy Romer (2006), responded to the assembly bill by saying that "the mayor's compromise is about power and money, not about children" (para. 3). There is no doubt that LAUSD faced severe problems, but the public fight between the board, superintendent, and the mayor only reinforced the idea that the school system didn't work.

With reports showing high dropout rates, and reports in the media that Americas' kids aren't getting the education they deserve, there have been plenty of suggestions for improvement. Schools have become ideological and political battlegrounds; therefore, what schools are actually doing is often lost in the smoke.

Politicians are not the only figures that criticize schools. Along with Gates, another influential critic of public education is investment banker Ted Forstmann who said that school systems performed poorly, and he wanted to open education to competition. His free-market ideology states that competition in education would be a way to weed out incompetent teachers. Near the end of a speech that extolled the virtues of competition in American education, Forstmann (1999) said:

> America was founded upon a completely different system: a competitive educa-
> tion system—without compulsion or government interference, in which parents
> were free to choose from many options—a system which served the country
> well and lasted a long time, until the government monopoly pushed it aside
> 100 years after its' founding.
>   Freedom, competition and choice will improve education. The current
> monopoly will ensure more failure. The public should give the present system a
> failing grade and refuse to promote it any longer (para. 18,19).

It sounds pretty good, but the problem is that it entirely skirts reality. America wasn't founded on a "competitive education system." It wasn't based on the freedom of parents to choose schools and education systems. It was based on the ability of parents to send a kid to school.

Education worked fine during the first 100 years of the republic. It was a competitive education system "in which parents were free to choose from many options." The first 100 years of American history will find the majority of the country in an agrarian economy. And what was the choice? Whether or not to go to school? Forstman is a highly intelligent person, but his argument is simply following "free market" ideals, but doesn't address the real problem of putting a better product in the classrooms.

When Forstman says, "The public should give the system a failing grade and refuse to promote it any longer," it is a call for change. It influences the public perception of education, its value and worth, and denigrates the efforts of everyone involved in education. Perhaps, however, that's the intention. At the very least, it helps promote the debate about educational reform.

As previously discussed, concerns about America's education system are widespread. Everyone has an opinion about the education system. Not only are schools ideological battlegrounds, many people thing they know how to fix schools. When *Frontline* (2000), a television news journal of current events, did a program on *School Choice,* some of its viewers wrote to share their views. Some of them are included here. In a letter from Antioch, California, Lionel Q. stated that teachers, parents, and the community as a whole rare esponsible for student performance:

> The issue of failing schools in America has been with us for quite some time
> now. . . . We have thrown untold billions of dollars at this problem for the bet-
> ter part of 20 years without addressing the real issue here: teacher and parent
> accountability. . . .

Bottom line here is, hold teachers and parents, the community as a whole, responsible for those funds granted to them by the Federal/State agencies, assuring once and for all that everyone has a stake and interest in the succesful education of our kids (para.1).

This view seems shared by Stan Wexler (2000) of Philadelphia, Pennsylvania who wrote:

Dear FRONTLINE,
Pogo said, "We have met the enemy and he is us." The problems of public schools are cultural, political, social and personal. The fractured "family" of morality, ethics, and values within our society are no longer of common interest. Selfishness, mistrust, laziness, blaming, and irresponsibility have replaced them. With no common vision among people, public schools are taking the fall. Few people will look at the real reasons why (Wexler, 2000, para. 1).

For Sarah Little (2000) the issue was a moral problem. Parents were failing and creating a system that "encourages mediocrity." This also impacts the gifted students in school by creating a poor environment.

I strongly agree with the previous comments that what passes as parenting these days is at least as responsible for the decline in achievement in American Schools.
I also believe our system encourages mediocrity. . . . we are working so hard to get to the students at the bottom, and we should be, that we are forgetting about the students at the top. Gifted students are seriously neglected in our current system. Our highest potential students are frequently not given the opportunity to reach their fullest potential. . . . (Little, 2000, para. 1).

The final letter discusses the role of teachers in the education process. Since *Frontline* had done a story about education, but didn't get teachers' input, teachers were a little upset. Michael Cole (2000) of Rio Rancho, New Mexico writes:

What the rest of America and apparently *Frontline* itself needs to realize is that any real, lasting public school reform has to involve teachers. Nowhere in your program did you interview a teacher about this issue. This is the perfect evidence of the problems with public education in our country; the people that work closest with children, those that know what works and what doesn't, those that are entrusted with this nation's children are ignored. When there is talk of real school reform it must include teachers or it is sure to fail (Cole, 2000, para. 1).

Cole's letter points out what is obvious in this chapter. It is obvious that teachers are the direct contact with the student, and the focus of any reform in education should end up in the classroom. However, this chapter showed that there is a great deal. Of waste in the education system that needs to be addressed so that the focus will be the classroom. We need a student-centered universe that focuses on the needs of the classroom; at present we don't have it.

This chapter has shown that educational system consists of many groups that have combined to create an inefficient system that wastes resources. There are school boards, district offices, county offices, state offices, and federal offices that can all affect education. The schools are also subject to legislators' demands as new laws affecting education are enacted. The inefficiency inherent in the educational process has created a self-perpetuating bureaucracy that drains resources from the classroom. The education system needs to be streamlined. A new, efficient system needs to be developed that uses real data to make decisions.

In an age of experts and specialization, the role of education is still primarily that of the craftsman teacher trying to perfect a product. A consortium comprised of educators and schools from states could create model lessons and optimize the learning environment. If present, such a group could coordinate studies of classrooms to find what techniques work the best in different environments. Teachers would still be craftsman, but they would be armed with the best tools possible.

A body of lessons could be developed that anyone could use (both home schooled and private school would benefit) that will demonstrate proven teaching techniques. If the system could be streamlined and administration pared down, a research consortium could be developed to find what will work best in schools. A system could be developed that helps remove uncertainty from the education process.

There are two major premises that will guide the reformation of the education system. In Chapter 4, the ideas Dr. Edward Deming are introduced and Chapter 5 introduces the concept of entropy as a guideline in the education process.

Chapter 4

A Better Way to Do Things

Destruction of schools. A public school in the United States is not operated as a component of a system. Optimization is obstructed by a city superintendent, a county superintendent, a school board (elected, shifting over time, no constancy of purpose), district board, local government, county government, state board of education, federal government, assessment by standardized tests of pupils, comparisons between districts and states

—Edward Deming, 1993, p. 74

4.A. EDWARD DEMING: TRANSFORMING THE FACTORY SYSTEM

Chapter 1 presented the argument that today's schools are based on the industrial model of the factory. Chapters 2 and 3 have shown that many attempts to improve school performance have been based on political, economic, or social beliefs rather than information based on how schools operate. It isn't difficult to make the argument that the *education system* has been affected by many parties whose motives are fueled by personal motivations more than educational excellence.

The high toll of public education on state budgets, and the public's dissatisfaction with the state of public schools, make education a perfect place to target lawmaker efforts. It is natural for state legislators to become involved in writing laws that try to affect or reform education. The legislative members of every state promote their ideals of what are intended to improve the education system. As we've seen, the tinkering from state politicians to change education's path hasn't produced a solution. Massive bureaucracies have been created in each state that siphon funds away from kids entitled to them.

Perhaps it's time to consider creating a single system that will maintain the focus on schools and learning rather than politics. A single good system of education based on research and efficiency is better than what we currently have.

Though education has historically been a local or state issue, the passage of No Child Left Behind has demonstrated that the federal government has the legal capacity to impose its will on American education. The specter of national education standards in the American education system creates a new path for the country's policies.

Since the federal government apparently has the capacity to set education policy, perhaps it a good time to look at the efficiency of our existing education system. Perhaps it would be best to streamline educational agencies to improve the efficiency of the American education system. One should ask whether an opportunity exists for states to combine or significantly reduce their education departments to free up more funding for local use. Not only could savings occur, but a national education system would allow for the formation of a national research effort that could develop better methods for teaching and school management.

If a single school system centralizes its efforts, then one could reduce redundant functions found at the state and district levels. This would allow for more money to be channeled into the classroom.

The education *system* needs to improve efficiency and allow for continuous improvement of the product delivered in the classroom. Can a system be developed that can optimize education processes and improve them? In previous chapters, efforts were made to show that the school system is based on a factory system. The next two chapters will suggest methods that have been used to improve factory performance and, presumably, can be used to improve schools.

The current chapter will examine methods used to optimize factory performance and evaluate whether schools follow these suggestions. The methods of Dr. William "Edward" Deming, one of the pioneers of improving factory performance, will be examined in context to schools.

Tortella (1995) explained that Deming's abilities as an organizational quality expert were the result of solid education and having the opportunity to exploit his talents. After earning a Ph.D. from Yale University (para. 4), Deming went on to work at Bell Laboratories where he was introduced to Walter Sheward, who introduced the concepts of statistical process control (SPC) in the factory and to company executives. Through his experience at Bell, he learned to use statistics to improve and form guidelines for business practices (para. 9).

In 1950, following World War II, Deming was asked by the military to help conduct a census for Japan. While working in Japan, Deming began to instruct people responsible for running Japanese companies on methods to use SPC to improve factory production. Japanese corporate executives were impressed by Deming's claim that improved quality would lead to lower expenses while improving sales. Using SPC in the Japanese factories was successful, and increases in productivity and product quality were coupled with lower costs. The improved products created huge demand for Japanese products throughout the world (Tortella, para. 11–14, 1995).

As Japanese companies began to sell more high quality merchandise, they began to take market share away from American companies (Ford, 2001, para. 1). In 1981, when industrial competition from Japan had cut into sales, market share, and profits, Deming (1993) was asked to examine the practices of Ford Motor Company. The three previous years the company had incurred $3 billion in losses (Ford, 2001, para. 1). Upon examining the company, Deming found that changing some of Ford's management practices could lead to a better product with less cost (Walton, 1986, p. 134).

After implementing Deming's principles, Ford improved and became profitable. The management principles that Deming taught were put into a book called *Quality, Productivity, and Competitive Position* (Deming, 1982) that introduced his "14 points" (p. 20) to improve quality in a system. In this chapter, Deming's 14 points for improving the management of organizations will be used to examine some of education's current practices and processes.

When examining the issues pertaining to American education, perhaps it is best to examine the system as a whole. One of the things that Deming (1993) provides is a definition of a "system":

> A system is a network of interdependent components that work together to try to accomplish the aim of the system. A system must have an aim. Without an aim, there is no system. The aim of the system must be clear to everyone in the system. The aim must include plans for the future. The aim is a value judgment. (We are of course talking here about a man-made system.) (p. 98)."
>
> A system must be managed. It will not manage itself. Left to themselves in the Western world, components become selfish, competitive. We can not afford the destructive effect of competition (p. 51).

Before examining Deming's 14 points in conjunction with schools, perhaps the first thing that one should do is examine what constitutes the American *system* of public education.

When Bill Gates discussed American education, his comments were not based on regions, but on the entire country. A comprehensive look at the education system should produce a system that produces results anywhere and everywhere. People who seek reform of the education system need to recognize what comprises it. Though teachers are the face of education, the American education system is created by, and subservient to, the wishes of legislators, the local population served, the schools, and society as a whole. To look at the system of education, you have to look at where and how decisions are made.

Any substantive changes to education will require cooperation between those who make decisions and the society they serve. Society has severe reservations about the American education system. There's good reason for this.

First and foremost is the fact that when a student fails or succeeds in the school system, he or she is absorbed into society. It is everyone's problem. Although the school system may not be able to control social conditions that hamper student learning, it is possible to modify the product produced in the classroom so that the best education is given in all places. A second reason for viewing the school system as a whole is because "economies of scale" favor such an approach. If the cost of something is shared among everyone, it costs less and saves money.

What will be examined next is finding a system that can improve all of education.

4.B. IS THERE AN ALTERNATIVE OR BETTER WAY?

A system is a network of interdependent components that work together to try to accomplish the aim of the system. A system must have an aim. Without an aim, there is no system (Deming, 1993, p. 50–51).

The previous chapters have shown that the *aim* of American education is anything but clear. With this is mind, it is important to have a framework to view the system that is examined. This analysis will begin by using Deming's methods to examine what the *education system* means. Some of the techniques developed by Deming to improve management were called "14 Points" and "Seven Deadly Diseases"(Walton, 1986, p. 34–36). Both consist of common sense methods that can be used to improve the performance of an organization if they're applied throughout an organization.

Many books have addressed Deming's methods when examining the issue of quality in the schools. Most books have proposed using Deming's methods to improve the education at the level of the school (Arcaro, 1995, p, 2–3), or district (superintendent) (Frazier, 1997, p. 58). These books tend to examine the issue of education from a local perspective and the "leadership" they look for is at the local level. These views tend to examine the issues of education in terms of the "super" leader. This would be a leader who takes it upon him or her self to transform a district using business techniques while performing all the normal duties of the job.

Adopting Deming's methods at the school or district level is not without merit. However, due to sample sizes in schools, it's difficult to obtain relevant data about the differences that one might find in a classroom situation. Even if there were differences in test results from the classes of two different teachers, the variables (time of day for instruction, for instance; different teaching styles) could be as responsible for variation as something a teacher is doing. The differences in test scores could be due to the kids, teacher's personality, or the quality of the lessons. How could one effectively test whether the lesson itself, or the teacher's presentation, is responsible for difference in learning outcomes? The sample size is too small at the school level.

Given a sufficient sample size, the school system can measure inputs (lesson, homework, reinforcement) that go into a class so that best methods can be evaluated and shared. A large scale study (state or national) could find factors or lessons that work best and then could be adopted across all classrooms. Deming's methods are designed to improve the actual day-to-day methods within the system and to build a system that will allow for continued improvement in the future.

One of the premises of using Deming's model is that one must understand the inputs and expected outcomes of a system to effectively manage an organization. Once one understands what one wishes to accomplish, one can determine the best ways to approach the goal (Deming, p. 5). To help identify these factors that go into a system, Deming used a simple flow diagram that describes the process. The first thing that must be understood is who the process is serving. It is only through knowing who the customer is and understanding what they want (or need) that one can find the best way to alter something (someone). Thus, consumer research is a key element of the Deming Flow Diagram (Deming, 2000, p. 4).

One of the nice things about the Deming Flow diagram is that it is simple and allows one to identify potential problems in a system. In regard to the American education system, one can ask whether there is a defined goal for American education. The input into the diagram (consumer research) is to create a product consumers want. The product will be utilized by society so we need to understand what sort of education system will best benefit society. Is it known?

With the public school system serving so many masters, the inputs into Deming's model are quite complicated. Who decides what and how subjects should be taught? From the previous chapters, we see that lawmakers and

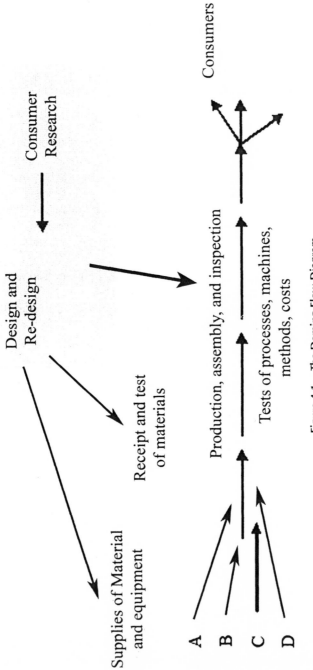

Figure 4.1. The Deming Flow Diagram.

state school agencies are both directly involved in developing curriculum and laws that affect various parts of the education factory. It might also be noted that the federal government also makes demands of both the state and local school districts that change how the system is run and structured. The presence of multiple *masters* violates one of the precepts of Deming's 14 points. To work effectively, it's important for an organization to set its sights on consistent goals.

In Deming's Flow Diagram, A, B, C, and D represent suppliers leading into the factory assembly line. In the school factory, the primary inputs into the system are students. One of the apparent problems with the current education system is that it's been unable to properly compensate for variations in student variables (family income and present education levels). Since schools have been unable to properly compensate effectively for parental factors that affect student and school performance, the system needs to find ways to effectively compensate for these problems. Perhaps more importantly, the system must develop a way to incorporate improvements into the system that reaches into the classroom.

The improvements have to be made in the actual delivery of product. On Deming's diagram, teachers work the assembly line where the actual education process occurs. Any system that is adopted must have the capacity to learn so that it can address problems with the current system and find ways to address them. The current system of education seems unable to do this.

As the most visible and familiar part of the education process, the teacher is the focus of most educational reform efforts. Perhaps the inputs (A, B, C, D) into the education process should gather more attention. For Deming, the beginning of the process of improvement begins with management's ability to make a product meet the needs of the market. As the previous section noted, there are lots of managers in the education system trying to adjust the processes in schools. These include people in government, education departments, and local education agencies all rearranging the design of education. This creates a problem because it violates the first of Deming's 14 points of management which refers to "constancy of purpose."

The previous chapter discussed people who have the misguided belief that they know what is needed to "fix" education. The argument presented by Deming states that to improve a system, one needs to understand the inputs and objectives of a process so that one can find ways to statistically improve it. Through the use of Deming's simple diagram, one is able to examine the inputs into the education process as well as the desired outcome. If processes are found to improve the speed or quality of the product, they can be employed in the system.

It is important to understand what the needs of kids are and then ask if the education system serving them can meet those needs. Do we have a systematic way to determine the needs of kids? The needs include socialization and knowledge to be a good citizen. Then, there is the idea of preparing people for successful futures. What is missing in this picture? Well, let's start with trying to define the customer.

A. student
B. parents
C. society
D. government
E. business (employers)
F. colleges and universities
G. all of the above

From experience, one can tell that the student is probably the most important customer. It also creates the largest problem in Deming's world regarding problems in the future. What will the future be for the student? What entity is best suited to determining the future needs? Is it the local school board? district office? state board of education? state department of education?

In Figure 4.1, if one considers that the shaded part of Deming's diagram is applied to education, one comes to the realization that there are many important factors that an education system cannot control. It is important to understand these elements because one needs to understand what can be affected in the education system.

The very first point Deming makes is to develop realistic expectations of what is wanted from the school system. Walton (1986) examines what Deming said about the customer:

> Draw a flow diagram. Who's your customer? What comes in? What goes out? Do you know your customer? Do you know what he needs? Almost nobody does . . . (p. 27).

This is an essential question in education. It pertains to the future of individuals and of the country itself. Ultimately, one would assume the customer is the student being trained and the society served. Colleges and businesses will certainly be interested in the outcome of students that move through the system, but they are not as affected as either society as a whole or the individuals being educated. The parent is an extension of the student, and government is an extension of society.

If you don't have direction and focus on what is to be done, you may end up with an education system that asks its customers for advice. An example is this letter by the California secretary of education. A message from Secretary of Education Dave Long (2007):

> We all know that a quality education can open the door to a world of opportunities and be the foundation for life-long success. Unfortunately, California's education system has resulted in a significant gap in achievement for many of our students. As a lifelong educator, I have experienced first-hand success with students and the challenges we continue to face:
>
> - Our best estimates say that one-fourth of children that enter 9th grade do not graduate.
> - Too many California children do not fare well against their counterparts in national and international standardized tests.
> - Too many students entering California's higher education system are underprepared and require remedial coursework.
> - Too many high school graduates who don't attend college are ill-prepared to enter well-paying career fields.
> - Too many schools do not provide a safe enough environment for children to learn and prosper.
>
> The next year and the months leading up to it will be an unprecedented opportunity to focus on our current challenges and place our efforts in some well-reasoned solutions. As the primary advisor to the governor on education issues, I am gathering input from students, teachers, parents, community and business leaders, administrators and others through a series of Community Leader Meetings to help identify these challenges of these troubling results as well as solutions that can lead to improvement.
>
> I am asking for your help. I want to hear from you regarding the challenges facing education today and ways we can work to ensure that every California child has access to a quality education. Please submit any thoughts or recommendations you have on education reform to edpolicy@ose.ca.gov.
>
> Thank you and I look forward to hearing from you.
> Sincerely,
> Dave Long
> Secretary of Education (Long, 2007, p. 1).

This letter from the leader of California's K-12 education system says a lot about the state of education. When a state's secretary of education says, "I am asking for your help," does it make you believe that management of the education system is sound? Put another way, would Bill Gates put a message on the Microsoft Web site asking for the public's help in developing their product? Though the letter does provide a list of problems facing education, it doesn't do anything to answer how to improve the situation. Since this is from the office of the superintendent of education in California, one might wonder, "Who is responsible?"

With federal and state laws subject to change, curriculums being revised at the local level, and lack of coordination at any level, it's difficult to see who's in charge. Teachers and principals are making things work in spite of the lack of concerted leadership in education, but one thing to be sure is that there isn't "constancy of purpose" in American education.

4.C. EDWARD DEMING'S 14 POINTS APPLIED TO EDUCATION SETTINGS

Edward Deming offered 14 key principles for management to transform business effectiveness. We've demonstrated that there are impediments to the *system* of education that prevent it from working efficiently. Rather than maximizing the product by making changes at the classroom level, the management structure tries to "will" student performance through mandates. Deming's mandate of 14 points to improve an organization will require one to decide on a *system* of education.

Deming's 14 points are management's guidelines to improve an organization's practices. Whether one is talking about the organization at the school, district, or state level, one needs to find methods that optimize how students are taught. The focus of education efforts has to be at the classroom level. What are the best ways for a teacher to deliver service to kids? How do you successfully get as many kids though a program as possible?

The first step is finding what works best in the classroom. Research showing the best methods to employ at the classroom or school level should be found. If proper data management and assessment systems were found, a principal might look at data during the 5th week of a 7th-grade pre-algebra class and say, "Ms. Johnson, the data from your tests indicate that a large number of your students don't understand long-division. I have similar data from the other two classes. Federal data shows that the 'XYZ' afterschool program should take care of 85 percent of the students in six weeks. Would you be interesting in teaching it?"

Such a program would prevent the students from failing the class. Rather than teaching the entire subject to students again, the students would be *salvaged* during the semester. What is more cost effective, teaching the entire class again or intervening as a problem arises? It's likely that many principals read this and say, "There isn't an information system available like that!" The reply is: "There should be."

With current technology, one could create a system to monitor classroom practices practically in real time. They do it in factories while producing products; are America's kids worth less than consumer products? One would hope not. The best school practices must be found, made available to teachers and administrators, and implemented. The possibilities are remarkable if one optimizes the school system, however, one needs to agree on a system.

It can all start with a simple idea: Deming's first point is that everyone should work toward a constant purpose. As previous chapters have shown, it isn't happening now.

4.C.1. Create Constancy of Purpose for Improvement

The last chapter showed that the education system does not have constancy of purpose or even leadership that has constancy of purpose. Walton (1986) describes Deming's constancy of purpose to mean a system that incorporates:

> (1) innovation; (2) research and education; (3) continuous improvement of product and service; and (4) maintenance of equipment, furniture and fixtures, and new aids to production in the office and in the plant (p. 56).

As one may notice, the object of Deming's attention was the "plant." In the current context, the *plant* is a school. The question is how one improves the products and services offered by the school. Is innovation and research being applied at the level of classroom to make the schools better? Are the processes being offered in the classroom and the school being improved on a continuous basis? These are the questions that Deming addresses in his first point, and it is an essential point for education to address.

With public education, different agencies at the federal and state level, legislators, district and site administrators all work toward slightly different agendas, and one wonders if it is even possible to create "constancy of purpose."

The words "constancy" and "purpose" mean moving toward a goal(s) in a consistent manner. With regard to constancy, it would involve having long-term goals in place to improve the product being produced. Is there a constant improvement of the product? Is there a mechanism in place to create improvement?

With regard to purpose, there are many groups with their own agendas. For instance, the groups that want to maximize school choice by pushing for vouchers and charter schools have constancy of purpose with regard to pushing the issue of school "choice," but that effort doesn't necessarily lend itself to improving the "system." In fact, it helps contribute to the fragmentation of the system.

There seems to be constancy of purpose to provide tougher "standards" for students to meet, but it doesn't necessarily translate to change in the classroom. There is purpose in evaluating annual test scores that are done at the end of the year. The underlying purpose of NCLB's annual tests is to give purpose to the process. Annual scores are supposed to hold people accountable. One should ask, "What are they accountable for?" Can an administrator or teacher actually say there's a wrong or right way to do things? Does the system have a way to fix the problem?

Constancy of purpose means that "change" is directed toward a specific objective. Change in the education system should have a definite purpose? Reform ideas such as school choice, tough standards, and annual tests are supposed to provide the best education to every kid possible? How?

What is common to vouchers, school choice, and charter schools is a desire to try something new. The main theme is the advantage of being able to shop around. If the schools are offering similar products in terms of classes and delivery, how will shopping around improve the quality of education? Do the teachers of a new charter school have new teaching methods that they've been hiding? If overrun with low income students and operated in a similar manner to *regular* public schools, the failure of charter schools can be predicted. What will be different?

Chapter 2 showed that school failure, can be predicted to a high degree. What is often overlooked is that success is also predictable. What is needed is to find methods that lead to success and employ them across the education system. What is needed is constancy of purpose to attain that goal. The system needs to find ways (plural) to overcome the disadvantages of students who grow up in less fortunate situations.

While we're at it, let's not pretend that the *good* schools are optimized either. They can also be improved since their teachers may have better working conditions, but they may not be using optimal teaching techniques. By constantly improving the system of learning at the classroom level, there will be more success in schools for everyone.

What is needed in the education system are small changes that are directed toward a larger goal. Not all change will necessarily be good for a school system. For instance, if one looks at the issue of charter schools, home schools, vouchers, and any other type of school, they all address personal freedom of the consumer. Let's just approve all voucher programs, charter schools, and home school programs. Complete choice for everyone. Now, here's the question? Why will this improve education? Under the same circumstances, these schools will still be faced with the same problems and methods employed by traditional schools. What will change?

The students will not necessarily change because the name on the school is different. As you open up the doors to new schools, they will soon have all the same problems currently facing public schools. Now what? You still have to find the best way to deliver the lesson to the student.

Some think that the way to improve the education system is through standardized testing. If one looks at the current use of standardized tests, one finds that classroom operations leading to test scores are long forgotten by the time results are received. Some are a year old by the time scores arrive. Are the results supposed to change the lessons that have preceded it? Would a teacher know whether their lessons were good based on these results? How would a teacher know which lessons were good and which to change based on an annual test?

Another current trend is one which wants to reform education by imposing tougher standards on schools and students. It is curious how imposing higher standards on the system will help a system that can't meet the low standards. Here's a suggestion: why not introduce the following Advanced Placement (AP) classes to serve as high school graduation requirements: physics, chemistry, calculus, micro- and macro-economics, government, and English language and literature (AP, 2008). If you can pass the AP exams in four areas (a mere three or better), you graduate. It's a crazy idea, right? The nation's graduation rate would probably be less than 5 percent, but the standards would be high! Would making the standard more rigorous improve education? Would it improve the nation if a majority of students drop out of school?

The answer is that higher standards don't improve education. One can change the standards without any change in the process in the classroom. High standards are good, but they don't address the issue of improving education at the level of the classroom. The same logic can be applied to the annual tests used for NCLB. Without a way to use the data to improve education, the annual tests mandated by NCLB can look at school performance, but there isn't a tool to use with the test to improve school performance. Then, there are those who feel that teacher's pay is the issue.

Higher teacher pay is supposed to improve education by bringing in highly motivated people who are smarter, will work harder, and therefore be better teachers. As a teacher, one always hopes for higher pay, but if there is higher pay for teachers, what will change in the system? Will teachers who are paid more suddenly find the right way(s) to teach because they've been drawn to the profession by higher pay? It would be nice to pay teachers more, but it will not necessarily improve the education that kids receive.

As Deming points out in the quote that headed this chapter, improving the system of education system means deciding on what you're trying to do and understanding what can be done to get to one's goals. When bosses are changing the system without identifying problems and solutions, there will not be a consistent goal to move toward. With education facing so many changes from various factions, it is difficult to "optimize" the system that isn't stable. There is little constancy of purpose.

The idea of finding constant purpose in education is good for the education system, however, it also requires goals that can be measured. If our purpose is to *educate each student to the best of our nation's ability,* it means nothing. It is too vague a goal. Politicians can say these things about what should occur, but what is more important is finding the way to make education better. The question we need to ask is, "How do we put the best lesson in front of each kid at the most appropriate time?" We need to streamline the processes in education, and put every resource possible aimed toward improving the classroom and school. That's where the operations occur; that's where the student is located.

If a unified education system is developed; the following are broad areas of interest that could be pursued: (1) a national "core" curriculum, (2) dissemination of the best methods to deliver the curriculum, (3) a system to continuous improve the curriculum and delivery, (4) alternative educational objectives to keep all kids interested in school, (5) methods to remediate students based on need, and (6) leadership to insure implementation of the aforementioned objectives.

Common Purpose

The issue of whether or not to pursue a national curriculum is primarily concerned with common sense. It could create uniformity among states and allow states to save money by eliminating redundant services. The states would still have the ability to choose what elements to use and, as with environmental law, could impose *tougher* standards if desired, but a basis of what should be leaned in subjects would be established. One of the advantages of such a system is that it would allow for a collective research effort that could provide information on the best ways to deliver and support the lessons in the schools.

The previous chapter showed that people at the federal, state, district, and local school levels are all involved in similar roles in education. There are specialists to tell schools how to comply with both state and federal rules on many issues. Every one of the issues detracts money and time away from the mission of education. One level of bureaucracy should be enough for anyone. Whether meeting the needs of special education, English learners, or curriculum, the system will function better to set a single standard. Serving multiple masters is wasteful and creates unnecessary bureaucracy.

The question one should ask is why should there be so many levels of bureaucracy to discuss what to put in a curriculum? Do students need to know different things in Oregon as opposed to Georgia to be successful? Do special education students in Vermont have different requirements than those in Tennessee? How can one develop a constancy of purpose unless one can agree on what should be taught? The idea is that the education system should be streamlined.

To exemplify this point, perhaps it would help to look at a basic skill that all students must learn to be successful: reading.

Wouldn't the best way to develop a comprehensive reading program be to: (1) determine what should be taught, (2) compare methods to help one teach, (3) find the best teaching method(s) through research, (4) determine the best ways to implement these methods in the classroom, (5) insure that the methods are available and used in the classroom, (6) obtain feedback to allow for improvement of the reading program to allow for continuous improvement of the product.

Since there would be a general consensus that reading should be taught, perhaps instead of having thousands of people continually reworking curriculum guidelines, the focus could be on developing and testing lessons in school laboratories across the country to determine lesson effectiveness. Small improvements into the lessons and materials could be worked into the curriculum, delivery, and materials to maximize their effectiveness.

One advantage of having lessons and the accompanying materials developed by the government is that they could be readily used by the teacher. This would preclude problems with copyright infringement and other problems currently experienced by teachers. A teacher would have the advantage of using materials that have been demonstrated to work. In addition to providing curriculum where it is needed, curriculum developers could also find out what materials are most needed by teachers and students. The primary advantage is that curriculum developers could understand what materials are needed based on usage by teachers.

Information about what is needed in the classroom could help the lesson development process. One could work on materials and lessons to begin a system of continuous improvements. As lessons are developed further, specialized lessons could be developed for subgroups that weren't served by the initial curriculum (English language learners, i.e., non-native residents).

Research in a national education system will allow one to examine different learning methods and choose the best. For instance, there are many programs that promise to help students learn to read, but there isn't a way for a district to unambiguously find the best way(s) to teach each lesson and to find benchmarks for intervention when the lessons aren't working. It may be that among some students or teachers, the "best" way isn't actually the best for a given group of students; therefore, other acceptable alternatives should be explored.

During the process of finding the best teaching methods and use of the best materials, one could also optimize the issue of time spent on classroom activities. How much time (on average) should be spent on each lesson? One could determine what types of learning works best to reinforce the lessons. If one were to set up a general system of education that revolves around improving the lessons taught to kids, those lessons could be transmitted to teachers, it would be a national system that would optimize teaching to read. Such a system would optimize the best way to teach each lesson, the best way to reinforce each lesson (home and class work), and then could be optimized by finding the best methods to help struggling students.

The leaders of school systems based on these ideas will have advantages that current educational leaders lack. Since the materials and best teaching methods would be available to everyone, the issue of how to guide and improve the product produced in the classroom could be improved. At the very least, then, the results of annual tests for students (which do delineate concepts taught during the year) could be tied to ways to improve lessons. The constancy of purpose must be to deliver better lessons and improve the conditions for teaching and learning.

As for those people who do not wish to partake in the public school, or who are absent, ill, or forced away from school, the lessons would be available in some form of electronic media. In fact, there isn't any reason why students couldn't have access to lessons delivered by expert teachers via some form of electronic delivery system.

This would create a common playing field in education, and schools in disadvantaged areas would have the capacity to deliver the same curriculum as the most affluent districts in the country. A system that focused on the development and delivery of curriculum would allow support programs to be built that would be built into the standard curriculum. The leadership at the local level would be responsible to made sure that students would benefit from the lessons by creating support services to help create success. The basis of improvement would be at the factory level (in the classroom where teaching takes place).

No comprehensive scheme for improvement will occur unless the system decides what it is trying to accomplish. Unless one figures out what one wants to accomplish, the rest of Deming's 14 points will not matter. One needs to have a purpose for the education system, and change should be aimed at achieving that purpose.

4.C.2. Adopt a New Philosophy of Cooperation (Win-Win)

The second of Deming's 14 points calls for an organization to adopt a new philosophy of cooperation. In Walton (1986), Deming said that "Point two really means in my mind a transformation of management. Structures have been put in place in management that have to be dismantled"(p. 59). It is a proactive management style, according to Gitlow and Gitlow (1987), where leaders anticipate failure in a system and are proactive in trying to anticipate and fix problems rather than merely reacting to problems after they've occurred (p. 32). This means that an organization must tear down impediments to improving the system.

This was done at the classroom level by two educators, Jaime Escalante and Rafe Esquith, who both built successful programs in areas where students were from low-income homes with high numbers of English learners. One thing common to both Escalante and Esquith is that both had to reject the philosophy of the system they were in and create their own philosophies. Both decided that traditional methods (and expectations) would ultimately lead to failure for their students, and they created their own philosophies for success.

For Escalante, a high school math teacher, he decided to measure success by having his students take and pass the advanced placement calculus examination. For Esquith, a fifth-grade teacher, his goal was to ingrain the seeds of long-term success. In *The Hobart Shakespearian* by Stuart (2005), Esquith has created an environment that promotes overall growth in all phases of his students' education. Among the many strategies he adopted, Esquith's program included an extended day in which fifth-grade students performed Shakespeare's plays (DVD).

In both cases, Escalante and Esquith decided to challenge the existing philosophy that said low-income students would fail. They both decided to create standards of excellence that flew in the face of traditional thinking and through hard work proved their points. Both had to create their own philosophies to achieve success—a point that Deming states must be done. In doing so, both developed their own "constancy of purpose" and then had to convince students and parents to buy into their philosophy.

Merriam-Webster (2008) defines *philosophy* as "the most basic beliefs, concepts, and attitudes of an individual or group" (online definition). A common element of Escalante and Esquith's educational programs was that they succeeded under challenging circumstances that normally produce failure. Both Escalante and Esquith were required to create philosophies that challenged the assumptions of the system. Both of them created "win-win" philosophies in situations where winning seemed improbable. The system they were in was failing, so both men created their own system.

The problem with the systems developed by Escalante and Esquith is that they are dependent on the *superman* teacher whose methods are not easily emulated. Teachers in a system don't start their days at seven in the morning and teach students constantly until five in the afternoon. These teachers do not represent the *norm* anymore than Albert Einstein or William Shakespeare represented norms in their fields. There are extraordinary people performing at a level that most cannot or will not.

Esquith and Escalante are examples of people that refuse to lose. What they both exemplify are the possibilities of the education system to both the school and the student. Since most teachers are not going to develop the work ethic that either teacher had, it is unlikely that their teaching methods will be directly applicable to current K-12 students. One aspect common to teachers like Escalante and Esquith is an intense desire to succeed. Both teachers were told that their students were hard-luck students who would be difficult to teach. Teachers like Escalante and Esquith do not accept failure easily. They looked for ways to intervene and prevent failure.

What teachers and students need is a system that will create success in their classrooms. That's what the *system* is supposed to do. It involves setting up programs that prepare students for their classes, setting expectations, and maintaining a good learning environment. The school sites are supposed to get this from each state's department of education or local school agency (district), but neither site has answers. The reason that teachers like Esquith and Escalante have been successful is not because of the system, but in spite of it.

Deming's principles call for a *win-win* situation between workers and management. Management must set the tone of a *win-win* attitude for whatever level of organization they run. Management's role in education is to find a system that creates success. Recall the letter from California's secretary of education that asked for people's suggestions. It doesn't portray leadership that knows how to successfully implement a successful strategy. Leaders at the state level should be able to go into a school and prescribe what needs to be done to improve every classroom.

Do the education leaders at the state level have the information to improve classroom performance? The answer is *no*. Have they come up with methods that will tell schools how to improve? Not in any appreciable way. One must ask, then, what purpose do they serve?

The *system* primarily consists of several million teachers dealing each day with the hands they've been dealt. The interactions between teachers and site administrators must create a win-win situation as well since they work in partnership. A principal's effectiveness at a school will depend on setting up conditions for student achievement.

The principal (and other administrators) function to insure that the best personnel are presenting the best lessons possible to meet the learning objectives. However, it is also important to set a good tone at a school. Stipek (2002) states that the culture of the school is important:

> Teachers can motivate students only if they themselves are motivated. They can make students feel valued and secure only if they feel valued and secure; they can foster enthusiasm for learning in students only if they are enthusiastic about teaching. The school culture can make or break a teacher in the same way that the classroom culture can support or undermine students' efforts to learn (para. 1).

The principal sets a tone around a school to both staff and students that can make or break a school. Without teacher motivation, the entire process of education can be quickly crushed. One of the reasons that it's important to find the best methods to deliver lessons is because teaching is theater. It takes a lot of energy and attitude to deliver those lessons. In order to make information seem fresh and important, the teacher must project drama into the classroom and make everything interesting to an audience that will not cheer and may be full of hecklers.

The win-win culture of a school means that people will feel part of a larger mission. Both faculty and students must embrace the idea that each widget coming down the assembly line is special. Every lesson is special. The principal has to set a tone that reinforces this idea.

It is essential that that a principal and the staff understand their roles in education. The principal's job will create conditions that create success in the classroom. This will include the teaching time, materials, and climate (next chapter) that optimize teaching. The teacher will agree to employ the best techniques in the best manner possible, and if an innovative idea is presented (and funding is available), teachers will be encouraged to try out new ideas. Innovation is an important part of continuous improvement, and a school that is moving toward a goal is more likely to have a staff that feels a sense of satisfaction.

4.C.3. Don't Depend on Mass Inspection

Walton (1986) recorded Deming's thoughts on the issue of *mass inspection* when he said, "Inspection with the aim of finding the bad ones and throwing them out is too late, ineffective, costly" (p. 60). In spite of this, one of the key components of NCLB calls for mass inspection of schools. The scores recorded on the annual tests aren't even used to evaluate students in a meaningful way; they are used to evaluate the schools the students attend.

To understand Deming's attitude toward mass inspection, a good example is the operation of a simple machine in a factory. Let's suppose that a drill-press operator is supposed to put a hole precisely in the middle of a metal plate (within 2 1/100th of an inch). Mass inspection would call for every single plate to be inspected after being drilled. Another method, called "spot inspection," would call for testing to occur at intervals (every 10th plate). For Deming, the idea was to make the factory process so good that the product could be assumed to be passing. The failures in the process (quality of plate, drill bit wear, improper placement into operation) would be anticipated and addressed before the process started, and this would eliminate the costly need to inspect each piece. It would also lead to less failure.

When applied to public education, mass inspection has less value than it does as a factory process. Kids who fail are a year behind before the mass inspection occurs. Of course, the tests that teachers give in their class measure knowledge of a subject, and if there is intervention when failure occurs many of the students can be *salvaged*. Does the school system build methods to rehabilitate failing students? Yes—it's called summer school. What would be better would be a system that anticipates failure and intervenes before the damage is done.

This would be done by scientifically determining where the failure points are in the system. Suppose parts are damaged due to worn drill bits. Deming would favor anticipating the failure of the drill bit and changing it. The process wouldn't wait for failure to occur; it would anticipate it. If one knows where failure will occur, then it's possible to intervene during the process.

In the field of education, inspection or testing is a huge component of the process. There are lots of examples of mass inspection during the education process. Standardized test are taken every year by each student, but do they help improve the student? More importantly, do the tests that teachers give students periodically help define where intervention should occur? At the elementary grades, they often do. At the middle and high school levels, there may not be any intervention to prevent failure. This is a failure of the system.

In Walton (1986), Deming opposes mass inspection because it's: (1) expensive, and (2) a process that is designed right to begin with will not need inspection. In other words, if you understand the process, you can predict failure in the process and prevent it (i.e., the drill bit may wear out after every 200th part, and it can be replaced with a fresh bit). Obviously, one cannot compare a classroom lesson with a drill bit, but if the lessons are studied sufficiently and understood, one will be able to anticipate where failure will occur. Generally, this is the idea behind a quiz, but how often does failing a quiz lead to intervention?

Generally, failing a quiz is a wake-up call for the student. The student failing a quiz is told that they must study harder or risk failing the test. The motivation is to put the onus of failure on the student. It is an idea that Deming absolutely hates.

What is desired is a system that is maximized to produce a successful product. Perhaps that's why Deming (1993) does not like the idea of grades in a classroom. His view is that students who are graded will put their emphasis on the grade they receive rather than on learning the material. He is in favor of abolishing grades (p. 149) and eliminating the process of comparing schools on the basis of test scores (p. 74). Although Deming is correct in his assessment that grades can detract from the learning process, they do function by allowing students, teachers, and parents to assess each student's strengths and weaknesses. They can also help pinpoint areas where students need additional help.

The idea that "being graded" will have a negative influence on learning is shared by some people who choose alternative schools for their children's education. The problem with the alternative schools is that students will sometimes fail to master difficult and useful subjects such as algebra. Students who are given alternatives to classes may drop the material because they are challenged or will not learn the material very well. Part of the education process is learning to persevere and to overcome challenges. It's a good lesson for life. A counter-argument to Deming is that the education system needs the tests rather than the student.

Deming's points regarding mass inspection runs counter to the aims of NCLB, a law that requires students to be tested on an annual basis. The reason that NCLB calls for mass inspection (2nd to 11th grade mandatory testing) is to find areas where schools aren't doing the job. The idea of mass inspection means that everyone being taught is inspected to see that they are meeting a stated goal or requirement. The results of the tests may give clues to places where improvements should be made, but the kids who need the improvement have already moved down the assembly line.

States are currently mandating that students take both state tests to meet NCLB standards and a test to measure minimum compliance for graduation. The test of basic skills is given by each state and is called the High School Exit Examination (HSEE). It is an example in which legislation has helped compromise the education system. Since the standards for minimum compliance for math and language arts skills aren't incorporated into the annual subject tests given at the end of the year, high school students spend more time taking standardized tests. The result of the HSEE is that students must get a passing score in order to earn a diploma. Those who do not pass are identified by the standardized tests as low achievers who do not have basic skills. They are placed in remedial classes to help them learn basic skills.

There are at least three problems with education's use of the HSEE as a mass inspection system. The first problem is that it finds out who hasn't made the grade when it is too late. In California, the HSEE is given in the 10th grade to measure for 8th-grade competency. A student that doesn't pass HSEE as a high school sophomore is clearly deficient in academic skills. Instead of getting trained for job skills, the student continues along the education system's factory line toward a future that is not favorable.

A second problem with the current mass inspection system of state tests is that the tests can be meaningless to the student. With the exception of the HSEE, which is required to earn a diploma, the state subject area tests (algebra, biology, English) have no bearing on whether the student passes, or doesn't pass, his or her class. A student can fail the subject area tests, but it will mean nothing to the student in terms of grades. The incentives for students, especially at the upper grades of the K-12 system, are minimal. Since a student has no stake results, a prudent question is whether the tests should be used to evaluate schools? If the tests are important enough, shouldn't a student's success or failure matter to the student taking the test?

As soon as students realize that students aren't subject to any penalties from failing the subject area tests, many don't try, and moreover, many won't give their absolute best effort. Thus, states spend a lot of time aligning curriculum and standards to match state examinations that are relatively meaningless to the students taking them. Of course, students confined to a desk for a certain amount of time will usually try a test, and may even do a reasonable job, but will they do the job to the best of their ability? Thus, standardized tests can be used to compare schools, but they are not well designed to do so.

The third problem regarding mass inspection testing is that it reinforces the idea to students that testing isn't important. This undermines the entire school system. A school district can take an entire week of its instruction time to administer tests, but since students know that the tests are used to evaluate schools, there's no personal incentive for students to do well. If you're a teacher, it is difficult to read too much into the test results. What then is the benefit of the standardized test in today's school?

There are three groups that may benefit from the standardized tests. The first are parents who may shop around for their child's school based on test scores. The second group gaining benefits from standardized test scores are real estate agents who can steer families toward neighborhoods with higher-achieving schools. The final group that benefits from standardized tests are people that create, distribute, and work with the tests. The tests provide jobs.

When Deming states that an organization needs to cease dependence on mass inspection, it is because a properly run system will do (teach) what is needed. The students are evaluated during their classes, and if the system of education isn't working at that level, fix it. How will the education system be helped by measuring the output using a poorly designed test? By the time the test score information is available to administrators and teachers it is historical data and serves no useful purpose to either the student or the school. As Deming said in Walton (1986), "Quality comes not from inspection but from improvement of the process" (p. 60).

The standardized tests weren't designed to improve the process. They were designed to examine the end product. These tests are poor tools to measure the education process, and they certainly aren't a basis for constructive change of the education system. The analogy of how this test works can be seen by someone who measures the weight of vegetables grown in a garden each year and uses the data to try to increase yield. Unless one knows what went into a process, it's difficult to know how the end-product is affected.

4.C.4. End the Practice of Awarding Business on the Basis of Price Tag Alone

The fourth of Deming's maxims for success; "End the Practice of Awarding Business on Price Tag Alone" (Walton, 1986, p. 62) seems puzzling. The idea behind using criteria other than awarding business on price tag alone is that it pays in the long run to find a single supplier who fulfills one's needs rather than shopping around to find the best price. The reasoning considers that in the long run, one's business will profit more from long-term relationships and excellent quality, than trying to shift suppliers to save a few dollars.

Deming's point runs counter to most people's experience because we are usually shoppers (consumers) looking at an end product. As such, we make decisions about quality and price when we determine what product to buy. We hope that the product we buy is good, and if it isn't, we re-think our attitude toward the company that produced the product. For instance, if we buy a car that is a "lemon" from a particular company, it's likely that we will dismiss that company from consideration. For a company, losing credibility in the market will result in a loss of sales. Ultimately, a company could go out of business if poor product quality ruins the company's reputation.

With regard to schools, the idea should be put forth that incorporates research about classroom and school performance into products that are selected. A top-quality research program that addresses what works with respect to books from publishers, as well as products from other educational suppliers, should be developed. The research showing results from different suppliers should be made freely available so that schools and districts can make scientific choices based on data rather than salesmanship. This should help provide the foundation for better lessons for everyone (public, private, and home-schooled).

A top-notch research program for K-12 classroom education will be expensive to implement. It will not be inexpensive to distribute the findings to all the schools in America. But, a program based on finding all the small steps that lead to success will provide a template for long-term success in the schools. There are no easy answers, and what it takes to succeed is hard work and effort.

It is presumed that relying on research rather than sales pitches would improve the product that is placed into the classroom. This would keep the focus on continuously improving the lessons that work, rather than opting for the latest fad.

4.C.5. Constantly Improve the System of Production and Service

The quest to create a system that includes Deming's fifth point is one of the largest obstacles to the improvement of public education in the United States. Even if leaders could agree on a course of action and a new philosophy was adopted, how would one instill continual improvement into the process of education?

The entire focus of a comprehensive plan to change education must be focused on the process of exchanging ideas between the instructor and the student. In today's world, how will this occur? Is it the principal's job to exhort teachers to teach harder, smarter, or create better lessons? Should this occur as part of a daily pep talk as a principal tells teachers to, "Go out there and teach your hearts out!"

It might be effective as a pep talk, but perhaps the best way to insure that schools teach proper lessons is to insure that methods used in classroom have already been proven to work. This doesn't mean that everyone will teach the same way, but it does mean that there will be an understanding of what has worked with a particular group of students.

Will knowing what someone else has used to succeed help teachers with their own lessons and presentations? One would have to believe that this is definitely a "yes." There is no doubt that examining methods that another teacher has used to be successful will help teachers in the classroom. As teachers understand what works in the classroom, and know the best ways to present material, learning in the classroom will improve.

Knowing what works in the classroom can serve as a foundation to evaluate and plan lessons. What Deming is trying to instill into the system is constant improvement. That would mean that a teacher that has "perfected" a lesson would still look for another way to improve his or her lesson.

One of the most cost-effective ways to study and archive lessons is through a central education body. Such an agency could have the position of collecting and evaluating lessons that are used to improve the education process, where it may not be practical to share teaching practices across a school, or even a district to find what works. Schools do not have the resources to document and evaluate the lessons. Such actions if left to a district would be prohibitively expensive. However, if the costs and benefits are shared across the entire state, or, preferably, the country, a system of continuous improvement of the education system is possible.

Moreover, the role of facilitating the collection and evaluation of lessons would seem to be a perfect job for the federal department of education. If the government is able to create a central electronic depository that is responsible for creating and distributing successful lessons, the system would continue to improve as long as new and better lessons would continue to be added. When better lessons were verified to be better, automatic updates could be sent to interested parties. As long as teachers continue to create and share their lessons, the element of continuous improvement would be built into the system.

The ability to find and package lessons that work best in the classroom is a key component of improvement in the school. As teachers continue to find methods (other than lessons) that work, continuous improvement will be built into the system. Likewise, methods that improve the operation of schools need to be continuously improved. Administrators must also develop and share strategies to improve the way schools operate to help maximize learning. Further discussion on this point will occur in the next chapter.

4.C.6. Institute Training and Retraining

When people seek to improve the education system in the United States, one of the first things often cited is the need for better teachers. In the American Federation of Teachers (AFT; 2008) Web site, an article states that "teacher quality is the most important school variable affecting student performance" (para. 1). The AFT goes on to state its belief that "it is the Union's responsibility to improve teacher quality and improve the teaching profession" (para. 1).

One wonders how a teacher's union can improve teacher quality, particularly in light of the fact that unions are often cited as responsible for creating the impediments to getting rid of poor teachers. Whether it's the union, politicians, or citizens, the most visible sign of teaching is the classroom teacher and, therefore, all of them seem to cite the need to improve teacher quality as a key toward improving education. Yet, if one believes (like Bill Gates) that the *system* of education is the problem, then the teacher is probably not the place to start change.

In Walton (1986), Deming states that workers are responsible for only 15 percent of the problems in a system, and the system is responsible for

85 percent of what happens in a given system. Since the system is the responsibility of management, the fault for systemic problems is with management (p. 94).

With respect to teachers in education, teachers are both managers of their classrooms and workers. How does one go about systematically training teachers? It goes without saying that training and retraining in an organization is absolutely necessary to create a smooth operating system. One must ask how the bosses in the education system (school board, superintendent, state and federal legislators) as well as local site managers (principal) integrate training and retraining of its teachers in the education process.

What is unique about the public school system is that it hasn't optimized the processes of education. The teacher has far more than 15 percent of the responsibility for the success of the system. The teacher in the classroom *is* the system. The teacher currently doesn't succeed because of the education system, but in spite of it. That is why successful teachers are often considered rebels.

With all the chiefs coming into the picture, the teacher may not have much effect on the system of education unless they buck the "system" and create their own program. When teachers like Jaime Escalante, a high school math teacher (Matthews, 1988), fifth-grade teacher Raef Esquith (Stuart, 2005), and English teacher Erin Gruwell (Graveness, 2007) buck the system, they do show what is possible with a subset of the student population, but they are not part of the "system." All of the celebrated teachers created their own systems, and with the tightening of standards, one risks a great deal by doing so. It essentially represents developing a system that goes against what your school and the status quo is doing.

The "uber"-teachers such as Esquith and Escalante are the one's that are often cited as having the methods to induce excellent results from their students. The charter school movement is being based on this idea that being freed from structure and bureaucracy will make a difference. The difference was made by using good methods, taking lots of time, and an attitude of refusing to fail. As wonderful as these teachers are (and were), their methods are not directly applicable to a system. The system didn't support their efforts so they created their own way to get things done.

The uber-teachers aren't the answer for the system because a *system* revolves around the norm. These are not *normal* teachers. What can be learned from the great teachers are the factors that might be incorporated into a system to improve it. The system hasn't developed a system to compensate for the "inputs" that affect education in low-performing neighborhoods. There are teachers that show if the right influences are put into the education system, it can work.

A study by Mayer, Mullins, Moore, and Ralph (2000) stated that having good teachers through content-area knowledge, experience, proper (classroom) assignment, and continued training are the best predictor of student improvement at the school site (p. 5). The study somewhat contradicts itself since it states that teaching doesn't seem to improve after five years (p. 13), yet the level of improvement levels off after five years even though teacher-training presumably continues (p 16).

It appears however that demographic figures such as parental income and education levels seem far more important than *teacher quality* when examining academic success. The current education system has not incorporated methods to compensate for the exterior factors that affect local education systems. Once it takes care of improving the processes inside the education factory (lessons), more attention can be applied to external factors. Teacher training is an important aspect of this process.

Another important factor in improving a system is stability. What is probably a common occurrence in schools around the United States is that a principal will run a staff meeting at the end of the day and delivers the latest "top-down" education suggestion. The experienced teachers in a staff meeting will roll their eyes while the latest and greatest proposal is rolled around. Some of the older teachers will whisper, "If you wait long enough, you end up back where you started. Back in the old days they called it 'xyz,' but it's the same old thing."

The old teachers will be little changed by what they've heard. They've created lessons that they know will work for a given unit, and they understand how to deliver the information to their students. These teachers are still within the "system" since they haven't gone out and tried to challenge the authorities. How do you create a system that incorporates new ideas and freshness into a school setting?

Any reform efforts to improve schools will have to begin with teaching methods. There is a lot of hype about using scientifically-based (research-based) curricula that is "standards-based." Generally, the discussion here revolves around what should be taught (standards), not what has been proven to work. It means that someone has gone to all the trouble to figure out all the factors that one should know in each class. If you're a huge market (like California), the publishers will even write the names and numbers of the standards on the pages of textbooks, a practice that is just stupid.

To please legislators, the standards are incorporated into books as if knowing the state standard is important. An analogous situation occurs when learning to drive. Is knowing the vehicle code numbers important for knowing how to drive? Unless you're a police officer writing a citation, the name and number isn't important. What is important in a lesson is the information being transmitted, not the name and code of the standard.

What a reader might ask is what this has to do with "training and retraining." They are examples of waste that is put into the education system. If you're going to train someone, make sure it's important and that it contributes to the goals of educational improvement. Change without a firm reason is wasteful and destructive to morale in an organization.

Teacher Training

Although teacher *training* programs have been established in colleges and universities in the United States, the real training for K-12 teachers comes from being in front of students (student teaching) at the schools. Of course, a teacher doesn't have a lab to determine what will work and what won't. In the classroom, the teacher tries to find what *works* for each class. It is during the interactions with a class that the "real" experience and knowledge of the craft of teaching is acquired in what Deming (Walton, 1986) would call learning on the factory floor (p. 94).

In essence, the modern school is a factory that employs people who begin in apprentice positions (student-teachers), and then they are thrown into a classroom with a "sink or swim" mentality. Kindly department chairs and colleagues may help the new teacher in their vocation, but generally, the impetus is on the teacher to create their own lessons that meet standards and for finding the best way to teach a lesson. That isn't really a scientific way of doing things. With so many people teaching the same subjects, the same principles and ideas, why doesn't someone determine how best to approach teaching? That process of optimization of how to teach a lesson is sorely missing from the education process. Where do teachers learn to begin the teaching process?

The universities and colleges oversee the training of K-12 teachers; however, there is quite a bit of agreement that the process could use improvement. In a report titled "Educating School Teachers" authored by Levine (2006) of the non-partisan Education Schools Project, the inadequacies of teacher training programs were highlighted.

> Today, the teacher education curriculum is a confusing patchwork. Academic instruction and clinical instruction are disconnected. Graduates are insufficiently prepared for the classroom (Levine, p. 26)

Levine (2006) stated that alumni from teacher education programs (both administrative and teachers) were surveyed about 11 skill areas needed by teachers, and only 40 percent on average felt that that the universities were doing well or moderately well (p. 31). The only area of the 11 surveyed where a majority of school administrators said that the faculty were adequately prepared was "knowledge of subject matter" (p. 33). What is ironic is that knowledge of subject matter is not taught by departments of education in teacher education programs. The subject area (e.g., biology, history, English, math) is taught in other departments.

The training of teachers moves the student-teacher through a state-dictated curriculum that provides some background information about basic education techniques. Walton's (1986) book about Deming's methods begins the chapter regarding training:

> All too frequent are stories of workers who learn their jobs from other workers or who are forced to depend on unintelligible printed instructions. Often there is little training or none at all. Just as often workers don't know when they have done their jobs correctly (p. 62).

How does this apply to education? Well, in the teachers lounge, if a new teacher is lucky, a teacher will share lesson plans that have worked for them. If the district has a mentor plan, there might be some ideas of what will work to teach a particular lesson, but mostly, one tries to teach the lesson as it was taught to you.

Most teachers figure out what works in a classroom on their own.

What that means is that the teaching methods are not optimized. For many of the lessons, the teacher will try to go through the book, put together lesson plans, and hope that something works. To their credit, textbooks have a lot of support in them, but they don't show how to do the job.

The student-teacher (or any teacher for that matter) is probably presenting a lesson that is similar to those found in thousands of classrooms across the country. That same information is being presented to an audience again and again and again. It is a factory. If that teacher knew what lesson had been presented to allow a class to result in great scores, would he or she be interested in what was done? Would veteran teachers want to know the "best" methods? One would hope so.

It is imperative to determine the best way(s) to teach lessons that maximize the transfer of information from teacher to student. The teaching, testing, and practice methods need to be optimized so that the classroom is as effective as possible. The optimization of individual lessons should be done by teachers and education specialists that determine the best way(s) to deliver, reinforce, and assess the transfer of lessons. There should be statistical analyses of methods under classroom conditions to determine what lessons work the best. The study of lesson development should not only study what works best (or worst), but also for what population of students. That is what the role of education departments and universities should be if they want to have a positive affect on K-12 education.

If student-teachers were given models of what they should be doing in a classroom and why each event is important, it would immediately set a standard and a set of expectations for new teachers. There would be support for the lesson the new teacher was planning to present. The new teacher wouldn't have to guess what works best, the information would be available. This could lead to some positive effects in the teaching profession.

One effect might be a higher retention of teachers in the profession. An Alliance for Excellent Education (2005) report estimates that it costs $2.2 billion to replace the 1,000 teachers per day who leave the profession, and the figure becomes $4.9 billion (para. 3) when adding in the losses from finding replacements for teachers who transfer to other schools looking for better working conditions. Thus, losing teachers from the profession represents both a loss of experience and an economic loss to the education system.

Training teachers for K-12 settings occurs each day in the K-12 settings. The teacher learns how to impose their will on classes by trial and error, and what methods get them through the day. As they learn class-control techniques and incorporate the delivery of a lesson, a teacher improves to a standard he or she can live with. The system of education has not created an ideal lesson or ideal class control methods. The teacher makes his or her own standard.

The education system experiences a large turnover and losses of experienced personnel. By its very nature, one should expect the education system to do a good job training its personnel. However, [g]iven the fact that the education system offers little:

1. Constancy of purpose (violation of Deming's first point)
2. Depends on mass inspection (violation of Deming's third point)
3. Has no internalized method to constantly improve product or service (violation of Deming's fifth point)
4. Is on shaky grounds with respect to creating a win-win philosophy (Deming's fifth point)

Would it be surprising to find that the education system doesn't do a good job achieving Deming's sixth point regarding teacher training and retraining? When one looks at the state of training in American education, one finds that most teachers are prepared for teaching by universities and colleges that teach educational theory. Within the program, most of their training (student teaching) comes from being paired with a teacher for a semester and then learning the ropes from that teacher. The student-teacher is given a few weeks or months of classroom control (or lack thereof) and learns to adapt to the situation.

Suppose one were to follow a student-teacher of science into a classroom; what would they be doing? First, let us explain what is being expected of the teacher. He or she is trying to give a performance that will teach a crowd of potential hecklers (student audience). It is analogous to a comedian learning that he or she will need to learn their craft in front of a tough audience. It isn't the easiest assignment since both parents and students have little confidence in the student-teacher and want the headliner (regular teacher) to remain in the position. Luckily, the student-teacher is so naïve that he or she doesn't even recognize this aspect of the situation.

The first thing a student-teacher should learn is that there really isn't a down moment in a classroom. The planning for your day begins with ensuring that students are entering your classroom in an orderly manner. You never know what animosity has developed in the hallway or playground, so while you're writing notes on the board for the class, you're also quite aware of the tone of the students as they enter. As a teacher, you should have the students doing something while you take roll to allow you to do your job. It might be something like copying the assignment for the day from the board.

What one may or may not hear in a college or university course is that control of the classroom is a continuous activity. One must combine the lesson plan into the system of crowd control. Of course, as a student-teacher you don't realize this at first, but come to appreciate the lesson. You're worried about delivering the material, delivering the facts correctly, pausing to take questions. Unlike the comedian playing the nightclub, you may have to use some of your "act" to insure that Bobby and Susie are paying attention. Imagine if a person at a nightclub had to pause to see if the audience really understood his or her jokes? The teacher will have to develop a test that will see whether the kids were actually tuned in or not.

So, the bottom line is that the material being taught is only one of several things that a teacher considers when planning a lesson. There are many other factors to consider. What is the best reinforcement to teach the lesson? That means, planning out how many problems to give, how much time to use reviewing materials already covered, and then what is the best method of testing. This is a question faced by teachers every single day when they go into the classroom. It isn't really taught because: (1) an individual teacher has no way to test for the effectiveness of his or her homework or testing policies; and (2) teachers usually don't have the time to go to the bathroom, much less think about the effectiveness of homework and tests.

The bottom line is that the school system could do a lot to help teachers but doesn't. When Deming's sixth point about training and retraining is applied to school systems, it doesn't do the job.

So, in a nutshell, the student-teacher (or experienced teacher for that matter) receives little practical training during her or his experience during college. Once in the classroom, there is some support, but much of the improvement in teaching technique comes from finding what works. The process of teacher training is currently a trial by fire and there's definitely room for improvement of the system.

4.C.7. Adopt and Institute Leadership for the Management of People, Recognizing Their Different Abilities, Capabilities, and Aspirations

> The job of the leader is to accomplish the transformation of his organization. He possesses knowledge, personality, and persuasive power. (Deming, 1993, p. 119)
>
> It is the responsibility of management to discover the barriers that prevent workers from taking pride in what they do. The workers know exactly what these barriers are: an emphasis on numbers, not quality; turning out the product quickly rather than properly; a deaf ear to their suggestions; too much time spent on rework; poor tools; problems with incoming materials (Edward Deming in Walton, 1986, p. 70).

In the adoption of leadership in education, the central idea is to place people in positions that will improve a system. The preceding pages have called for materials and lessons that are geared to the classroom. However, a school is a dynamic place offering a great deal of service to a variety of constituents. The leaders of a school should be pushing for goals that have been identified to be important for success. The goals are not numerical based on achievement tests, but smaller steps at the school and classroom level that will lead to better performance. A principal of a school must identify how to best apply limited resources to improve production.

What is the role of leadership for the schools? At the national level there is a secretary of education who heads the department of education that functions by: (1) establishing policies for giving out financial aid; (2) collecting and disseminating research about America's schools; and (3) preventing discrimination in the schools. Thus, the federal department of education doesn't set education policy. At the state level, each state has an education department which is headed by a Superintendent of Public Instruction and a Board of Education. In some states, they call the head of the education department a commissioner, but titles notwithstanding, there are 50 agencies that try to accomplish the goals stated by the Massachusetts commissioner of elementary and secondary education, Mitchell D. Chester (2008):

1. Qualified educators for every public school and classroom
2. High standards for what all students should know and be able to do in the core subjects
3. Adequate resources and support services, used well by schools, districts, and communities
4. Valid, reliable assessment and accountability systems for students, educators, schools, and districts
5. Timely, useful information to stakeholders
6. Efficient agency management (para. 3)

Since Massachusetts has stated its education department's goals so well, perhaps it would useful to examine each function.

Although it may be unfair to lump every state department of education under the goals described by Massachusetts, it would be fair to say that most states have similar goals. Each state takes care of licensing requirements or *qualifications* for its teachers. Why couldn't a single licensing agency provide teachers with a national license? Teachers would have more mobility and free market forces could help determine salaries rather than union activity. Do 50 bureaucratic agencies move better than one?

The same question can be asked about the second standard set by Massachusetts' Education Department that calls for creating *high standards* for students. The idea of high standards in the curriculum can be done easily, but is it really able to be enforced in the classroom? A discussion of using advanced placement tests as the graduation requirements was mentioned previously. Is it really necessary to have 50 states coming up with essentially different version of "high standards?"

The third role of the state education department is to provide adequate resources and support to schools, districts, and committees; it merely puts them in power of delegating resources. The other aspect of this is auditing (the "well used"), which also utilizes resources. Again, one might ask if a single entity couldn't provide both these functions (delegating of resources and auditing) more efficiently. It would also create common guidelines for funding America's schools.

There is no doubt that states spend a lot of time making up, administering, and analyzing test data. The fourth item covered by the state is to provide tests to students. A national standards test would allow schools to be compared on common bases. It should be possible to lower the administration costs as tests are used throughout the country, rather than on a state-by-state basis. There is also little doubt that a national test would prove to be just as effective for less overall cost than state exams.

The fifth goal of the Massachusetts' Department of Education calls for timely delivery of education information to stakeholders. The stakeholders would be students, parents, teachers, administrators, state representatives, and taxpayers. Again, a single agency or a regional agency could deliver information to *stakeholders* just as well and with less expense.

Finally, the last goal is to make sure that the state's department of education is using its own resources efficiently.

Is there anything on that list that couldn't be done through a single agency? Do one need 50 of these agencies doling out funds to 14,000 school districts? It seems that most of the jobs done by the state education departments are redundant. It takes a lot of money to run a large state agency, and one of the issues with educational leadership is cutting costs to make a better product. Unless the advantages from a state department of education outweigh the costs, they should be discarded. Leadership involves using resources efficiently, and the education bureaucracy needs to pare down redundancy to channel money to students.

School leadership is a national issue. It starts with a commitment to make the issue of education important. It involves transforming the culture so that the country feels that the role of education becomes important. Leadership is leading the teachers into a mission to educate students who believe in the cause. Leadership is not about setting standards and benchmarks, it is the process of analyzing how to use available resources to achieve success. At the local level, the district superintendent sets the tone for how a district operates.

The superintendent of a school district can influence how resources in a district are allocated and place people into positions to lead. A visit to districts advertising to hire superintendents in the American Association of School Administrators (2008) shows the following common requirements that districts look for: 1. knowledge of finance; 2. ability to communicate with stakeholders; 3. knowledge of curriculum; and 4. strategic planning (Career Center, various descriptions). The superintendent serves as a means to insure that the district is meeting its requirements to the community. Perhaps the most important aspect of the superintendent's educational mission is to coordinate the district's school toward becoming a coherent organization.

The key toward improving a school district performance is to have leaders that are united in purpose and interested in instruction. According to Shannon and Bylsma (2004):

Leaders in improved school districts are described as dynamic, united in purpose,

Involved, visible in schools, and interested in instruction. Leaders provide encouragement, recognition and support for improving student learning (p. 16).

In line with Deming's philosophy, one sees phrases like *united in purpose* and that has clear similarities to *constancy of* purpose that is the first of Deming's 14 points. A superintendent is therefore making sure that an overall agenda is being followed by a district. However, the person who is associated with putting a face on the overall learning process of a school is the principal. A superintendent may set the tone for a district, but the school factory is fine-tuned by the actions of a principal.

The job of the principal is to maximize the allocation of resources at the school, but there are limited staff members and limitations on time. The principal is also responsible for setting up conditions (discipline and conduct) that permits the school to work toward its objectives. With the myriad of activities in a school, how resources are deployed in the school are critical. The principal should set a tone with the staff so that expectations can be met. In meetings with the staff, the problems that interfere with the school's mission (learning) have to be addressed.

The principal of a school has to choose the battles with a great deal of discretion. With limited resources, each choice to pursue a course of action will leave another choice on the sideline. A document prepared for a U.S. Senate meeting by Schnur (2007) stated that "nearly 25% of the in-school factors related to student achievement can be attributed to the quality and effectiveness of the principal" (para. 1). The report goes on to say that schools showing improvement: 1. use data effectively; 2. create teams that manage projects well; and 3. develop a school culture among students and adults that reinforces personal responsibility and aspirations (p. 4). So, the bottom line is that a good principal can make a difference in school performance.

The principal, then, can set the tone for the classroom experience. The principal is the eyes and ears of the education system at a site. Principals are held responsible for success or failure of a school (failure mainly), while they carry out the system's goals. Does the education system have a matrix or prescription for principals to follow to run their schools? Shouldn't the education system understand what a school should do to be successful? Why should the actions of principals make up to 25 percent of the difference in school performance?

The school system as a whole should have the answer for how best to address school improvement. Instead, as with teachers, the idea is that a great

leader will make the difference. This is problematic as is shown by the following quotation from management theorist Peter Drucker (1993):

> No institution can possibly survive if it needs geniuses or supermen to manage
> it. It must be organized in such a way as to be able to get along under a leader-
> ship composed of average human beings (p. 26).

As is the case with teachers, the function of the school system is to find
proven ways to help schools operate better. The principal of a school should
have methods at their disposal to help the school achieve its objectives. What
is probably more important is that the principal set a positive tone for teachers
and students.

Once people finally figure out what education should do, managing the
people that teach should seem simple shouldn't it? How hard can it be to
teach? This thought crossed my mind while watching a rehearsal for my
daughter's dance company for the winter dance performance. They were
doing a run-through of performance pieces for an up-coming show, and
since there were too many people in one room, the main teacher and some
of the dancers went to a second studio to rehearse some of the choreography.
Remaining behind were some young dancers and three teenage dancers, who
were given the task of leading younger dancers in warm-up exercises.

The three teenagers selected to lead were more interested in their personal
business than in the task they'd been assigned, and the warm up (usually a
directed exercise that the teacher leads) disintegrated into chaos. The three
girls all had the necessary training to lead a warm-up exercise (ability to show
students the moves), and had the leadership capabilities to do so, but none
had the determination to properly warm up the class. The warm-up exercise
wasn't taken seriously by those who led it, and the culture of the studio didn't
stress the importance of the warm-up exercises. The warm-up turned into a
waste of time.

This was an issue of culture. My daughter's dance company wants to
make the dancers "feel good" about themselves and about dance, but the
details of teaching dance are sometimes left behind. The students go through
the paces, but instructors do not take pains to correct dancers who do not
use proper technique. Perhaps one of the reasons for this lack of emphasis
on dance technique is that the studio focuses on making the dance class an
enjoyable experience, and continuously correcting dance elements would
discourage some of the dancers from attending the studio. Having fun is part
of free market economics.

In contrast to the "free market" dance studio, my daughter also took classes
at a ballet studio where classes were structured toward getting techniques just

right. At the ballet studio, techniques stressing the right and wrong aspects of each student's movement were examined and dancers were corrected. The dancers were taught structure, and variability between dancers was in correcting technical issues the less formal studio would overlook.

At the ballet studio, *fun* is not the point. Proper dance is the point, and enjoyment is a by-product of doing well. It occurred to me that if three of the dancers ("high school aged") from the ballet company had been given the task to "warm up" other dancers, they would have spent the time constructively. The culture is different.

They would have known that there was a "right" way to perform the warm-up, and it would have been taken seriously. The difference is in the culture developed at the "laid back" studio (feel good, don't discourage) versus a studio devoted toward perfecting technique. What one finds at these two studios are actually problems inherent in the public education system. This is another example of market forces at work. The dance studio that encourages self-expression is the better capitalist. Students are less likely to drop out. The ballet company adheres to higher standards and better teaching, but is more likely to discourage the dancers.

Ironically, the attitudes expressed at the two dance studios have a lot to do with public education. Public education not only needs to transfer information from one generation to another, it must also instill acceptance of a culture that values hard work to achieve a goal. In the ballet school, there is an acceptance by students that ballet is a rigorous pursuit, and some students willingly put themselves through pain and difficulties to move toward personal goals. When our current education system increases standards, it results in an increased rate of drop-outs.

The mission of public schools is to teach everyone. America's schools are being asked to perform at high standards (like the ballet studio) while providing an accommodating education that makes students feel good. The students whose parents have enjoyed the benefits of higher education buy into working harder toward a goal. The parents support their kids moving toward higher education as an inevitable event. Students who come from the culture of the ballet studio understand where the rigors of a dance education will take them. Their parents are living examples.

The same cannot be said of students in lower-income, lower-educated households where the fruits of education aren't apparent. How does one create a culture that makes students want to make sacrifices and succeed when examples of success are not readily apparent?

Disadvantaged students whose parents haven't enjoyed academic success are less likely to buy into a system of sacrifice than students whose parents enjoy an affluent lifestyle. Thus, schools with a population of students whose parents haven't pursued higher education and who are less educated often lower standards to try to keep students in the schools to fulfill the mission of higher graduation rates. Like the *free market* dance studio with *lower* standards, a school can cater to fulfilling the wants, but not necessarily the needs of its students.

What is apparent is that the two issues, needs and wants, are culturally dependent. One of the primary things you must attempt to create in an education system is a culture. The culture created will embody the expectations that one has for the members of the culture. As a culture, educational systems often reflect the community that they are derived from. They shouldn't, but they do. The reason that scores are so dependent on demographic information is because the schools reflect the cultures around them.

Schools must create dreams for students to aspire to, and society needs to actively support those dreams. Our schools don't do a good job of creating tangible goals for students. Kids will work toward goals when they understand the reward. The kids from middle-class to wealthy families who are well educated already have built-in inducements to promote education. In these families, plans to attend college coincide with the birth of their children. The expectation of educational success is part of their lives, and when they attend upper-crust public or private schools, they've already bought in to the program.

The wealthy school has a clientele that is more like the ballet studio. A young ballet student will push her or himself though instruction because they understand what the eventual payoff will be. They can look at students in higher level dance classes to see where they're heading. Like students in ballet, students from affluent families go to schools that re-affirm success among their peers. They have role models and peers to follow right into the gateway toward college.

In most low-income schools where parents have less education, spending twelve years moving toward the prospect of college is predicated on a huge leap of faith. Without immediate role models in their family or a large number of peers that are moving toward college, the student can easily find reasons to eschew the education system. Students still try to find reasons to attend school, but they are often non-academic in nature; sports, activities, and socializing take precedence over academic achievement. When financial pressures are added to the mix, students who are not academically successful may look to help out with finances rather than continue school. Students will tend to look toward short-term gains over hazy, long-term objectives.

Ironically, one of the *free market* effects that is not done very well by schools or society is marketing education. This is where one can learn something from a dance studio that tries harder to please everyone. A dance company cannot alienate its clientele because it wants to impose standards. A perfect dance instructor who merely follows the letter of the law and doesn't make the lessons fun will result in less dancers. The egos of dancers are massaged a little more, the discipline is sacrificed a little bit, and the company survives and thrives as a business by keeping their clientele happy. For all the talk of standards and goals, the real issue should be marketing.

The great teachers like Esquith and Escalante (and many others) manage to meld the high standards of the ballet studio with the fun of learning. Both worked in schools and districts that had slackened expectations for kids. What the teachers had to do was create a culture in their classrooms that differed from the prevailing cultures of the students' school and community. The leadership wasn't merely throwing the right information on the chalkboard, it was making students believe that what was said was important enough to sacrifice to earn. This brings us around to leadership and the idea that a principle should set the standard.

The basic idea here is that education can either reflect the society that is already present, or it can serve as a means to create a new and better society. The person who is the point person for creating a new culture at the school level is the principal. The principal's role in the school is to utilize people to not only fill the school with able-bodies to teach, but also to place people into positions where they will impact the school's culture. When Deming says that leaders must manage people and "recognize their abilities, capabilities, and aspirations," it means putting people where they'll do the most good. For a school, that refers to using the staff to build not only classrooms, but a culture that shows students the importance of learning. The principal has to strive to set up a culture that students want to emulate.

For a school, the principal should create and reinforce the idea that working hard in school will take one to the American dream. Most principals today are so overwrought with paperwork and meetings (see point 9) that setting up a culture at the school is beyond them. The role of principals should be in looking at how to improve the school, rather than in how to please their bosses. The current trend toward standards-based curriculum misses the target. It creates a culture where reporting information is important, rather than teaching and learning.

If the education system is going to improve, the education system must support the leaders at the school site. The job is to move resources into place so that learning can be maximized. The other equally important job is to act as motivators to keep students and staff moving toward higher goals in education. In essence, the principals will have to have the time and flexibility to increase standards while keeping everyone on board. What the principal needs is a computer-management system to help allocate his or her teaching and space resources to meet the education demand of the student population.

The principal should be able to look at results from a test and say, "Hey, these kids need intervention now." Scheduling an intervention program could correct problems with students before the entire semester becomes a bust. Is the technology for such a program available? Yes. It is used in manufacturing to schedule manufacturing and delivery of resources. It is another example of what the system should be doing to help education, but doesn't. The principal could spend more time rallying resources and the troops to get the job done. If the principal is managing resources to get the job done, it should involve putting the best people into areas where they're needed in a timely manner.

Anyone who works in school long enough becomes aware that administrators are often more mindful of the needs of their superiors than the needs of teachers or students. Who can blame them? That is how our system is set up. Rewards flow from the top. The superintendent is trying to keep the community happy, principals are trying to keep the superintendent happy, and the superintendent is kowtowing to the school board.

The administration is supposed to produce educational leadership, but what are the tools they can use? Does the system depend on the "great leader?" Even great leaders are going to want the best tools and technology at their disposal to improve education at their school.

When Deming states that on organization needs to institute leadership by recognizing the *abilities, capabilities, and aspiration* of its workers, there's a problem. There is at present, no systematic way to maximize the abilities of a teacher in a classroom; the system should help the person use their abilities to do a better job. Capability refers to the ability to get something done, and to its credit, the NCLB act has tried to insure that each teacher knows his or her subject area. The third item, "aspirations" is the wish to achieve a particular goal, and although all teachers aspire to teach to the highest level possible, is there even a clear meaning of what teaching to a high level refers to?

4.C.8. Drive out Fear and Build Trust so that Everyone can Work More Effectively

In order to implement a system that encourages continuous improvement, people in the system must feel confident that they can bring up problems in the organization without fear. If an employee is afraid of bringing up problems because a "superior" doesn't want to hear bad news, then improvement is more difficult. Since the Deming model asks for worker ideas in promoting positive change in an organization, an environment of trust must exist.

Fear is an emotion that can come from several places in an organization. Most people can understand the inhibitory effects that fear might have on an employee. An employee that has been reprimanded might have the feeling that they're being persecuted and become resentful. Such an employee would be less likely to share productive insights about the organization that could be valuable. How might fear affect the leader of an organization?

To examine fear in a school system, a district with a perfect storm of problems was found in Winona, Minnesota, a small city located adjacent to the Mississippi River—the Winona Area Public School (WAPS). Winona Area Public Schools (2006) serves a student population that is rather homogeneous by many standards with 88 percent White, 5 percent Black, 5 percent Asian, 3 percent Hispanic, and 1 percent American Indian. The system served nearly 3,800 students in 2006–07 in the District Overview (p. 1). Unlike most districts suffering from problems due to growth, WAPS is struggling with declining enrollment and revenues and operation costs that continue to escalate.

The reason that the employees in Winona's school district must live in fear is due to declines in student enrollments and, therefore, revenues. This leaves the teachers confronted by a climate of fear due to potential layoffs. According to a Minnesota planning report (Minnesota Planning Perspectives, 2000), between 1989 and 1999, school districts in Minnesota decreased from 435 to 360 schools due to closures or mergers (p. 6). Winona's schools faced the same problems in 2001 as state funding was lowered and more area funding was needed.

According to Fiecke (2005), in 2001 the first levy (tax referendum) was put before voters when budgetary shortfalls, declining enrollment, and less state funding saw an operating deficit for WAPS. Though the voters approved the measures, WAPS was still strapped for funds (para. 2).

In June 2004, in response to the financial problems of the district, WAPS hired a new superintendent named Dr. Paul Durand to head the schools. The superintendent faced immediate financial pressure on his new job and was faced with cutting programs from the moment he took the job. He was faced with lobbying for additional taxes from the community (levy) in 2005 (para. 3). WAPS wasn't alone in the state since 83 of the state's 343 districts asked for tax levies to bridge school operating funds. One would not say that Durand took over the school system in the best of times.

Though primarily hired to lead the WAPS through the financial crisis, Durand also faced NCLB sanctions. Although Minnesota is recognized as having a good public school system, the state didn't meet the requirements for NCLB because it failed on one portion of Minnesota's state assessment to meet NCLB (failure to have enough proficient special education students pass in reading). Thus,

Minnesota didn't meet the Adequate Yearly Progress (AYP) goals governed by NCLB. As Johnson (2007b) reported, Winona was like many districts across the country that didn't make the AYP of NCLB, but unlike the state of Minnesota that failed in one category, WAPS failed in multiple categories.

During his tenure, Durand saw that several minority groups measured for Annual Yearly Progress didn't make their stated goals. In the case of Winona's district, any group of similar people with more than 40 members was measured, and if they performed poorly on the Minnesota Comprehensive Assessment (MCA-II) test it would cause the entire district to fail. Thus, as shown in Table 4.1 (2007 AYP, 2007b), the district failed although 83 percent of the students met minimum testing requirements (Johnson, 2007).

With the spending cuts, WAPS was also forced to spend time and resources to try to plan for remediation of the groups that had failed AYP guidelines. By the time these results were published, there had been many things for Durand to contend with.

When he took over the district in 2004, cutting costs were one of the options being explored, therefore, Durand's loyalties were initially slanted

Table 4.1. State of Minnesota: AYP Progress for 2006-07 for Winona Area Public School System.

| | AYP Status: Not Making AYP – Corrective action | | | | | |
| | Reading | | Mathematics | | | |
All students	Part. Rate	% Profic.	Part. Rate	% Profic.	Attendance Rate	Graduation Rate
All students	Yes	Yes	Yes	Yes	Yes	Yes
American Indian/ Alaskan Native	-	-	-	-		
Asian/Pacific Islander	Yes	No	Yes	Yes		
Hispanic	Yes	Yes	Yes	No		
Black	Yes	Yes	Yes	Yes		
White	Yes	Yes	Yes	Yes		
Limited English proficient	Yes	No	Yes	No		
Special education	Yes	No	Yes	No		
Free/reduced price lunch	Yes	No	Yes	No		

Source: Test results are from the Minnesota Comprehensive Assessments—Series II (MCA-IIs). They are the state tests that help districts measure student progress toward Minnesota's academic standards and meet the requirements of No Child Left Behind.

The Mathematics Test for English Language Learners (MTELL) is a computer-delivered mathematics test in grades 3–8 and 11 with simplified English that reduces the confounding effects of language on mathematics performance.

The Minnesota Test of Academic Skills (MTAS) is Minnesota's alternate assessment based on alternate achievement standards. The MTAS is part of the statewide assessment program and measures the extent to which students with significant cognitive disabilities are making progress in the general curriculum.

more toward the school board than the needs of the school's employees and students. Singleton (2004) reported that the new job called for cutting $2.4 million in costs from the $40 million school budget. When interviewed, Durand said:

> And in a state climate of tightening budgets, school districts have to "efficiently utilize the resources you have. You can't always go and ask for more. Sometimes you have to, but you can't start from there."
> Durand said he'd focus on building relationships in his first few days as superintendent—and throughout his tenure.
> A trusting relationship with the school board is the basis for strong relationships with staff, he said (para. 24).

Fear is generally derived from dread about prospects for the future. The present and future of WAPS looked grim from a financial standpoint since Filke (2006) reported that enrollment numbers had dropped from 4,400 to 3,800 over the last five years, and the next five years the enrollment was project to continue falling (para. 2). Although Durand said that he wanted to build "strong relationships with staff," it was something that he failed to do.

As one blessed with luck, during Durand's tenure in Winona, the costs for public education were shifting from the state to the local level through the use of levies as evidenced by the following information from Parents United for Public Schools (2007).

The primary role for Durand as superintendent for WAPS was to keep the district operating through a fiscal crisis. While Durand was faced with

Table 4.2. School District Aid, Property Tax Levy, and "Grand Total" Revenue in Inflation-Adjusted Dollars

	Adjusted dollars per pupil in FY 2003 and FY 2007.[1]					
District Name	FY 2003 Per Pupil in Const. FY 2007 Dollars				FY 2007 Per Pupil in Const. FY in 2007 Dollars	Change from 2003–2007 Const. FY 2007 Dollars
District	Years	AID	Levy	Revenue		
Winona	(2003)	8741	664	9406	Projection value of 2003 spending determined by value in 2007 dollars.	
	(2007)	7618	2036	9654		
	Difference	−1124	1372	248		

Source: Funding for 2003 is projected into 2007 dollars. Therefore, "real" revenue per student has increased by $248 due to increases in the levy (tax) assessed on local schools.
[1] Parents United for Public Schools, St. Paul, MN. "School District Aid, Property Tax Levy, and "Grand Total" Revenue in Inflation-Adjusted Dollars per Pupil in FY 2003 and FY 2007. www.parentsunited.org, <parentsunited.org/sites/ .../2003-2007_Grand_ Total_Revenue- District.pdf>

trying to raise new revenues from the community, he was simultaneously cutting costs. One of the ways for school districts to raise money in Minnesota is to call for more taxes. Termed a "levy," it is a ballot measure that schools traditionally used to raise money for "extras" that might be needed for schools. As an article by Baske (2007) on Minnesota's school funding explains:

> At one time, the so-called excess levies were a way for school districts to pay for niceties beyond the basics covered by state allowances. Increasingly, school leaders say the local taxes go for essentials such as textbooks, supplies and teacher salaries. State dollars currently pay 78 percent of education costs, down from a high of 86 percent six years ago (para. 5).

Thus, as the brunt of higher costs is passed to local voters, one of the jobs of the superintendent is to sell tax levies to local residents. A superintendent from Albert Lea, Minnesota describes the situation:

> Unfortunately, our state government is pretty much telling our school districts that if you want a quality school district you have to go to your voters," said Albert Lea Superintendent David Prescott. "Some of our voters are angry about not being able to decide other tax increases, so they take it out on school districts (para. 7).

Durand successfully lobbied for levy twice, thereby avoiding layoffs, but during his tenure he became criticized for an inability to communicate with his staff. When local teachers approached the local paper to voice their displeasure at the lack of communication between the school district office and teachers, it violated one of the stated goals of Durand's stewardship as superintendent: to build relationships.

Three years after starting the job, a local reporter, Johnson (2006), reported discontentment about Superintendent Durand among some of the district's teachers. They asked for their complaints to be aired in the local newspaper. The paper began the story by saying:

> A culture of fear and miscommunication permeates the Winona public school system. Some blame the superintendent and the school board, but others say there's nothing new or unique about the problem (para. 1).

The local community voiced its displeasure with Durand's lack of communication skills by replacing three school board members (Johnson, para. 12). This quickly dissolves the continuity that was established between Durand and the school board. Durand has said that a "trusting relationship with the school board is the basis for strong relationships with staff." As this is being written, another levy asking for more money from the locals continues that shows that "efficiently utilizing the resources you have. You can't always go and ask for more," shows that things haven't gone as well for Durand as he'd planned.

What does this all have to do with fear? Here, it seems interesting to see how fear might arise in an organization. Unless Durand was born without a neurological system, "fear" probably became his middle name during this time. One of the reasons might be the changing conditions he faced from the first day on the job. The prospect of firing employees and reducing the schedules of others is difficult. Ending extracurricular programs (music, football, etc.) is difficult. Asking an aging population for more tax money is also not an easy thing to do.

What is the constancy of purpose in Winona's school system? Superintendent Durand's is to create a fiscally sound structure. He's had to ask taxpayers to cough up an additional $1,372 per student out of their pockets, and each time he asks the voters for money, he threatens school programs and teachers' jobs.

The teachers are concerned about their jobs because of the threats to cut the budget. They will, therefore, be rather reluctant to come forward with valid criticisms of the system. Teachers would not feel comfortable about trying to change the system. In an organization like WSAP, the constancy of purpose in their actions is to survive to live for another day. Superintendent Durand will face each election cycle with two budgets in hand: one for maintaining the current system and a second plan for laying off employees and cutting school programs.

Durand is responsible for making plans for the future, but he's been hired to take care of fiscal issues. Is it possible in such a condition to drive out fear and establish trust in an organization? Are all the employees working toward a similar goal in the district?

When Bill Gates (2005) spoke about problems with the school system, he said "It is the system." (para. 2). If one looks at this example, one could see that fear of all the outside pressures (local funding, NCLB, school board; shifts in funding) were defining issues in the superintendent's actions. In the case of Winona's schools, the composition of the system helped create fear within the system. The superintendent must also be fearful since he is hired by the board, and three members of the local board of education that hired Durand were voted out of office during Durand's tenure. This also adds to the element of fear. In the case of Winona, the superintendent is suddenly faced with three new board members. The superintendent's policies that were created to please the previously elected school board may not be valid anymore. The superintendent's job suddenly has as much long-term stability as a piñata at a kid's birthday party. There's not much constancy of purpose except to survive.

Research shows that a superintendent can have an effect on student performance and that it depends on creating goals for the district they lead. Waters and Marzano (2006) identified five characteristics that districts implement that lead to better student achievement. The five areas involve: 1. collaborative goal setting; 2. setting specific goals for staff members to action; 3. board alignment and support of district goals; 4. monitoring of goals to see the level of progress toward district goals; and 5. proper allocation of resources to support district goals (3–4). If one examines the situation of the WAPS, all five would have been difficult due to the lack of stability facing the district.

Fear in an organization is normally caused by the unknown. In the case of Winona, the teachers don't understand the details of what the superintendent is trying to achieve. Therefore, they feel that speaking out about matters that they feel need to be addressed will lead to personal persecution. As described by the article by Johnson (2006) covering the story:

> Several teachers said they are not heard, and that opinions different from the school board and administration are not only unwelcome, but grounds for punishment (para. 20).

This is the fear that Deming says will create problems in an organization. Building trust is a key toward success in an organization. Using Deming's method, the key is to end fear so that ideas from within an organization can be used to improve it. If there is fear in an organization it will be costly. Poor methods will continue to be used when employees fear that speaking out suggestions to improve how things are done will be held against them. This is exactly what is found in Winona's school district.

4.C.9. Break Down Barriers between Departments, Abolish Competition, and Build a Win–Win System of Cooperation within the Organization

In the school factory, there isn't a huge chain of command that exists between the management (principal and vice-principal) and the production workers (teachers) in the classrooms. One may or may-not like the managerial style of his or her school, but for the most part, a principal of a school doesn't visit or say anything other than "Hello, how's it going?" Usually, departments (or grade levels) cooperate among themselves to set up protocols for running the school based on guidelines from the state or district.

If the school systems had lessons that were optimized for the classroom setting, one of the school management tasks would be to insure that conditions for success were optimized for each classroom. This topic will be discussed in more detail in the following chapter, but what one might consider now is the burden of leading a school under current conditions. To address the needs of schools, one needs both time and resources. Principals of schools have neither.

To understand the difficulties of running a school, you might try to imagine a principal's job. The United States Department of Labor (2007) publishes job descriptions describing a principal's role as follows:

> Educational administrators who manage elementary, middle, and secondary schools are called *principals*. They set the academic tone and hire, evaluate, and help improve the skills of teachers and other staff. Principals confer with staff to advise, explain, or answer procedural questions. They visit classrooms, observe teaching methods, review instructional objectives, and examine learning materials. They actively work with teachers to develop and maintain high curriculum standards, develop mission statements, and set performance goals and objectives. Principals must use clear, objective guidelines for teacher appraisals, because pay often is based on performance ratings.

> Principals also meet and interact with other administrators, students, parents, and representatives of community organizations. Decision-making authority has increasingly shifted from school district central offices to individual schools. School principals have greater flexibility in setting school policies and goals, but when making administrative decisions they must pay attention to the concerns of parents, teachers, and other members of the community.

> Principals prepare budgets and reports on various subjects, including finances and attendance, and oversee the requisition and allocation of supplies. As school budgets become tighter, many principals have become more involved in public relations and fundraising to secure financial support for their schools from local businesses and the community.

> Principals must take an active role to ensure that students meet national, State, and local academic standards. Many principals develop school/business partnerships and school-to-work transition programs for students. Increasingly, principals must be sensitive to the needs of the rising number of non-English speaking and culturally diverse students. In some areas growing enrollments also are a cause for concern because they are leading to overcrowding at many schools. When addressing problems of inadequate resources, administrators serve as advocates for the building of new schools or the repair of existing ones. During summer months, principals are responsible for planning for the upcoming year, overseeing summer school, participating in workshops for teachers and administrators, supervising building repairs and improvements, and working to be sure the school has adequate staff for the school year.

> Schools continue to be involved with students' emotional welfare as well as their academic achievement. As a result, principals face responsibilities outside the academic realm. For example, in response to the growing numbers of

dual-income and single-parent families and teenage parents, schools have established before- and-after-school childcare programs or family resource centers, which also may offer parenting classes and social service referrals. With the help of community organizations, some principals have established programs to combat increases in crime, drug and alcohol abuse, and sexually transmitted diseases among students (para. 3–7).

If this description of requirements doesn't make you want to jump out and get an administrative credential, then you're not alone. For the amount of responsibility in the position, a site administrator has to deal with keeping facilities running, students, faculty, parents, and the community at large. For both the elementary and secondary school principal, there are many after school functions that fill one's time. It isn't surprising, then, that it's difficult to find people who want to be a principal. A government job that provides one with long hours, high stress, and relatively low pay when compared to the private sector isn't exactly what one dreams about growing up.

A principal's day is described in an article by Guteman (2007) that describes the current shortage of principals:

> So far today, among many other things, you've spoken into a crackling megaphone at a school assembly, listened to a phone message in which a parent yelled about parking rules at drop-off time, added four new students to your already overflowing classrooms, helped one teacher with a science-curriculum question and another with an email problem, met with the school site council, worked with the PTA to keep a canceled after-school arts program alive, fetched children in time for the late bus, snuck home for a quick dinner with your extremely forgiving family, and then (once your meal was quickly scarfed down) slipped out to explain to the local neighborhood association why the upcoming construction project to repair your school's long-disintegrating playground won't inconvenience them as much as they fear.
>
> In your free time (stop laughing), you've been able to focus on education, which is what originally brought you into this job (para. 2–3).
>
> Welcome to a day—and night—in the life of a public school principal.

What does all this have to do with developing a "win-win system by abolishing competition and creating a system of cooperation" in the organization. Let's suppose that this is a typical day for a principal. What does it say about the organizational structure of his school? One could say that the principal here is very busy, but is he working to improve the product? Deming is quoted by Walton (1986) to describe what the principal was doing:

Putting out fires is not an improvement. Finding a point out of control, finding the special cause and removing it, is only putting the process back to where it was in the first place. It is not improvement of the process (p. 67).

One might be charitable and say that he was "problem solving," but how will today's effort result in improvement? This description of a principal's day is but one day, and there may be days will less chaos, but there is little here to suggest that there is a method to improve the product. He did manage to clarify a question about science curriculum, and save art classes from being cancelled, but that is an attempt to maintain the status quo. What would be a "win-win" situation that would improve a school?

We've previously discussed the waste in the school system. Thousands and thousands of schools across the United States all run generally the same. The primary function of the school is teaching. The principal's time and effort should be substantially devoted to that end. From the descriptions given above, how much time is devoted toward the mission of learning?

Why ask this question? As the United States Department of Labor (2007) description of the principal's duties said:

> Decision-making authority has increasingly shifted from school district central offices to individual schools. School principals have greater flexibility in setting school policies and goals, but when making administrative decisions they must pay attention to the concerns of parents, teachers, and other members of the community (para. 4).

What is true is that the principal is preparing a budget, setting up class schedules, and dealing with students, teachers, and parents. The principal must also account for having teachers who are teaching the subject areas, but to say they are experts in each subject area would be stretching the truth. Is the support system at the district office and above doing its job?

Deming is asking for someone to create a "win-win" scenario. The win occurs when the maximum amount of resources reach the student. A previous section noted that California claimed to spend $10,000 per student, but only about $7,500 reached the various districts. Out of the $7,500, a little more than half actually goes toward direct educational expense. So, out of the $10,000 spent each year in California for K-12 students, about $4,600 tracks to the student in terms of service. That is primarily in the cost of teachers and support personnel at the school site. So the question is, how is the student supposed to win in this scenario?

The student must be the focal point of the education effort. Students that perceive education as a gateway to college are motivated to do well, but there's a large population that isn't buying the story. The principal, teachers, custodians, and every other person in the district exist to serve the student. So, how does the student win when the system only delivers about 60 percent of funds that are intended for education. How about funding students who do well? The money's there if we cut out the waste.

The chart (Figure 4.2), "K-12 Education," from the Governor's Office in California shows per pupil spending for K-12 education (Governors Budget, 2008). According to Ed-Data (2006–07), the districts in the state reported spending an average of $8,345 per student (based on Average Daily Attendance [ADA]). The direct educational expense delivered to students was $8,117 per student (ADA) (Ed-Data, 2007). The Governor's report shows expenditures of $11,279 total spending per pupil (Governors Budget, 2008).

California's Department of Education had a budget of $57 billion in 2006–07. That accounts for spending of $9,300 per student for the state's 6.3 million students. However, that represented the "non-categorical" (funds not assigned to specific spending category) spending in the budget. There was also a "categorical" (funds designated to specific uses) spending component that added $14.4 billion to the state's education costs. Now, when school districts report spending an average $8,195 per student, one is left to wonder where and how the difference between $11,279 and $8,195 was used.

The point of the question concerning the principal regards the cost of maintaining a bureaucracy to support the schools. For instance, Riverside Unified School District reported $8,251 per student in revenue for 2006–07

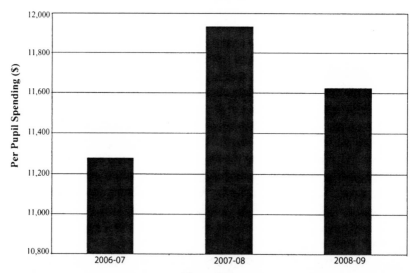

Figure 4.2.

and reported expenditures of $7,823 per student. Finally, the state requires the report of "Current Expense of Education per ADA" and the number is $7,648. In the other districts in the state, they averaged $8,195 per student. Is this the best way there is to report aggregate financial data for the K-12 school system in California?

The data for the non-categorical funding shows a difference of $1,105 per student between the general funding level and the amount of funding that was delivered to students. With regard to the "restricted funds," one might guess that higher reporting requirements would entail more administrative costs, however, the bottom line is that when they're added to together, the revenue is only $8,251 per ADA (student). Total spending per pupil reported by the governor's office was $11,279. That's $3,024 per student or 26.8 percent of the revenues being used somewhere other than the schools. One might claim that it's used to support administrative expense, but, there's already district administrative expense that's reported for the $8,251 per student.

Do you think that by combining the expenses and cutting out the "middle man" (state), do you think that more money could reach the student? Let's not stop there.

There are over 14,000 districts in the United States that are running administrative offices that are similar to the one shown here. How much can be cut out of downtown offices that don't serve students and put those people back on campuses. While one's at it, one should look at the county offices of education that are designed to serve areas that haven't formed localized school districts. It is another area where savings could be achieved but cutting out positions that do not directly serve students.

Can the local district budgets also be cut?

There is the question that anyone would ask at this point. Based on the information from the previous section regarding Winona, Minnesota, one can tell that the school districts are facing economic despair. Voters are being asked to spend more and more money to support education, a product that is often criticized for the quality of its schools. How then, is it possible to cut expenses from the school system?

If you look at the functions of the principal in today's school, it's obvious that the place where change is going to take place is at the school. Many of the functions that are currently done at the district level (finance, computer services) could be optimized in another location and shipped off site. With the extra money saved, more people could work at the school site and make a difference with the student.

It appears that there are two choices that are possible. The first choice is the most likely, and that is to continue down the same path the nation is currently on. The current path is to continue to treat education as an entity that can either be saved by new legislation or an army of uber-teachers and administrators who enter the profession and save it. The second choice is to recognize that the current system isn't working on several levels and try to fix them.

The first is to try to adopt economies of scale that share costs and bring down expenses. If the option to try to fix the schools is tried, the first suggestion would be to standardize curriculum in schools.

A national curriculum would establish agreed upon parameters of what should be taught. As discussed previously, this curriculum and the lessons associated with them would demonstrate how best to teach ideas. When a lesson is judged particularly valuable, it can be added to a lesson bank for history. Thus, at any time, a teacher or student could examine excellent examples of lessons prepared by the best teachers in the country. This represents a starting point since it places the focus of education on learning in the classroom.

If lessons are taken care of at a central location, the role of the state and part of the district office can be downsized. The system can benefit from economies of scale. The same thing can occur for testing, and test results can be quantified by a central scoring entity (perhaps the stripped down federal department of education). Suppose that the system of education is pared down and $1,000 per student can be added to money spent at the school. Will that make a material difference?

This is where the breaking-down-barriers and the "win-win" part of Deming's point comes in. If money is shipped directly to the school and the principal has more discretion over spending it, a huge barrier is removed between the district office and the school site. Principals who can plan their own objectives can listen to teachers' ideas for improvement and decide which ones to try. That's a win based on breaking down barriers and working with staff. Here's the other idea that affects the student.

Every student who "tries" on the year-end examination will have $1,000 deposited into an account in their name for every year they take the test. The fund will apply to future education costs at an accredited school. As long as the test is taken with reasonably good faith each year, the education fund will have $1,000 deposited in it. It can earn interest at a money-market rate and becomes available upon graduation. It's a win-win idea because it helps incentivize the students and makes the assessment test more valid.

4.C.10. Eliminate Slogans, Exhortations, and Targets Asking for Zero Defects or New Levels of Productivity

According to the American Heritage Dictionary (2000), the word "slogan" originated in Scotland where it was used to refer to a battle cry among clans (American Heritage, 2000). One might feel that Scottish leaders might want to say a few inspiring words prior to battle to help get followers ready to slice and dice the enemy. A few well chosen words might inspire one for a battle. However, in modern a modern factory like a school, Esquith's (2007) book *Teach like Your Hair's on Fire* may be a great title for a book, but it isn't likely to inspire teachers over the long term.

In an article by Good (2006), some of the popular slogans showing up in school settings include: "It takes a village," "Every school a good school," and "Leave No Child Behind" (p. 35). The article on school slogans was written when his local district started using the motto, "Believe and Achieve." The slogan was plastered on walls, tee-shirts, and on announcements that went home to parents. The author states that the slogan shifts the discussion from the backs of administrators to the students who are powerless to change the system (p. 35).

Deming (1993) was not in favor of slogans because they don't fix problems, they merely create resentment. Slogans such as, "Take Pride in Your Work" or "Do it Right the First Time" (p. 44) only create resentment among workers since they imply that the worker could have done things better. If the problem is inherent in the system, and the worker is given an impossible challenge, he or she will not be able to respond to the challenge. The article by Goode (2006) supported Deming's contention about resentment. When the school district employed the slogan *Believe and Achieve,* local teachers responded with *Believe and Deceive* (p. 1).

The real problem in schools is not the presence of slogans, but the use of slogans in the absence of substantive changes to the system that create improvement. One wouldn't suppose that a slogan would hurt, but always remember: one teaches children not subjects.

4.C.11. Eliminate Numerical Goals, Numerical Quotas, and Management by Objectives. Substitute Leadership

The passage of NCLB created numerical quotas for schools to reach for years. Until a school reaches the level indicating proficiency for a school or district, each school, district, and state is placed under a microscope. This has resulted in more paperwork for schools, more time spent working to send reports to middle managers, and therefore, less money and time devoted toward the classroom. According to Deming, numerical goals detract from the mission to improve the system.

This is a thought that is counter-intuitive to most people. We've been sold on the idea that creating numerical goals gives a person or organization something to strive for. Deming (1993) asserts that:

Anyone can meet almost any goal by:

- Redefinition of terms
- Distortion and faking
- Running up costs (p. 44)

Since the implementation of NCLB, schools, districts, and states are required to show improvement according to standardized tests. Since there isn't a uniform test for everyone, each state creates its own assessment and then chooses "proficiency" levels for students taking the test. A redefinition of the standard would mean that the test would be adjusted to make its requirements easier to attain. It appears that this is exactly what has happened.

A report by the Cronin, Dahlin, Adkins, and Kingsbury (2007) examined how states have responded to testing requirements of NCLB, and they found that redefinition of terms was rampant. Since states are supposed to create proficiency by the year 2014, some have responded to the requirement by "lowering standards" for proficiency. The report shows 8 of the 26 states studied had lowered their proficiency standards, and that 70 percent of overall test gains in math, and 50 percent of reading gains had been due to relaxation of test standards (p. 7).

This directly supports Deming's contention about redefinition of terms. Another report that supports the redefinition of terms is the graduation rate which is one of the criteria used to evaluate public high schools by NCLB. According to the Alliance for Excellent Education (2007), states are currently using five methods to calculate graduation rates. The variation between "actual" and reported rates show lower drop-out rates by an average of 11 percent and one as high as 30 percent (p. 5). This may represent "distortion and faking" by the states, but as Deming states, it is merely natural when the system of education is looking to meet targets.

Lewin and Medina (2003) show one way that districts are distorting or faking graduation rate data is through *pushouts,* a term that refers to students who are being dropped out of schools to help increase graduation rates (par. 1, 11). In their study, New York students over the age of 17 who were deemed unable to graduate were forced from schools. This is a method to insure that graduation rates aren't affected. Since N.Y. Education Law (2008) states that students are eligible to attend school until they are 21 (§ 3202 (1)), the practice is also illegal.

In some cases students with excessive absences may be dropped from school rolls legitimately, but it is a convenience to the school, not to the student. The intent of the law and the system of education is being sacrificed in order to meet a numerical goal.

The basic idea is that numerical goals can guide practices that are detrimental to improving the system. People try to play games with the statistics rather than dealing with the problem at hand. One needs good data to understand where problems exist and how to approach them.

4.C.12. Remove Barriers That Rob People of Joy in Their Work

Deming (1993) defined the system as "a network of interdependent components that work together to try to accomplish the aims of the system" (p. 50). For Deming, a workforce devoted toward continuous improvement of the workplace is a happy place. There is one fact that cannot be denied in an education setting; they can be happy places. In spite of everything one hears about "the kids today," they are worth any hassles of the job.

When Deming discusses barriers that "rob people of joy in their work," he's refers to getting rid of the annual rating or merit systems that rank people and create competition and conflict in the workplace. The presence of teachers unions has made the "ranking" of employees a moot point. What seems to be lacking in the education system is firm direction or commitment to a goal. The aim of the school should be to maximize the education process given the resources available.

As previously discussed, teachers often feel left out of discussions on school improvement and principals are so busy running schools that time for their systematic improvement is lacking. Upper management has to be responsible for finding ways to optimize the school system. That is their primary job. We need people to find the best ways to accomplish school goals and find ways to provide the information to teachers and principals.

As we find the best ways to deliver lessons, research has to be made available to give principals the tools to make decisions for school improvement.

4.C.13. Institute a Vigorous Program of Education and Self-Improvement

The idea that education has to constantly improve should be an inherent part of the K-12 education system. If you examine most school districts, they will have courses that provide teachers with the knowledge needed to run a computer and how to deal with special needs children (either gifted or special needs). However, there usually isn't a comprehensive program to show teachers how to improve teaching skills in their disciplines. One of the reasons for this is that each district must meet the needs of prior legislation.

Districts spend a great deal of time to bring people into compliance to meet the needs of specific groups. In many cases, money has been set aside for specific training, and the training is designed to help the meet the requirements of a specific law. Examples of state-mandated funding include training for English learner programs that cover techniques to present material to non-English speakers. These programs, like many others, are governed by meeting civil rights legislation. Teachers are put into workshops to learn words like "scaffolding" and a host of acronyms that allow teachers to talk about the problem, but there isn't a comprehensive curriculum to cover how to bring English learners to a proficient level (FEP–Fluent English Proficient).

This is pointed out, not to demean the aims of programs to help disadvantaged groups, but to show that the limited resources of schools are not in response to need, but in response to legislation. So, one must ask if current methods in any approach are an effective way to "establish a program of education and self-improvement." These programs don't meet the needs of the site; they meet the needs of legislation.

The drain of time and resources that "outside influences" can impose on the education system is tremendous. If you really want an example of a legislative nightmare, the situation for English learner students is an example. In 1974 Congress passed the Equal Education Opportunities Act (1974), which states that an "educational agency" must take measures to overcome language barriers (Sec. (f)).

While federal law said one thing, California voters enacted Prop 227, a ballot measure enacted by voters in 1998 to insure that all K-12 instruction was in English. When enacted in the California Education Code (1998), the law prescribes that students receive no more than one year of instruction in a "sheltered immersion classroom." The bottom line here is that the law tells the education community how to teach. Not only that, but the law enacted by California might also be at odds with federal law. Can one imagine that at Microsoft someone would come into Bill Gates' office and say, "Mr. Gates, guess what?

"I don't want to guess."

"All right I'll tell you. It's illegal now to use multiple programming languages to create code for software."

"Are you kidding?"

"No. We've decided that all new programming should be done in Microsoft C++. It's the law."

"Well, I'm happy," Gates forces a smile, "that you've chosen a Microsoft product, but, we soft of like to match the best programming language to the application at hand. Like I said, C++ is great, but we use a different language for Web-based application. Then there's. . . ."

"How hard can it be? Isn't it all about ones and zeros? Come on now, you're a smart guy and you'll figure it out. It's the law now."

Of course, such an event could never happen. Our economic system is built on the premise that Gates or his competitors need to use the best products possible to produce the best products possible.

Self-improvement in teaching should also be based on education. It would be a wonderful thing to for teachers to analyze master lesson plans that can help them re-think their current teaching strategies. If you have the best tools, and then find ways to get them into the teacher's hands, management will make sure the teachers are using them. No company in the world would improve its productivity if they are forced to use techniques that don't work. Using Deming's method, one begins with the unambiguous goal, "Everyday, students will receive the best lessons possible." Management's job will be to create classroom dynamics on the campus that support the teacher.

The continuous improvement of teachers will come from providing them with techniques they can use. Isn't that a simple concept? Here's another concept that is often lost in schools, and that's incentive. If the best ways to teach are available for a given level of student, then teachers who demonstrate some mastery of material (particularly those in teaching areas where specialists are in short supply, such as math and science) can be compensated for their efforts. For instance, if there's a current shortage of mathematic instructors and an art teacher decided to learn how to teach an algebra class (to mastery—as exhibited by a rigorous exam), he or she could be compensated for filling a need.

There may be people who feel that such a system would be unfair in some way, but under the current system, one can get additional compensation for gaining a masters degree in a subject that isn't even related to what the person teaches. So, a mathematics teacher can gain a masters in physical education and gain a large increase in compensation. How such a policy serves education is difficult to discern, but that is how the current system operates. In education, the training of teachers has to be aligned to the needs of students.

4.C.14. Put Everybody in the Company to Work to Accomplish the Transformation—the Transformation Is Everybody's Job

Many schools and districts practice top-down management styles that don't allow for a great deal of input into the "transformation" process. Schools and "school systems," such as district, will argue that everyone is already doing the job. However, in the top-down management environment that currently exists in schools, the primary motivation is to fulfill the needs to please the manager to whom you are beholden. If you're a teacher, you try to understand what the principal or vice-principal wants you to do.

If the requirement is to write something on the board to meet a district policy, then you do it. For instance, one may have to write the name of the state's "standard" on the board. Now, writing something on the board may not improve education at all, but doing this will allow a teacher to approach their lesson with the knowledge they've fulfilled the rules. The administrator in the school can then visit the classroom and collect evidence that the "standard" is being written on the board. The superintendent can then tell the school board and the state department of education that a "standards-based curriculum" is being utilized.

4.D. FOUR OF SEVEN DEADLY DISEASES

When Deming discussed his methods to improve organizations, he also discussed barriers to success. He called them the "Seven Deadly Diseases." When examining the seven deadly diseases, four seemed particularly pertinent to education:

- neglecting long-range planning
- relying on technology to solve problems
- seeking examples to follow rather than developing solutions
- excuses, such as "Our problems are different"

It may seem premature to discuss problems that one might encounter when trying to improve a system prior to beginning the process, but Deming was experienced and some of these, and four of the seven items, seemed particularly important to education. The first item regards "long-range planning."

With *long-range planning* the first issue might be whether this applies to the schools or the students. Students who have long-range plans do better in schools because their goals are clearly defined. This will be followed-up in chapter 6 in programs like Advancement Via Individual Determination (AVID) that make sure that students are on-track. When their families don't have the criteria that promotes success, the school is trying to intervene so the students don't slip through the cracks. As far as the school system, the first goal should be getting rid of bureaucracy that doesn't directly support classroom instruction.

Duplicity of efforts at the federal, state, and local levels needs to be streamlined and funding applied to students. There are people who will argue that the problem is that government involvement in the public school system has created the problem. Not true. In health care, an equivalent problem exists since players in the middle (insurance companies) are taking disproportionate amounts of equity from caregivers. In the case of both education and health care, one of the first goals of long-term planning should involve a restructuring of the system that maximizes the benefit to those served. Goal one for long-term planning would be to cut bureaucracy.

The second issue will be *technology*. There are plenty of people who claim that technology will make teachers obsolete. These claims were made with the invention of the television, and they were repeated when the Internet and computer technology became commonplace. It might happen someday, but at this point, the education-related computer programs that have been developed haven't been impressive. As discussed in the final chapter, the successful use of computer programs in education is often determined by how much "human interaction" is involved in the process.

What is needed is to develop computer programs that aid the learning process and then to determine the best way to implement them. Again, there would be a role for the department of education in such an endeavor and these efforts could benefit every student in the country. Technology is not a panacea that will help education.

The third item calls for *seeking examples to follow rather than developing solutions*. Essentially, this axiom states that each site must address its own problems. There is quite a bit of irony if one looks at charter schools. One of the arguments used for promoting the charter school movement is that schools will be freed of the bureaucracy of the education system, thus freeing students and teachers to excel in the "free market" environment. The irony is that a second argument for charter schools is that once these wonderful schools show the world how education should be done, it will serve as templates for everyone to follow. Schools love to plagiarize each other's work. However, leadership involves coming up with solutions for problems inherent at each site.

This leads naturally, to the largest excuse in education, *our problems are different*. This isn't true. Everyone is facing the same problems. Schools are generally underfunded and barely getting by. Virtually all the test scores in the country can be predicted based on the economic status of students and the family education level. The truth is that schools face similar problems and that is why studies showing how best to approach lessons in education are needed. It is also necessary for the education system to be revised so that economic resources actually reach the kids who need them.

Chapter 5

Entropy: Education Is a System of Planned Chaos

"The main hope of a nation lies in the proper education of its youth."

—Erasmus

"Today, only one-third of our students graduate from high school ready for college, work, and citizenship."

—William Gates, 2005

Many people have expressed their frustration with American education. Most feel that the school system should improve, but many of the suggestions for improvement (standardized testing, school choice, higher pay for the profession) haven't addressed the process of how *the process* of education should occur. One of the ideas promoted by Edward Deming is that improving the process will improve the product. If Deming's methods were employed for a single system, changes in education would directly affect what is actually being done in the classroom or school.

Methods to improve education have traditionally targeted the teacher. The idea that improving teachers will improve education is quite pervasive. Although teachers are an important part of the learning process, they are essentially one part of a process within a larger system. The schools get students in kindergarten and spend the next 13 years trying to convert them into high school graduates. Teachers are at the workstations, but they don't control what comes into their classrooms. In some respects, this education process invites comparisons to a factory. As a factory system, American education is flawed in many respects.

Thus, teachers work in a flawed system. There are examples of great teachers rising above the system around them to produce great results. When those teachers leave, the system reverts to its original form.

As this book began, Bill Gates targeted American schools for improvement and suggested the education *system* was flawed. Teachers are the most visible link to students and, therefore, the easiest *targets* of criticism for education's failures, but Gate's remarks suggested a far more serious charge. The education system itself was at fault. It was ironic that several years later, Gates (2009) described teachers as the key to changing education. Thus, instead of creating a good system to deal with education's problems, Gates put the onus back on teachers. There's no doubt that teachers are important, but when examining the management of systems, people like Dr. Edward Deming suggest that a majority of a system's failures are due to management.

This isn't surprising. Since the education system doesn't have a systematic way to improve itself, it keeps rethinking the same information again and again. For example, when the National Education Commission on Time and Learning (1994) published *Prisoners of Time,* it stated eight goals that had been developed by state governors as goals for education for the year 2000. They were: 1. all children will start school ready to learn; 2. graduation rate of 90 percent; 3. students at 4th, 8th, and 12th grade will demonstrate subject-area mastery; 4. teachers will have access to ways to improve their skills; 5. U.S. students will be first in the world in science and math; 6. every adult will be literate and able to exercise the responsibilities of citizenship; 7. every school in the country will be alcohol and drug free; and 8. each school will create partnerships that promote parental involvement and to promote the learning needs of children (p. 12). Well, we're well past the year 2000, how did we do?

The only one of these items that appears to be true is that all children start school ready to learn. Perhaps the students didn't meet the aspirations of the governors, but one can be assured that they are ready to learn. With respect to every other objective on the list, education is still failing. It is very easy to come up with a list of things that schools should do to improve. What is needed is an approach to education that allows for improvements to be incorporated into the education system.

The previous chapter examined slices of the American school system by using Dr. Edward Deming's criteria for successful systems. The chapter suggested that American schools could be set up to find and adopt methods that would promote better teaching and learning.

In addition to a way to improve teaching methods, the education system should have a systematic perspective of the American classroom. The methods used to educate students should be measured for effectiveness under real conditions by an agency that specializes in education methods. Results of these studies that show what does and does not work should be directed to teachers and principals to use at school sites. Using statistics to find the best teaching methods and then providing them to teachers and school sites will improve the odds that excellent lessons are delivered.

The idea is that the school system should support the teacher by finding the best teaching methods. Even if the best methods were used by teachers, it wouldn't insure that all kids would learn. The previous chapters have shown that demographic factors have a large effect on student performance in schools. In this chapter, the common factors of low-performing schools are boiled down to a single concept: the examination of disorder or entropy. What will be examined here is what school management can do to help schools provide a better learning environment—what will give student the best chance to "beat the odds"

This chapter will examine a way to approach policy and practice in the education system. The data from the education system shows that the *odds* favor places where there is less disorder. This chapter focuses on the idea that limiting entropy (or disorder) in the learning environment is necessary in order to improve the education system. School management should not only provide the best methods for the classroom, but also the best methods for setting up the classroom and school for success. The current system is woefully negligent in this regard.

The following will show that using entropy as a tool to examine school sites can help improve school performance.

5.A. DEFINING ENTROPY

Entropy is a term that is usually used in the physical sciences to describe disorder in a system. However, it is presented here as a useful way to examine processes of education. Perhaps a good place to start with how entropy relates to education is to define the term. Some of the definitions of *entropy* according to The American Heritage's (2000) include:

1. the amount of disorder or randomness in a closed system
2. the measure of loss of information in a transmitted message
3. the tendency of all matter in the universe to evolve to a state of inert uniformity
4. inevitable and steady deterioration of a system or society

If one examines each of the definitions of entropy, each has a unique application to the educational system. It is the second definition concerning disorder that is most applicable to describe the education process.

The first thing to note about entropy is that it defines disorder in a *closed system.* For education, a closed system can be defined in terms of the classroom, school, local school system, or education system of the United States.

When discussing the education process, the following pages will show that the degree of disorder in a system is a factor that can limit success. This means that if the school setting is sufficiently ordered (low entropy), it will help provide an environment that will accentuate teaching and learning. Does the data support this?

Most schools reflect the neighborhoods they serve. The demographic characteristics of the parents often predict the eventual success of each student at a school. High income parents with high educational levels will devote (or have surrogates devote) more educational time and resources to their kids. At the present time, one can predict with reasonable certainty "the odds" of success in schools based on parental incomes.

The parents of students who've invested the time and effort in education create uniformity. When parents are able to devote a lot of resources toward education, the cumulative effect is to prevent entropy. Parents who put more resources into raising their kids will, on average, produce kids that are more uniform. They have been "formed" to societal norms more than students who receive less attention. When parents of students lack the resource of time and money to contribute to the education process, over time the student will tend to gain disorder or entropy. The affect of parental education can also affect the process since students without guidance in the education process are less likely to accept the need for education. Though the process happens to individuals, social conditions (poverty and wealth) group people together. Schools thus become high-income, low entropy schools or low-income, high entropy schools. Disorder in a system (society, school, classroom) can be ameliorated if sufficient energy or resources are put into the system to compensate for the lack of "order."

One of the large fears that parents face is in putting their children in a situation where the amount of disorder in a school or classroom will be detrimental to their child's education. Parents fear that their careful plans to avoid entropy in their child's lives (monitoring television, language, habits) will be overwhelmed.

Since teaching is a process that essentially creates order in the life of a child, factors that detract from creating order will affect the learning process. Whether it is in a classroom or home, parents and teachers use a sophisticated system of censorship and indoctrination to place *order* in a child's life. Energy needs to be directed toward a child to avoid disorder. Disorder is the normal order of things. Left to itself, a system will tend to move toward disorder. Teaching and education's role is to promote order and sufficient energy that must be put into the system to succeed.

The amount of disorder in a classroom is described in terms of two factors that sound paradoxical: (1) the amount of disorder students generate in the class; and (2) the disorder or lesson the teacher brings to the class. It's natural if you're wondering how a teacher brings *disorder* to a class.

To solve this apparent paradox, let's examine the classrooms that we've been exposed to in the movies to examine the disorder students bring to a class. At one extreme, the English preparatory academy (Eton, for example) would be an example of an ordered environment. The twenty or thirty preparatory school students are sitting in their seats, and although they aren't all clones of each other, they've all received proper training for the classes they're in. All have grown up in families that support education and most are from wealthier families. For some of them, classes will be relatively easy, and for others the classes will be difficult, but all of the students are capable of doing the work.

This means that the instructor of this factory (classroom) can present information that is appropriate to the level of the students. In the classroom, the inherent entropy (disorder) among the learning levels of the students is low. The capacity to present material to challenge them (create entropy) is high.

If the instructor is reasonably certain that his or her students have the skills to perform well, then, he or she can create challenging lessons. The presentation of challenging lessons and ideas will initially create "disorder" in the mind of the student. If a student is being challenged by a new concept (mathematical, philosophical, or otherwise), it initially creates disorder. It must be worked through and integrated into the student's mind.

The exposure to new information is disorder since it challenges what a student knows. When introducing a new idea into the classroom, the factors include the energy that a teacher uses to deliver the information and the energy that the student can devote toward understanding and integrating new information. In order for teaching and learning to occur, the teacher and students need an environment that is ordered so the information can be presented and then digested by the students. Learning must occur in an "ordered" environment.

A second scenario will be presented based on the Hollywood version of the American inner-city classroom. It looks quite different from the preparatory school classroom. The screenwriter creating the *ghetto* school must love writing the scripts since there are always stereotypical characters that look and act in specific ways. There are always a couple of gang-type kids in the class who are on the verge of leaving school. There will be a student who is supporting his mother and a student with a family member who is in a gang. There is always the brilliant kid who is disadvantaged and on the verge of dropping out. Unfortunately, from experience, these scenarios are not just fiction. An inner-city teacher can see these scenarios on a daily basis.

Usually, dropped into this *hopeless* situation is the *uberteacher* or super-teacher (Miriam Webster, 2008) who will overcome obstacles to transform the group of scary misfits into educated members of society. Generally, the teacher must overcome the anarchy of the classroom, gain the trust of the students, and have the students come to order. One of the things that usually happens during the story is that the teacher will sacrifice a great deal (marriage, wealth, health) in order to overcome the obstacles posed by his or her situation.

Does this situation follow the factory system? Is entropy a useful model when examining an inner-city classroom? As a matter of fact it is; it is a factory in disarray. The usual Hollywood image of the inner-city class shows it to be a disruptive classroom. The students are not interested in school and are disruptive of the teacher's attempts to educate them. The audience becomes aware that the well meaning teacher faces a huge obstacle.

The audience realizes that the situation has too much disorder to overcome. The poor teacher has entered a situation in which the entropy (disorder) is too high. There is too much disorder in the classroom to overcome to effectively teach. As a factory analogy, the English schoolboy situation represents a situation where the kids are coming to their "workstation" ready to be honed into fine, upper-crust members of society. In the situation for the inner city kids, the Hollywood scenario would search and find a way to identify with the kids, the kids would accept the teacher, and then the kids become great students. Let's examine if this demonstrates the idea of entropy in education.

First, the inner-city situation is a high entropy (situation) setting. The kids in the class are all having different problems. They vary widely in their education levels (level of preparation), and they create disruptions in the classroom. It is a situation in which teaching cannot occur unless the situation is ameliorated in some manner. When there is high entropy, the disorder is too high in the room for the teacher to present a lesson. Not only is the entropy (disorder) in the room too high, the education levels of the students make it practically impossible to find a lesson that will adequately challenge all of them.

In the movies, of course, the uberteacher manages to motivate and teach the kids in spite of differences in education level. This may be a good story for Hollywood, but it cannot be expected to form the basis of a factory system. The uberteacher puts a huge amount of energy into the process and finds a way to reach the children. Essentially, the story is inspirational because it is unlikely; it defies the odds. However, it also makes us think. If the right energy is applied to the class, education can succeed. Energy can overcome chaos. It is a great demonstration of the teacher overcoming entropy and shows what is possible.

For most teachers and schools, the happy ending for teacher and students would be fictional. In order for the teacher to be successful, enough effort (energy) has to be put into the classroom setting to overcome the entropy (disorder) created by the students. Then, the teacher is responsible for introducing new thoughts into the minds (entropy) of the student in the form of lessons and ultimately leads the students toward a more complete understanding of the world. The teacher is a master of entropy.

5.B. AREN'T DEMING'S METHODS ENOUGH?

The reason the subject of entropy is discussed here is because it provides a means of looking at a school setting with a defined purpose. There are two factors that must occur for learning to improve. One is that the delivery of the lessons must be maximized. To do this, one must measure what works under *real* classroom conditions and determine the best teaching methods. A second thing that management should do is create conditions that allow students and teachers to succeed.

If there is too much entropy (disorder) in a classroom, a lesson cannot be delivered. It is the school system's duty to deliver students to a classroom so that learning can occur. What level of entropy can a classroom accommodate and still function? That's a good question.

If one accepts the contention that the school is a factory, and K-12 education is an operation in a long-term process of producing adults, a good factory would place the right materials at the appropriate time so the operator could work. That's what the education system should do for the teacher. Entropy gives one a way to examine the education system. If you can reduce sources of entropy in a classroom, the instruction delivered can improve. Learning will improve.

Entropy is a measure of the disorder in a system, whether at the level of the state school system or in individual classrooms. Earlier discussions focused on legislative entities that are outside the school system whose actions create disorder. As an example, legislators might consider a law that would require every student to pass a year-long chemistry course prior to graduation. Is it a noble goal? Yes. A class that gives one a better understanding of the world around us and a foundation for a better understanding of how the world works is a noble goal. As a college preparatory class, it would also channel more students towards college.

How would such a law impact the system?

At the school level, one would need to build more classrooms with laboratories, hire more science teachers, and schedule students into the new classes.

The current algebra class requirement would force students to pass algebra in their junior year prior to entering the chemistry class. There would be great pressure to get students through algebra by their junior year.

According to Deming, adding a chemistry class is creating a new *standard* for schools and students to meet. As Deming said, people in systems tend to find ways to meet standards. One can predict that the chemistry class would become a place where either: (1) standards (content) would be dropped to prevent a drop in graduation rates; or (2) the class would be responsible for pushing down graduation rates. There would be increased numbers of drop-outs, and the school system would be blamed for the failures. The legislators were well-meaning in their desire to increase academic standards. They feel that increasing graduation standards will lead to a higher percentage of college-ready students.

The truth is that throwing a chemistry class into the schedule of students who are at the end of the K-12 education process will help students prepare for college and for life. The question that must be asked is, "Is a legislator's desire for more college-prep students (tougher standards) worth the increase in drop-outs?" The chemistry class was available before being legislated; it wasn't being denied to anyone. Would requiring such a class for graduation help improve education? The law adds a lot of disorder into the education system. The mandates for school do not revolve around the college; they revolve around meeting societal needs.

The data shows that the economic success of American citizens is positively correlated with college attendance. However noble the intent, one shouldn't lose sight that the goal of the education system isn't just related to college education. To improve schools, one must improve the processes that will allow students to take higher-level classes (such as chemistry) by their own choice. In the previous chapter, Deming's methods were examined as guidelines to improve the process of education.

This following example of a simple factory process will examine the sources of entropy in a factory setting. This example will then be applied to a school setting to show how the school system can decrease entropy.

5.B.1. Entropy and Disorder in the Factory

If a school is a factory, perhaps the best way to envision entropy is to see how it affects a factory process. Then, it may be easier to show how entropy can affect productivity while making parallels to processes in schools. In a factory, let's suppose you are at a workstation where you operate a lathe that cuts rounded pieces of wood of a specific length into legs for chairs. As operator of the lathe, you are responsible for cutting 600 chair legs per day. You need to cut each leg individually.

The lathe has a preset pattern that will cut the piece of wood after it is properly positioned for cutting. The operator is responsible for putting the piece of wood on the lathe, starting the operation, and then testing each piece to make sure that it meets specifications. The finished chair legs are each 20 inches in length when finished. At the smallest point, they have a diameter of one inch. The "sticks" that will form the legs arrive at the operator's lathe station; she or he must properly mount the piece to be cut in the lathe and must insure that the lathe is in proper condition to make the correct cut in the wood.

To be successful (make the proper parts), the lathe operator needs: (1) proper input materials; (2) successful placement of material in chuck (holds wood); (3) check for proper settings on machine to make cut; (4) proper tooling that is in good condition to prevent flaws during cut; and (5) periodic inspections to insure that the process is going well.

Each of the items listed will have the capacity to increase entropy in the process of cutting the wood. If the piece of wood is either too short (less than 20 inches in length), or with a diameter that is too small (less than 3 inches), the process cannot succeed. If the operator has to insure that the wood he or she receives is the right size, time will be wasted. Once the operator takes the material and places it into the machine, he or she has to insure that it is properly placed in the machine.

Then the lathe will be programmed to cut certain designs into the wood. Even if the instructions are correct, if the operator uses poor tooling to cut the wood, the operation will fail.

Finally, the last step is to periodically perform inspections to insure that the processes are working. Every one of the items listed is a potential source of disorder in the operation of cutting a chair leg. The success of this factory operation depends on: (1) quality of the input materials; (2) quality of the tools being used; and (3) skill or diligence of the operator. The strength of using Deming's methods is that it allows one to look at sources of error in a process and prevent them before they happen.

What if one applies the same criteria to analyze a classroom setting? The operator (teacher) has a group of students that shows up for class. Suppose it is a secondary teacher that's teaching algebra. Her or his chances for success are greatly improved if all the students already have the requisite math skills for the class. Those that do not will fail. Is this a process that is difficult to assess? Is it possible to assess students for having the proper skill level?

It isn't possible to learn algebra without basic math skills anymore than you can create a 20-inch chair leg from wood that is 18 inches in length. By placing the lower-skilled students in the algebra classroom, the administration has increased the entropy in the classroom. If there is too much entropy in the class, it will be impossible for the teacher to succeed. Yet, many kids are placed in America's classrooms without the required skills.

Is it the teacher's fault when the administration of the school has set up the teacher to fail by providing the wrong starting materials? Like a machine operator, a teacher doesn't choose what students arrive in his or her classroom. When students are placed in a class where the prerequisite skills are greater than those of a student, both the student and the class are placed in greater danger of failing. The entropy or disorder of the system has increased. This is part of what Bill Gates calls the *system of education* that is failing.

Returning from the classroom to the factory, we can see the effects of having the right parts in the proper place. In order to prepare for being processed, some unturned pieces of wood have been placed next to the lathe. Recall that the minimum length for a chair leg is 20 inches. Let's suppose that out of 30 pieces of wood delivered, five of them are less than 20 inches in length. The machine operator will get rid of those pieces of wood and they are recycled. Perhaps they can go to another operation where they can be turned (they can be made into shorter chair legs).

The irony is that the process in the factory can be improved by insuring that the pieces are all 20 inches in length. The factory benefits from using the 18-inch piece of wood for an alternate purpose. Although the machine operator would be foolish to try to make 20-inch legs out of 18-inch pieces of wood, a teacher is often expected to accomplish the equivalent operation in a classroom.

In a classroom with 30 students, there might be five students who don't have the requisite math skills to do algebra, who sit through the semester and will either be bored and disruptive, or bored and non-disruptive. In a factory, the operator isn't expected to make 20-inch legs from 18-inch pieces, yet our classrooms often expect miracles to happen. Although placement of students is the school system's responsibility, the teacher is the one who is responsible for the success or failure of students.

American teachers are often faced with having large numbers of students in their classes who do not have the pre-requisite skills needed for success. Thus, the education system has done a disservice to the student who could have been placed in the proper environment. It also does a disservice to students who've come to learn and whose efforts to do so will be compromised by students who've been misplaced in the classroom.

It is a situation that the teacher has little power to change. Students can sit in a classroom and waste the time of both the teacher and that of the student. To have students that aren't placed properly in classes will lead to decreases in the learning process for it increases the entropy of both the classroom and the school. It is one of the reasons that wealthier zip codes with less student variation outperform students who are less fortunate. It is an example of a function of the system that can only be altered by an administrator.

If one returns to the example of the lathe, we have yet to make a cut. The actual cut comes after proper placement of the material into the chuck and insuring that the proper settings are in place. This is analogous to the preparation and delivery of material from the teacher to the students. If the proper lesson is selected for the operation that is to be taught, there is a higher probability of success. What is required is for the proper place (classroom environment), and instruments (books, blackboard) to be in place so that the lecture can be delivered. The teacher is responsible for choosing and delivering the lessons.

The school administration should make sure that the environment and materials are as good as they can be. By environment, I mean the learning environment of the classroom. This is another way that the administration can cut down on entropy. At that point, the teacher must deliver the lesson effectively, assign proper homework, and reinforce the lesson properly so the students will remember the lesson.

When one finishes a product in a factory, the final operation will be to spot check the end product. In the factory, this will involve measuring the legs of the chair to insure that they meet specifications. The operator in the factory does this check to insure that the operation being done at his or her workstation is operating properly. With education, there are also unit tests, but the primary way a school is evaluated are by mass year-end tests.

Unlike the factory that can machine a part, measure it, and use it, the school must continually hone the student's mind. How much should the lesson learned in class be reinforced? We don't know? What is the optimal time and at what intervals should information be reinforced to maintain it? What's the most effective way of doing it? Teachers don't know this. Administrators don't know this either. That is why a central body should find the answers so they can be incorporated.

5.B.2. A Classroom Example: A Government Lesson

When teaching a government lesson, the teacher will have to introduce new ideas to the student (disorder) and provide examples that allow the new information to be integrated into the students' realm of experience (learning). If one is teaching the idea of three branches of government in a classroom, three essential elements have to occur.

The first is that that a student must have a fundamental grasp of the concepts that are being presented. The presentation has to be relevant to the student for them to understand it. The second is that there must be order in the class for new information (disorder or new information) to be delivered.

Finally, the new idea must be presented and integrated into the concepts that a student currently understands.

To demonstrate a lesson, the following will describe a government lesson. Suppose that one wanted to teach Baron de Montisquieu's enlightenment idea of having three branches of government (legislative, executive, and judicial) to help prevent tyranny in government. How can it be done?

A good teacher will begin the lesson by introducing metaphors that give students an appreciation of the enlightenment era. It was the enlightenment ideas that formed the framework of the American colonies quest for independence from England. At the very least, students must understand the idea that the era of enlightenment was based on reason and arose out of the dark ages. The thoughts arising out of the enlightenment era led to both a fundamental change in the rights of man and the responsibility of government to its people.

This first step is to orient the student toward the material so that they can relate to the information. In the preparation of the lesson, there is order, a process, and, like a factory, steps that allow information to be effectively transferred to students that have to be reasoned through by the student. Students must understand how this relates to them.

To do this, a teacher asks a leading question. Perhaps a teacher asks "What would happen to me (usually include students in example) if, during the reign of Henry VIII, I deeply offend the King by protesting against him? Could he have me (us) killed?" After reminding them about the fate of Henry's wives, students generally are on board (they love drama). Then, fast forwarding in time, the teacher will offer, "Now, what if we go to Washington to protest. We make a big sign that says discouraging things about the president. Low and behold, the presidential motorcade drives by and your sign hits the president's nerve. The car is stopped and several secret agents, who can place a bullet in one's eye while doing a pirouette, are with the president."

Students like the prospect of themselves or especially their teacher facing agents with guns drawn.

You ask the class if the current president of the United States could order a secret service agent to have a protestor killed. Students will affirm that the president cannot kill a person because he or she is subject to laws. The teacher get's the class to agree that a massive shift in philosophy has occurred, and using a time line, it becomes easy to relate the philosophers' enlightenment ideas to the American Revolution. Finally, one is able to discuss the reason for Montisquieu's separation of powers. It was an enlightenment idea to safeguard people against the re-emergence of tyranny.

One can ask the students about their concept of democracy and explain that right cannot be taken for granted. They assume democracy is the rule since it is the environment that they've experienced, and to teach effectively, you must challenge this notion (create entropy or disorder), and then recreate their world so that the ideas behind democracy are instilled into their experience.

Once the importance of the enlightenment is established, the braches of government can be explained. The role of the judicial, executive, and legislative branches are described. The concept of "checks and balances" is explained to show how any one branch avoids gaining too much power.

The point here is that teaching a lesson should be a well-crafted set of ideas that systematically builds upon a student's existing knowledge. It must be made relevant to the student and must be delivered with structure, purpose, and reinforcement. There isn't a single best way to deliver a lesson, but there are some great ways. For both beginning and veteran teachers, having the expert lesson modeled would be extremely useful. Teachers do not have time to perfect lessons for everything they teach; however, the lessons exist. There are people who create "perfect" lessons that cleverly use metaphors and integrate the emotions of the student like a Hollywood movie.

There's a process to teaching. There are great lessons and knowledge of subject matter is a weak beginning of the process. The delivery of a great lesson can have as much depth and forethought as a scene in a motion picture. Teachers use metaphors to bring ideas to life and it isn't easy to come up with great ideas. Perhaps that's why Darling Hammond (2000) found that inexperienced teachers are not as effective as experienced teachers, but research has shown that after five years of teaching, the benefits of experience level off (p. 9). This is likely due to a teacher falling into a "comfort zone" for things that are perceived to be working.

What teacher's do is develop decent lessons, but they probably aren't the best. The best lessons need to be discovered through research, developed, and made widely available. There is a need to provide teachers with the best examples of the best lessons; there *are* superior ways to teach. As a factory owner, one would be obliged to find the best methods to produce the best products. Our schools should study ways to put the best teaching processes in the classroom. The school system needs to find the best ways to deliver new knowledge to American students.

While the idea to develop a single curriculum and to master methods of delivery may sound like a crazy idea, the alternative is to have a system that continually tries to re-engineer itself with each new group of teachers. With the advent of the Internet, high speed servers, it makes perfect sense to develop lessons that teachers can use to model their classroom instruction.

Once the system begins to take care of issues of delivery of material in the classroom, one can take aim at the myriad of other influences in the education system.

5.B.3. Optimizing the Classroom

Once the curriculum and lessons have been prepared, the actual school site can be engineered to insure that the lesson has more impact. For instance, the administration can make sure that conditions in a room are appropriate, materials are present, or that the proper students are in the class. One of the problems that teachers face in the classroom is trying to teach students who will not benefit from the instruction being offered. Most importantly, the administration could insure that students are taking a class they will benefit from.

In general, there are two types of students that do not benefit from instruction: (1) students who already know the material from previous instruction, and are, therefore, bored; and (2) students who do not have the requisite knowledge to learn a lesson. The first example comes from a student who has already covered the material, knows it, and is not challenged by a lesson. This student is not engaged by the lesson and doesn't learn. This is a student who has the potential to be disruptive to the learning process. A second type of student that doesn't benefit very much from classroom instruction is due to insufficient pre-requisite knowledge.

A student without sufficient pre-requisite knowledge of subject matter will not be engaged by the material and will likely tune out. The student who is disengaged from the learning process has a higher likelihood of being disruptive to the learning process. Some researchers such as Galindo-Rueda and Vignoles (2004) have argued against "ability grouping" or "tracking" of students as a bad practice (p. 6–8). In Europe, these tracks will determine the type of education that one receives. What is argued for here is proper placement of students in the classroom, not necessarily ability grouping to maximize learning. (There is great controversy among researchers about this. British policy shows that moving to a "mixed" system of school from a selective grammar school system had reduced educational achievement of the most able students, but had enabled wealthier students of lower ability. The data suggest that the "high end" achievement is less, and the distribution of educational achievement is less, because diminished results from "high end" students are mitigated.)

It is important for students to be grouped to some degree in order to match the lessons to the students' abilities. The Deming model allows one to study factors that make learners more compatible. If after studying student groupings sufficiently, one could determine the class composition of students that would be optimized to promote learning in a classroom. If a commitment was made to create a scheduling program that would create a master schedule for schools based on both student attributes and requirements of the school, it would benefit the system of education.

Schools need to find the attributes about kids and learning that can be used to appropriately place kids in school. Information about individual students that is objective and reliable is solely lacking. Each student should have meaningful data that can be used to properly place the student, list strengths and weaknesses, and properly place them in appropriate classes. Not only should this information be available, it should be in a form that is easily transferred from one location to another.

Whether one likes it or not, information follows people as they progress through life. Teachers know that large numbers of students do not take standardized tests seriously. The students' say it's because "They don't mean anything." It's true. The current standardized tests used to evaluate schools mean little to many students. The reason is because the data has little influence on a student's life. The tests do not help or hurt the student and don't help the teacher to help the student.

One should be able to pick up a kid's file and know whether they have the requisite reading and math skills to succeed. The factory or school, if set up right, would set up a system that not only looks backward, but forward as well. Data should be used to predict what the students need for success. If the data is worth collecting, then it's worth using. Tests should have the ability to place kids in classes. The current testing system does not.

Applications of Entropy Analysis as a Tool to Examine Educational Settings

Teachers are masters of entropy. In fact, the ability to channel entropy effectively might be the true mark of a great teacher. In a classroom, one of the things a good teacher does is gain the student's attention at the beginning of class and then channel that attention toward the desired lesson. What this does is reduce the entropy (disorder) in the classroom to allow for a lesson to occur. Teachers establish routines that students understand to lower classroom entropy.

It isn't until the teacher has a low-entropy classroom that he or she can introduce the lesson. The transfer of information will occur best when outside distractions are minimized. New information is presented in the form of a lesson (disorder) and the teacher integrates that lesson into what is already known (order). This is true whether there are ten different activities going on in the classroom, or it is a group silent reading activity.

Teaching Students to Read

The National Education Association (NEA) states that a debate about the best method to teach reading is on-going and that: "There is no one way to teach reading that is effective for all students. The teacher is the key to successful reading" (NEA, 2007, para. 8). Does this mean that all teachers should employ multiple techniques or does it imply that no single method works best? In the 1990's, the battles over reading styles were being fought between *whole language* and *phonics or basic skills* proponents.

According to Shanahan (2006), during the Clinton administration, the president appointed people with the task of understanding what the research said about the relative merits of phonics and whole-language reading instruction (p. 5). With the multiple types of instruction available, the data implied that the burden of teaching reading is essentially related to the teacher's knowledge of the subject. How does one insure that the best methods are reaching the children?

In a Report of the National Reading Panel (2000), the panel studied results covering several aspects of reading development. They performed a study comparing whole language versus *basic skills instruction*. With respect to vocabulary development, the results were:

> Explicit and implicit approaches to vocabulary were found to be effective throughout the grades, so the panel concluded 'Vocabulary should both be taught directly and indirectly.'

The panel studied phonics and found that it helped students pick up reading faster in grades K-1, but by the second grade (and beyond) phonics did increase word recognition, but didn't seem to affect reading comprehension (p. 4–24).

Not surprisingly, there is disorder in the interpretation of the results. At what point does whole language replace phonics as a teaching strategy. What is the test to determine when whole language should be used? How are the two methods applied together? Studies have shown that both methods work at different times during the child's development. Obviously, it would be nice to know the best ways to employ reading techniques in the classroom. With a skill as important as reading, why not determine the best combination of both methods as students mature? At the level of the lesson, it would be advantageous to know not only what methods, but what lessons work best.

The source of disorder with regard to reading instruction comes from bias in research. Schools and teachers cannot get a good read on when or how to use the reading techniques. Rather than study how best to use one reading method or both methods combined, proponents are entrenched in support of one method over the other. The study of reading methods seems to suggest that integrating both methods would be best. One of the ways to reduce entropy in the classroom is to come up with the best method. One must do unbiased studies under actual classroom conditions to understand how to optimize reading methods.

Research should not be based on marketing one idea or the other, but by what works best in the classroom.

One Parent Family

This is a societal issue that affects the school system. It is known that students in single-parent households have a more difficult time than students from *traditional* homes with two parents. Amato (2005) found that compared to children from two-parent households, single-mother families score lower on achievement tests, have a higher incidence of substance abuse, and lower self esteem (p. 77). Barton and Coley (2007) found that the United States leads the world with 31 percent of American children living in one-parent homes in 2004 (p. 11). With regard to single-parent households the Educational Testing Systems (ETS) report states:

> First they need to determine whether children raised in single-parent house-holds are different from those who grow up with two parents in the home in ways that affect learning and academic success. And, if they do, researchers need to then clarify *how* they differ. They must then disentangle the factors that contribute to these differences, which involve separating factors related to low income from those that are entirely due to a growing up in a single-parent family (p. 8).

What the ETS report makes plain is that most of the factors about the effect of one-parent families haven't been studied yet.

What interventions would improve student achievement in single-parent households? What needs to be done is to identify the source of disorder in the life of students from single-parent families and find the most effective means to intervene. Moreover, how would you address students from one-child backgrounds (from outside the school) that would lead to improved learning for students?

In a long-term process, one must look for ways to intervene to remove disorder from the process. Legislation can help lower the problems that are common to one-parent families. Whether it's examining the effect of subsidized day care centers or after-school facilities, it is obvious that one-third of the country's children (and parents) could use some help. Students who are unsupervised are more likely to have problems in school. When nearly a third of a country's population is at risk, the proper response would be to seek methods to help mitigate the risk.

School Uniforms

The wearing of uniforms to school in public schools has gathered interest across America. It is an issue that doesn't affect society in any way, and is a choice left to the school. In some ways, this issue is nonsense. There is a school uniform called a *dress code* that is in place in each school. However, where students and parents do not take measures to follow the dress code, the issue of school uniforms is raised. It creates problems for both the school and classroom level by creating a distraction.

Walker (2007) released a research brief that discussed the advantages and disadvantages of wearing school uniforms. The question to examine is whether or not students' clothing choices distract from the mission of learning at schools. Here is their list of reasons for having school uniforms:

- increases students' attention in class because they are not concerned about what others are wearing and peer cattiness
- improves classroom behavior because they have a sense of safety
- aids in higher academic performance because they feel safe in the learning environment
- helps prevent school violence, especially in the form of stealing expensive and/or significant clothing and/or jewelry
- levels the socioeconomic playing field
- provides a sense of community
- builds school pride
- makes the school physically safer because outsiders can be readily identified
- reduces the wearing of gang attire (p. 1)

As a teacher, it's not only the disruption in classes caused by too little coverage or wearing of gang-related clothing, it is also a matter of enforcement. Each school has a dress code, and each staff member is supposed to enforce it. Each staff member of the school is forced to make daily decisions as to whether or not dress codes should be enforced. This takes the focus of the institution away from learning and toward games with the students. The staff of schools can spend a lot of time enforcing dress code issues. If a staff member has to deal with dress code issues, it detracts from the mission of education (higher entropy) and will reduce learning.

From the student standpoint, the primary mission of the school is to learn. One could make the argument that "dressing for success" is a part of life, but the students who are generally violating dress code provisions are not looking to impress Wall Street. The truth is, even with school uniforms, people will try to flaunt the rules, but the extent of the violations will be minor in comparison to enforcing a dress code. There will be less distraction and more attention to learning. School uniforms lower entropy in the school and environment and are good for schools.

Entropy, Private Schools, and Vouchers

This is an issue that is so entrenched in partisan politics that the education value of the issue is practically lost. A voucher is an example of *free market* economics that is supposed to give parents greater opportunity to send their children to the school of their choice. The idea is that the government takes in tax money for education, and then redistributes it to people who do not want to use the *free* public education system. The voucher is a tool that allows the parent to receive a payment to help defray the expense of sending a child (children) to private school.

An example of how the voucher program might work is described as follows. If the parents feel that they can get a better education at a private school, they can get a *tuition voucher* that can be applied toward the cost of a private school. For instance, suppose one hopes to attend Princeton Preparatory Academy, a fictitious school that costs $14,000 dollars per annum. The parent might receive $5,000 per annum to help defray the costs of the private school.

One of the problems with vouchers is that data shows that when adjusted for demographic factors, statistics show that private schools don't really outperform public schools. However, a school where tuition runs $14,000 a year will have parents that have the shared characteristics of disposable income and the willingness to use it for education. That will help to insure a low entropy environment for students.

One might argue that a person who sends their child to an elite school isn't entitled to a voucher. Although a private school might be partially subsidized by the government, the voucher program will primarily provide significant help to private schools with lower tuitions. The very expensive low-entropy schools (American versions of Eton) will remain out of reach for most Americans. A voucher might open moderately priced schools to the middle class students, thereby creating more choice and alternatives to local public schools.

It is difficult to determine how many students (parents) would forsake public schools in favor of private schools if vouchers were available. The cost for *day students* at elite private schools was examined using data from the Boarding School Review (2008). The results showed day student tuition for elite schools, such as Phillips Academy at Andover, $30,500; Deerfield Academy (2008), $28,200; or The Hotchkiss School, $30,900, and other schools costing over $20,000 per annum for non-boarders; there would be little effect other than giving mom and dad a little help with the tuition.

If a school accepts public money, then the school becomes subject to the "open" admissions policies inherent in public schools. For the private schools that charge tuition in the $5,000 to $10,000 per annum range, the open enrollment would probably shift the problems inherent in the public schools to the private school. The constitutional question that must be asked is whether taxpayer money should support religious schools and violate the secular clauses of the Constitution. One assumes that schools with mandatory requirements to study religion would not be eligible to receive vouchers (separation of church and state).

The question that must be answered is: *how would public and private schools be affected by the initiation of a voucher program?* Most likely, for mid-priced schools (tuition over $10,000 per annum), opening the door to more students would probably increase the entropy of the schools by allowing a larger population to attend. On the other hand, the schools would also have a greater population of students to choose from and therefore could be more selective in choosing students. One factor that would be common for all the private schools would be higher costs due to public oversight.

The low-cost private school that tries to compete with public schools without significant financial input from parents would suddenly find itself subject to regulation and oversight that would drive up their costs. In the less-expensive private schools, evidence shows that schools having the same demographic pool to draw from would probably have similar records of student achievement as public schools.

From the standpoint of entropy or disorder to the system, the introduction of vouchers would probably not have an effect on the education system. However, the damage to the traditional public school system could be severe in certain areas.

The problem with vouchers is that they really don't address education, but address an economic principle. Although Adam Smith's free market principles have transformed the world, it is unlikely a private school receiving vouchers could develop a winning formula for school success. If a private school defies the odds in a competitive system, it will probably raise its rates to reflect its success. It might be reluctant to share its methods with the world. As far as sharing educational methods through the system of education, vouchers accomplish little.

The Research on Class Size

As mentioned previously, class-size reduction is one of the issues that teachers' unions use as the centerpiece of their legislative efforts. It is a central issue that relates to education costs since smaller classes result in more teachers and more classrooms. Intuitively, one feels that class size is an important issue, but studies of class size provide conflicting conclusions about student performance. Hoxby's (2000) data suggest no significant effect from smaller classes (p. 1273), though Mosteller's (1995) study showed the positive effects of smaller classes on K-3 populations that boosted student achievement (p. 123).

States have acted on data showing that smaller class sizes in the early primary grades (K-3) are effective and have enacted incentives to limit lower grade class sizes. The effects of class-size reductions at higher grades have produced conflicting results. A RAND study by Stecher, McCaffrey, and Bugliari (2003) of California's Class Size Reduction (CSR) program disputed that significant gains resulted from smaller class sizes in K-3 (p. 1). Most data supports small increases in achievement where smaller classes are employed. This is not unexpected when analyzed from the perspective of entropy.

The question to ask is whether there is substantive change in a classroom due to CSR that will improve student scores? Will a teacher significantly change what is taught? The answer is probably "no." One would reason that in classrooms with "good" teachers, class control and disruption are minimized. Having 10 extra students per class will not change the content or delivery of the curriculum. The students will gain from more teacher interaction, but the students are likely to receive the same curriculum. If during the employment of CSR, specific learning activities were employed to take advantage of smaller classes, the results would probably be more dramatic.

The data from CSR suggests that in areas where there is highest disorder (low income, high EL populations, low parental education) are the areas where reducing class size has had the most effect. Consider the analogy to the factory. If one were working at a machine and that was used to process 30 parts per hour, lowering the pace to 20 parts per hour would allow one to take more care, but if an operator still performs the same functions, improvement may not occur. In a situation where one is processing 30 parts per hour amid chaos and disorder, having to problem solve while processing the parts would create more errors. In the high entropy example, improvement can occur since there is less entropy in the system.

A highly disordered setting will allow for greater improvement with a simple solution like class-size reduction. Once disorder is reduced in the classroom, changes in the process (lesson) need to occur for substantive improvement to occur. When CSR is introduced into a *normal* classroom, its effectiveness will relate to how much the system is changed to take advantage of smaller class size. One might think of an education process as an assembly line. There are instances where CSR might improve the education process, but under *normal* circumstances, CSR by itself will not result in substantive changes in student performance.

5.C. LOOK AT THE BOOKS: LEXILES AND THE PONY EXPRESS

During a department meeting at our school, one of the science teachers was discussing the difficulties of teaching students using "district approved materials." The problem was that the textbook's reading levels were higher than the reading levels of most of the students using them. The discussion was directed toward methods of teaching students whose first language wasn't English; a group designated *English learners.*

One of the staff members asked, "Why don't you use a supplemental text?" This suggestion was countered by other faculty members who explained that the teacher wasn't able to use anything but a district-approved textbook, and of course only the district-approved textbook was going to meet the guidelines of the state. The staff member who wanted to bring in supplemental material persisted in insisting that supplemental materials were feasible. She said that we should use a "pony."

The term "pony" did get a laugh, but then the teacher explained that a pony was a teaching aid and defined by Merriam Webster's online edition to be:

A literal translation of a foreign language text; *especially:* one used surreptitiously by students in preparing or reciting lessons (Webster, 2008).

The rest of the staff members at the meeting explained that not only were there no funds for supplemental texts, it was a violation of district policy to use such devices. There was a bit of argument about the use of materials, and one staff member, after listening to the argument, finally got up and walked out of the room. It was a signal to all that the discussion was essentially nonsense.

If you analyze the foregoing discussion, it was a case where all three people were correct and the system was wrong. First, the teacher described the new textbook as inappropriate for most of the students it serves. It happened to be an earth science text. Most students were struggling mightily with the state-approved science texts because the reading level of the text was beyond that of the students using it. The teacher told the audience that more bad news seemed to be on the way. The new textbooks that were being examined were even worse.

The second teacher who spoke of the "pony" or supplemental texts was just doing what teachers, or anyone for that matter, are taught to do: find a solution. The teacher should try to find ways to make the information accessible to students. The teacher said, "Give them a pony," and of course most of us were baffled. But she was also right to try to find a solution. The problem is that it wasn't a solution because teachers were forbidden from using non-approved texts. Management had made the mistake of choosing the wrong text for our students.

The teacher who walked out of the meeting was also correct. Here was a situation where a teacher had brought up a legitimate complaint, a solution had been offered, but was shot down as illegal. Management (at district and state levels) had set up a set of circumstances that made teaching practically impossible. There wasn't a rational discussion going on about how to improve things since the possibility of change had become a moot point. This is a perfect example of the adverse effects of top-down management.

One would think that *experts* would help the school systems with outside consultation. As Deming pointed out, changes have to come from within the system, and the experts aren't politicians, school board members, or parents who think they know how things *should* be. Deming said that a system operating without clear intent would not operate effectively. A good example of this comes from the textbook-adoption process. If there was ever a process that has inadvertently locked the abilities of educators, the textbook-adoption process is certainly a single example of a damaging top-down process.

California's selection of curricular materials is a prime example of top-down policies that create disorder in the learning process. The state has mandated that districts use state-approved textbooks. Districts are allowed to choose from the state-approved textbooks, but then students must suffer if their choice is poor. Influenced by calls for "tougher standards," the textbook-adoption committees must find books that meet curricular standards that have been influenced by university requirements. This leads to textbooks that are written at a high-reading level that is beyond that of many of the students who take the classes.

A school district is then courted by publishers during the textbook-adoption process. The district then picks one book for a particular grade level and this book will serve all students who take a particular class. There are some exceptions for English learner students, but in general, the teacher has to teach with the materials provided. There is a valid economic reason for this process since books can be purchased in bulk. However, by eliminating other textbook sources, schools can create a situation that impedes learning a great deal.

To examine how the appropriateness of a textbook might influence a student's learning if the book is written at an inappropriate level will be discussed using Figure 5.1 as a reference. The point here is not to show how the learning process works, but to show how an education system needs to use data from real student to make decisions that affect the classroom.

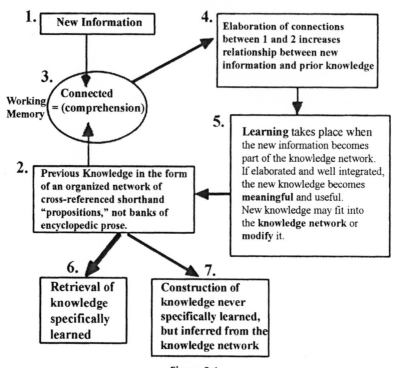

Figure 5.1.

Most efforts to introduce new information to a person (Fig. 5.1) occurs at the level between (1) new information and (3) the student's working memory. We have discussed the issue of having proper prior knowledge and its affect on the classroom. One must also examine the issue of new information (1) when it is presented at a level that is beyond the understanding of the student. How is a student supposed to integrate new information (create connections) into their "working knowledge" (3) when they don't understand the presentation. New learning (5) becomes difficult for students who connot make meaningful connections to either prior knowledge (3) or (1) new information. Obviously, When there is lack of either prior knowledge or inappropriate materials, it creates a challenge not only for the student, but for the classroom teacher.

Teachers in environments where more kids have the requisite skills to learn the material will normally have a higher rate of success then teachers with students who do not have appropriate academic skills. The same can be said for class materials. A teacher given a textbook that is beyond the abilities of many in the class will face steep challenges when trying to prepare lessons

Table 5.1. Theoretical TABE Scores for Two Classes: Class A, a "Good" Class for a 10th Grade Level Reader; and Class B, a "Lower Ability" Class

	TABE	Class A		TABE	Class B	
(Greater than grade 10; or less than grade 7 reading level)						
	score	>10	<7	score	>10	<7
1	12.9	1	0	12.9	1	0
2	12.9	1	0	12.9	1	0
3	12.9	1	0	11.2	1	0
4	12.9	1	0	10.6	1	0
5	12.9	1	0	9.8	0	0
6	11.5	1	0	9.6	0	0
7	11.1	1	0	9.5	0	0
8	11.1	1	0	9.3	0	0
9	10.9	1	0	8.9	0	0
10	10.9	1	0	8.7	0	0
11	10.5	1	0	8.5	0	0
12	10.5	1	0	8.4	0	0
13	10.1	1	0	8.4	0	0
14	10.1	1	0	8.2	0	0
15	9.6	0	0	8.1	0	0
16	9.5	0	0	7.5	0	0
17	9.4	0	0	7.2	0	0
18	9.3	0	0	6.8	0	1
19	9.2	0	0	6.6	0	1
20	9.0	0	0	6.2	0	1
21	8.9	0	0	5.8	0	1
22	8.8	0	0	5.3	0	1
23	8.6	0	0	5.0	0	1
24	8.2	0	0	5.0	0	1
25	7.6	0	0	4.3	0	1
Avg.	10.37			8.19		

Source: Cut-offs are shown where 10th grade reader is appropriate, or where students are reading three grade levels below the 10th grade text. Note in high level class, all students are within three grade levels of 10th grade reader while in lower grade, eight students will have difficulty reading.

that are appropriate. Where there's more variation and entropy (disorder), there is more challenge to the teacher.

Let's take a look at two randomly generated classrooms. One is from an affluent neighborhood, the second from a neighborhood with less favorable demographics. The idea is to look at relative-reading levels of two classrooms to see how effective a book at the 10th-grade reading level would have in both a "high-scoring" and "low-scoring" classroom. What effect will using a 10th-grade textbook have on learning in each classroom?

The following is a hypothetical classroom from two settings. How much difference can the class structure have on the education that occurs?

Table 5.1 represents the reading levels of each student in two classes. Each class has 25 students; the first has an average reading level of 10.4 and the second an average reading level of 8.2. One would think that perhaps there isn't a great difference between the two classes. The average reading level of the two classes is only separated by 2.2 grade levels. How much of a problem could this create in the learning process?

If the textbook chosen for a given class has a reading level of 10.0 (beginning 10th grade), there are dramatic differences in the two classrooms. In the higher reading level class, Class A, 10 of the 25 students (40 percent) read at or above the appropriate reading level. Perhaps more significantly is that all of the students in the class read within three grade levels of the textbook. Thus, all of the students can participate in learning using the materials.

This is not the case with a class whose average reading level score is at 8.2 (beginning 8th grade). If Class B is given the same textbook as Class A, four of the 25 students (16 percent) read at or above the grade level of the text. More significantly, seven (7) students (32 percent) read more than three grade levels below the chosen text. This would mean that approximately a third of the class would have difficulty comprehending the classroom text.

What Does This Mean?

It's difficult to put into exact terms what having a text that is beyond the reading level of a student will do to the learning process. If someone cannot compre-

Table 5.2.   Lexile Levels For Books, Grades, And Median Levels For Each Grades 1–12

Grade	Reader measures (Interquartile range, mid-year)	Text measures (From the Lexile map	Approximate Mean Lexile level
1	Up to 300L	200L to 400L	?
2	140L to 500L	300L to 500L	375
3	330L to 700L	500L to 700L	515
4	445L to 810L	650L to 850L	627
5	565L to 910L	750L to 950L	737
6	665L to 1000L	850L to 1050L	832
7	735L to 1065L	950L to 1075L	900
8	805L to 1100L	1000L to 1100L	952
9	855L to 1165L	1050L to 1150L	1010
10	940L to 1210L	1100L to 1300L	1075

Figure 5.2. Typical Reader and Text Measures by Grade; Lexile by Metametrics. By "mean" Lexile level, it is the average between the two reader levels. The Lexile company does not use "means" in their data, however, grade levels were constructed to show the necessity of proper reading materials for students.

hend the material, will they be able to learn? A company called Metametics, Inc. (2008) has created the Lexile® measure to examine the reading level of books. Lexiles examine the difficulty of words and sentence complexity of works and use this to create a scale that measures below 200L, for beginning reading material, to over 1700L for advanced text (p. 3). An example of a Lexile chart (Table 5.2) is shown that has been modified to show approximate average (Mean) Lexile levels for each grade.

For teachers and parents, the Lexile numbers allow one to choose reading materials for instruction and pleasure that will provide the correct level of difficulty to challenge a reader (p. 4). The idea of Lexiles is directly applicable to the classroom. For a student who struggles while reading a particular textbook, the change to a text that offers the same material with less confusing language will allow that student to comprehend the material better. For example, let's suppose that a 10th-grade teacher is doing a biology unit on photosynthesis. A typical 10th-grade biology textbook measures 1200L, while the range of students in the class can vary from 800L to 1400L. This means that 1200L text won't fit all the students.

To give the reader an idea of what the Lexile reading level of a high school text might be, several popular books with Lexile measures fall between 1100L and 1200L. These books, taken from the Lexile Framework for Reading (2008), are written at a 10th-grade level. They include *All the King's Men* by Robert Penn Warren, *Animal Farm* by George Orwell (1170L), *Arrowsmith* (1160L) and *Babbitt* (1110L) by Sinclair Lewis, *Beowulf:* A Student's Edition (1190L), *Bleak House* (1190L) and *Great Expectations* (1200L) by Charles Dickens, *Candide* (1110L) by Francois Voltaire, *Catch-22* (1140L) by Joseph Heller, *Turn of the Screw* (1140L) by Henry James, *The Trial* (1170L) by Franz Kafka, and *The Republic of Plato* (1170L) by Plato (Web site search engine).

If you've read *Candide* or *Catch-22,* you realize they are very readable works. However, one must remember that you aren't going to be evaluated for detailed comments about the readings the way a student might. When the text's content is chemistry or biology, the concepts of the material are keys to understanding, not whether the sentences are longer and larger words are used to explain things.

The choice of an appropriate text for a class is an important matter. Unless local districts have the flexibilities and budgets they need, school districts can be burdened with books for years that have inappropriate reading levels for many students. The Lexile guidelines provide that a student who reads at the 1000 Lexile level will be able to read a book that is 50 points higher or 100 points below the Lexile level of the student. The Lexile level of the reader is one where they comprehend 75 percent of the material covered in a book, *matched* to the level of the reader. The idea is that the books will be challenging, yet comprehensible. Books written at higher levels or levels too low are not appropriate for a student.

What does it mean for the classroom? As discussed by Metametrics, in a 5th-grade classroom, there will be readers that are 250 Lexile points above and below the normal 5th-grade average.

The significance of Lexiles is important because it measures whether a book or reading will be accessible to the learner. Thus, there are more difficult books (higher Lexile levels) associated with better readers. Both readers and books are given Lexile scores, and the match between the two can determine how well-matched the curriculum is to the learner.

The use of Lexiles is a tool that can provide appropriate reading levels to students and reduce the entropy of the learning environment.

5.D. TIME AND THE FACTORY SYSTEM

There is one aspect of the school-operation process that would baffle anyone who sets up a factory. The education factory seems to disregard the factor of time when planning its classes. Some schools have altered the traditional concept of time by block scheduling, but it is still creating a mold that the education process is supposed to fit into. In a factory, as an item moves from station to station, there is the realization that not all operations take the same amount of time to perform. Not schools. Generally, there is equal time spent for each class no matter how easy or hard the class is.

Think of a factory doing the same thing. Suppose there is a difficult cutting process that requires a great amount of time due to multiple cuts that take 10 minutes per part, and a second operation that can be done in one minute. The factory schedules machines needed and parts to be produced based on the time it takes operations to occur. Factories adjust their schedules to meet the needs of the product being built. Unfortunately, schools haven't adjusted to this element.

For those who dislike the factory analogy because it compares a child to a product, there is no disagreement on that point. The point is not to dehumanize the process of education, but improve the process. This is also agreement to the fact that the complexities involved with preparing a child are diverse compared with manufacturing an inert product. Thus, it is unfair to compare the operation of producing a child to that of creating something from an assembly line.

What is stunning when making this comparison is that students aren't processed as well as products developed in a factory. The concept of time is very important to any business, yet upper-grade schools seem oblivious to the concept of time. Contrast the factory to both the junior and senior-high levels where students move from class to class and sit in class for a set amount of time per day. If each class is considered a place where the child's mind is being formed (a workstation), doesn't the school system understand that not all operations take the same amount of time?

If one doesn't know how much time each operation should optimally take in a classroom, then how can one properly schedule the time to complete a task successfully? If schools actually knew what they were doing, when asked how much time should be devoted to each subject, a principal should be able to look at a list and provide an answer. It should show upper and lower limits (hours or class periods) for learning specific areas. The concept of time is important for employees. We get paid based on units of time worked. Our productivity is measured in terms of time. Yet, our schools cannot say for certain how much time each lesson should take. Do American students spend enough time studying core subject areas? When compared to international students in core subjects, United States' students do not study the core subjects as students from other countries.

When the National Education Commission on Time and Learning (1994) published *Prisoners of Time* in 1994, one of the findings was that students in the United States do not spend as much time in school as students from other countries. According to the study, educational progress in the United States is shackled by the fact that the American students spend less time studying core academic subjects than their counterparts in Japan and Europe (p. 25). This coupled with a larger curriculum in many core subject areas means that American students get less coverage of core material than students of other countries.

If a national effort was designed to develop curriculum and its delivery, one could tailor the needs of time to student learning. Many will argue that such a system would cause a scheduling nightmare and it will be more difficult to track kids at an educational setting. However, with the computer technology currently available, creating differentiated schedules may be difficult, but there are certainly algorithms that can be developed for the job.

A First Look at What We Can Learn from High Achieving Schools by Kimmelman and others (1999) examined results from the Third International Mathematics and Science Study (TIMSS). Kimmelman (2004) found high-achieving Asian countries had a much longer school year than American schools. Yet the Asian students total class time was similar to that found in the American school. The high performing countries curriculum appeared to deliver a higher quality curriculum that was more "coherent and deep" (p. 1).

In A First Look, Kimmelman and others (1999) also found that lecturing was used more often by teachers to deliver knowledge in science and math at high scoring schools than in American schools. One might propose that American teachers dislike lecturing to their classes. Another likely explanation is that there is so much variability among American students in math classes that preparing a single lecture doesn't work well. It makes sense that a teacher would rather create a lesson for a single group than to make multiple lessons for smaller groups in each class. One would guess that American teachers are trying to cope with the variation in ability levels. This could also partially explain why American teachers were asking less questions about reasoning than foreign teachers from high performing schools. This is not to provide an excuse for American teachers, but it does show how a system can affect how a teacher approaches the task at hand.

Student Time Devoted to Learning

Another key factor which should be analyzed is the amount of student time devoted to teaching and learning. Thus, there is no doubt that student learning time is the most valuable resource in the educational process. But is there a relation between the time devoted to instruction and to out-of-school learning activities and students' performance? This is the question which we address in the following.

In Haahr, Neilson, Hansen, and Jacobsen (2003), students were asked how many minutes there are, on average, in a class period. They were also asked how many periods they had spent in their school in the preceding week, in total. From Table 5.3, it appears that there are large differences in time devoted to learning in the countries studied. The figures were obtained through simple multiplication of the average length of class periods and the average number of periods in the preceding week, the assumption being that the preceding week was typical for an average school week in the school year. In addition, students were asked to indicate how many hours in the preceding week they had spent on various forms of learning outside the classroom setting.

Both Korean students and Finnish students do well on standardized tests. (One of the interesting similarities is that both Finland and Korea are countries that have rather homogeneous populations. In terms of entropy or disorder, both offer learning environments that would be favorable.) However, they are on the opposite ends of the spectrum on hours spent on educational tasks. What is not known is the best way to use time. What are the factors that allow the Finnish students to do well in less time? Thus, a good start for

Table 5.3   Instructional and Out-of-School Learning Activities for All Subjects Per Week.

	Total instruction	Total instrc. out of school	Total instruc. School & home
Korea	37.1	12.8	49.9
Turkey	28.0	17.6	45.6
Greece	26.6	18.3	44.9
Italy	28.0	12.8	40.8
Latvia	26.2	14.0	40.2
Ireland	28.3	11.2	39.5
Spain	27.0	11.9	38.9
Hungary	24.8	13.4	38.8
HK-China	28.3	9.2	37.5
EU Average	25.5	9.4	34.9
Luxembourg	24.8	9.9	34.7
Slovakia	24.6	10.0	34.6
Austria	27.9	6.6	34.5
Belgium	27.4	7.1	34.5
Poland	24.9	9.6	34.5
Portugal	25.8	7.8	33.6
France	25.6	7.9	33.5
Canada	25.5	7.7	33.2
Iceland	27.3	5.9	33.2
United States	25.2	7.9	33.1
Japan	25.7	6.4	32.1
Germany	23.3	8.3	31.6
Netherlands	24.9	5.9	30.8
Czech Republic	24.3	5.8	30.1
Finland	24.7	5.0	29.7
Denmark	22.5	6.6	29.1
Norway	22.6	5.9	28.5
Sweden	22.9	5.1	28.0

Source: PISA 2003 dataset, student self-reports (Haahr et al, 2004, p. 164).

the study of a proper education is to determine the amount of time to properly prepare students for life.

The study of foreign students showed that there were issues with both time and methodology that could be worked out. The data imply that aside from better teaching methods, there are also more efficient ways to present material in schools. Trying to find ways to deliver a higher quality lessons that teach in less time is something that should be built into the education process. Instead of focusing on the lesson, in NCLB our education system tries to change the teacher.

The opposition to NCLB says a great deal about how difficult it is to make any changes to the education system. There are some components to NCLB that would seem on the surface to make perfect sense. The law contains a provision that requires teachers to demonstrate subject-matter competency by holding a college degree in the subject they teach by demonstrating expertise on a test. For new teachers, the requirements are normally met in their pre-service training. For experienced teachers, the requirements must be met by complying with the provisions of their state's HOUSSE (High Objective Uniform State Standard of Evaluation).

The older teachers use a combination of coursework and experience to qualify in a specific subject area. The entire idea makes sense; people should know something about what they teach. Yet, it was not an idea that was embraced by either teachers or administrators.

A study from the National Council on Teacher Quality (2004) showed that the response to HOUSSE has been less than enthusiastic. Instead of developing rigorous standards for veteran teachers, many states are ducking the issue. The University of Pennsylvania's Richard Ingersoll estimates that one in three classes in high-poverty schools are taught by teachers who did not even minor in the subject they teach (p. 1).

In cases where the teachers do not have sufficient knowledge to teach a subject, putting a subject specialist in a class is a good idea. Yet, the system didn't welcome the change with open arms. In a letter, Dr. Paul Kimmelman (2004) said that:

> Notably, for many years, school leaders often said that if only they had the leverage to require teachers to meet higher standards and change teaching practices, they could improve student achievement. Then along came NCLB, and the response was that the requirements are too cumbersome, expensive, and pejorative for experienced teachers (para. 11).

This is an example of the school system putting the onus of instruction on the teachers. However, it is a hollow argument. It asks for changes from teachers (higher quality people), but does the system show the best ways to move forward? It would be similar for a coach to ask for the best players and then expecting them to win.

The school system has to play a part in improving schools. In Kimmelman's article he states that school leaders "have pleaded for greater leverage to change instruction and curriculum to increase effectiveness" (para. 12). In the third chapter, we discussed changing curriculum, but people have been changing the curriculum for years. What is needed in the educational system are instructional techniques and conditions that work. That is what will improve the classroom.

Thus, NCLB set up an arbitrary standard, and consistent with Deming's expectations, the system tries to find a way to get around it. Teachers are responsible for delivering the curriculum, but an expert physicist at a university might prove to be the worst high school physics teacher in the world. The point is that setting arbitrary standards for part of the education system will not address the process of education.

5.E. EDUCATION CHOICE AND NCLB

No government ever voluntarily reduces itself in size. Government programs, once launched, never disappear. Actually, a government bureau is the nearest thing to eternal life we'll ever see on this earth! (Ronald Reagan, *A Time for Choosing,* 1964, para 31–32).

One of the problems with large governmental bureaucracies is that they are considered impersonal and unresponsive to the needs of those they serve. The word has a negative connotation and a two of Webster's dictionary definitions include: "3. government characterized by specialization of functions, fixed rules, and a hierarchy of authority; and 4. a system of government marked by *officialism,* red tape, and proliferation." Taxpayers also dislike bureaucracies because they tend to gobble up resources like a monster without providing evidence of a tangible product or service. With the exception of the military, the largest government service provided in the United States is the public education system.

The Bush administration waged a campaign to reform public schools in the United States using PL-107-110, or No Child Left Behind. The administration has promoted a free market ideology as the key to the reform of public education. Part of the sales pitch for NCLB is that knowledge about school performance will give parents more information to choose schools and more ability to make choices. Eventually, in the perfect world, the laws of supply and demand would get rid of all the bad schools and the methods of the good schools would be spread throughout the land. In theory, this should reduce entropy because *ordered* schools would replace the disordered ones.

One of the facets of NCLB is that it mandates that children in public schools with poor test scores will have access to alternate school sites. The practice, called *school choice,* allows the parent to pull his or her child from a neighborhood school that is performing poorly and place them at an alternate site. If a school (or district's) performance continues to be poor, the school can be taken over by the state education department. The law is intended to

Table 5.4 Number and Percent of Students in City, Suburban, Town, and Rural Public Elementary and Secondary Schools with Membership Who Are Eligible for Free or Reduced-Price Lunch, by State or Jurisdiction: School Year 2005–06 (States With More than 1 Million Students)

State or Jurisdiction	Number of Students	Total Percent Free-or Reduced Price Lunch Eligible	Number of Students	City Percent Free-or reduced Price Lunch Eligible	Number of Students	Suburban Percent Free-or Reduced Price Lunch Eligible
All Reporting States	47, 957, 376	42	14,223,123	54.9	19,465,550	32.7
Arizona	1,018,457	47	498,231	52.0	303,775	38.8
California	6,124,988	49	2,731,256	54.2	2,877,847	44.8
Florida	2,614,228	46	664,016	47.5	1,495,259	45.4
Georgia	1,591,307	50	240,151	66.2	701,427	45.0
Illinois	2,076,435	37	640,415	62.2	1,017,381	24.9
Indiana	1,030,592	36	274,299	55.3	320,374	28.7
Michigan	1,660,823	36	430,821	56.0	719,111	25.6
New Jersey	1,363,174	27	136,920	47.7	1,098,957	25.4
New York	2,739,709	44	1,165,786	72.0	1,101,031	20.5
North Carolina	1,408,709	43	347,273	46.8	275,167	36.4
Ohio	1,834,479	32	392,141	57.7	818,688	23.9
Pennsylvania	1,794,967	31	364,704	63.1	880,096	20.6
Texas	4,451,130	48	1,922,722	54.9	1,433,371	39.4
Virginia	1,210,963	31	293,163	43.6	499,882	22.5

Source: The calculation to determine free lunch eligibility is to multiply $20,000 (poverty level for family of four) times 1.3 to get $26,000. This number is multiplied by 1.85 to get $37,000 (free lunch eligibility level).

give people access to better education by giving parents more choice and to protect them from underperforming schools. But does it?

Would a person in most schools that will be "closed-down" actually have access to alternate educational opportunities? The Health and Human Services (HHS, 2006) poverty threshold for a family of four, according to the federal government, is a $20,000 annual income. A person in poverty is considered to be in a family where the annual household income is less than $20,000 (para. 5). Neal McCluskey (2006), a policy analyst with the Cato Institute, said that since NCLB was failing in its mission to deliver qualified teachers, school choice was the real answer to the problem:

> So what's to be done? The answer is actually pretty clear. We must open our minds and do something other than consistently create more layers of government. We must, in fact, take power away from government by letting parents choose their children's schools and bypass the special interests (para. 17).

The answer according to McCluskey is to lower government interference and let the free market make the best choices. The fact that NCLB helps open the door for school choice seems to escape the attention of free market advocates; however, lets look practically at the question of school choice for a household of four living in this country.

The Preamble to the United States Constitution (1787) argues that the function of government is to "promote the general welfare" of its citizens. The Tenth Amendment of the Constitution says that individual states can promote items (such as education) that are not covered specifically by the Constitution. The states, therefore, have the responsibility for setting up and operating schools. The question relating back to NCLB is whether increasing choice and shutting down local schools is really a way to promote the general welfare.

In chapter 2, the data shows that low-performing schools were invariably found in low-income areas. Will the economics of school choice work for low-income families who are socioeconomically disadvantaged?

In California, the state breaks out "socioeconomically disadvantaged" students as students where either: (1) neither parent had earned a high school diploma, or (2) the student participated in the free or reduced-price lunch program, also known as the National School Lunch Program (NSLP). To qualify for NSLP, a student must meet the poverty guidelines as outlined by the Child Nutrition Porgrams–Income Eligibility Guidelines (2006):

> The following are the Income Eligibility Guidelines to be effective from July 1, 2006 through June 30, 2007. The Department's guidelines for free meals and milk and reduced price meals were obtained by multiplying the year 2006

Federal income poverty guidelines by 1.30 and 1.85, respectively, and by
rounding the result upward to the next whole dollar.

Using this data, unofficially, an attempt was made to determine whether the
poor could actually afford to take advantage of school choice.

The poverty level for a family of four in 2006 was defined as $20,000 per
year. For students from a family of four to be eligible for free meals under
NLSP, the student's family must earn less than $26,000 per year. According
to the Food Research Action Center (2006), to qualify for a reduced price
lunch, a child in a family of four must earn less $37,000 per year. This family
of four would earn $3,083 or less per month for reduced lunches and $2,167
per month to be eligible for the free lunch program. In Table 5.4, the numbers
show that there is a massive problem.

To put the numbers in perspective, in the Riverside/San Bernardino/
Ontario, California area, the median monthly income is $4,638 per month,
and the wage needed to afford a two-bedroom apartment is $36,440. To
earn $37,000 per annum, two parents would have to earn $9.25 per hour
working full time. Are parents who can barely make payments on an apartment (or are unable to) going to have a lot of choices regarding school
sites? If their local school is performing poorly, will parents have the means
(transportation) to get their children to alternate school sites? Will the parent be able to drive six miles twice a day for 180 days to get their kids to
an alternate site?

It would only amount to 2,160 miles, but that would mean 86 gallons of
gas and another $215 toward expenses (assumes $2.50 per gallon). To many
Americans, $215 ($21.50 per month based on 10 months of school) would
not be an issue, but for people living in the areas where there are poorly performing schools, money could represent a significant issue for them. This is
assuming that the family has a working vehicle to transport the kids. Thus,
school choice is a great idea, but it probably is impractical for many of the
lower income families that are likely to benefit from NCLB.

The socioeconomically disadvantaged tag also can be applied to households where neither parent graduated from high school. Since there is a high
correlation between education level and income, families without the skills to
finish high school are expected to understand education data to find the best
school for their child.

The administration has tried to come up with ideas to fix America's
schools. To the administration's credit, they were able to get NCLB passed,
but what does the law actually do to reform schools? NCLB mandates that
states identify and take control of poorly performing schools. It gives parents
the ability to choose a different school if their local school is not performing

well and promotes the development of charter schools, which are publicly funded alternatives to local schools, as a means to give parents more choice than the local school authority. Most of the premise of NCLB is directed at letting the market fix (or weed out) failing schools and giving parents more choice for their education dollar.

The law primarily creates a standard. It looks for specific performance and ultimately threatens poor schools with closure. The problem with NCLB is that it is predicated on the philosophy that the market should dictate what education does. A free market tries to fulfill customer desires. NCLB has the strong test emphasis—a certified teacher in every classroom and the choice to try out the novelty shops (charter schools) if desired. It threatens to close the school that isn't making the grade, but there is nothing substantive about improving the process of education.

NCLB is an advertisement that masquerades as policy. It gives the consumer the illusion of action, but does little to actually alter the process of education. Like many things sold in the free market, it doesn't necessarily give us things we should have. It is a law that is predicated on threats and exhortations to meet numerical goals.

Holding the public education system accountable for its performance is good, but NCLB is another example of an outside entity that prescribes what should be done without specific goals. Proponents of NCLB will say that the introduction of charter schools will solve these problems because it will promote innovation. People that support the charter school movement will find data that supports their argument and schools that work. In line with Deming's findings, a super teacher or principal is not something that can be replicated throughout the education system. It is imperative to create a system that has the capacity for continuous self-improvement. What NCLB did was introduce disorder into the education system.

Although NCLB may have created chaos and disorder, its most important legacy may be that it makes a single, efficient system possible. As discussed previously, as long as states take federal funds, they are obliged to follow federal law. This opens the door for educational reform; but reform to what?

What should be done? NCLB has ushered in the possibility of reorganizing school bureaucracies to make them more efficient. Federal law could mandate minimum standards for academic achievement across the United States. As with environmental regulations, a local jurisdiction would have the capacity to make the standards more "rigorous," but hopefully they would resist the urge to do so.

The real idea is to improve the learning process so the students know more. It is making changes in the everyday process of education that will make a difference—not legislation, nor exhortation, but improvement of the learning process. A common curriculum would save money by reducing redundancy and by putting effort into programs developed at the national level that address all levels of instruction for all levels of learners. Realizing that the states maintain the responsibility of running and funding education systems, the federal function should be seen as a way to study and make the best teaching methods available to teachers.

The department of education could develop statistical methods to find the best ways to teach and the optimal conditions (time, methods) using a system such as the one outlined by Deming. One could thereby determine the best ways to approach learning. The best methods used by teachers throughout the country could be identified and used in the classroom. The best methods for storing and distributing student information could be developed. In short, the focus of efforts would return to making the classroom the focus of the education factory.

In the end, this would lead to less disorder in the teaching process. Teachers could practice their art as masters of entropy.

Chapter 6

Enemies of Change? Bureaucracies, Education, and Money

Men are not prisoners of fate, but only prisoners of their own minds

—Franklin D. Roosevelt, 1939

President Franklin Roosevelt's phrase discussing the power of positive thinking has been a central tenet of American thought. The truth is that despite positive thinking, circumstances can create barriers that make people *prisoners of their own minds*. Education's role is to provide a pathway that illuminates new vistas in life. It is supposed to be one of the keys that can free people from poverty, but data shows that most of the time, it doesn't.

Obviously, if everyone had the same educational opportunities despite their background and personal circumstances, the department of education in California wouldn't brag about schools that *beat the odds*. The fact is, in the land of opportunity, the chance for a good life is firmly stacked against the poor and uneducated. It is education's role to create a bridge that allows people to escape poverty and provide a greater chance for opportunities in life. If schools are to fulfill this ideal, the change in the education system must be directed to the classroom. Changes have to make their way to classrooms to be effective because that's where the students are.

One of the central ideas of this book is to increase learning from the classroom up. Though the teacher of the classroom can have profound effects in his or her guidance of students, the key is to provide ways for the average teacher in any school to improve the product they deliver. It is the school's job to put students in classrooms that are ready and able to learn.

The ideas presented in this book are simple:

1. recognition that schools operate on factory model
2. redundancies in education need to be reduced to focus more resources to the school and classroom
3. a system of continuous improvement needs to be developed for lessons to optimize the classroom experience
4. Administrators should function to create classrooms and sites that minimize disorder (entropy) so that teaching can occur
5. schools need to have reporting systems that provide timely information about student progress
6. parents and communities where schools reside need better information about school spending

The primary goal of this book is to find ways to examine and improve the approach to education that will eliminate waste and maximize opportunity for kids. That being said, there are many groups that have interests in maintaining the status quo who will argue against structural change to the education system. The next section discusses an organization that is on a crusade to save education.

6.A. THROUGH THE GATES . . .

The Bill and Melinda Gates Foundation (Gates Foundation) originally focused their attention on the problems inherent in public schools, but have become frustrated by the resistance to change from the education bureaucracy. In fact, their early efforts were concentrated on funding small "utopian and communitarian movements," but Cline (2006) reported that according to a Gates Foundation spokesman, the efforts were abandoned because their efforts didn't produce results (para. 1). Blankenship (2007) interviewed Melinda Gates, who discussed that the Gates Foundation found that putting money into schools didn't insure that change would occur. As Blankenship said of the Foundation's struggles with school success in the article:

> that without working up the administrative ladder in school districts and with state and federal policy makers, they couldn't make the changes stick (para. 22).

The problem in education was succinctly identified by Bill Gates when he gave the speech prompting this book: "It is the system."

Improving American education is a large element of the Gates Foundation mission. One of the areas that the foundation has focused its efforts has been to improve high schools that are at risk. Through the use of grants, the focus has been to form small schools. A large focus has been forming small charters and breaking up high schools into smaller units—smaller high schools, as summed up by a document produced by the Gates Foundation (date unknown) describing the benefits of small schools. Some of the reasons given were:

> Anonymity: high schools have doubled in size in the last generation resulting in overcrowding and reduced student and teacher interaction.
>
> Isolation: Many teachers see over 150 students daily and have little adult contact.
>
> Low expectation: only one of four to six tracts prepares students for college.

The final reason was that large schools were difficult to change due to large staffs. Yet, one wonders how one would eventually create change throughout the "system" if one is worried about the opponents ("interest groups") that would stand in the way (para 2, *The Reason Why*).

The Gates Foundation document goes on to make a number of claims about the evils of larger schools and the idea of giving each student "an adult advocate." There are many compelling arguments for small schools. Some of the arguments found in a previous chapter would champion the small schools. The schools will have less disorder and have lower entropy. However, the truth is that most districts cannot afford small schools. The doubling of the size of high schools has been due to the increased costs of building and operating smaller schools.

The small-school paradigm makes sense for it allows for the elimination of disorder that can distract the learning process. However, with a maximum school size of 400 and small classes (15 students per class) there would be 27 teachers. Even with one counselor and two administrators, the salaries without benefits would run roughly $1.9 million and $2.8 million with benefits (using a figure of $60,000 per annum per teacher, $180,000 for two administrators, and $75,000 for a counselor and figuring a 50 percent markup for benefits, $1.87 m $\times$ 50% + $1.87 m = $2.8 million). Thus, one is spending over $7,000 for teacher salaries per student, without counting facilities, school supplies, utilities, and the myriad of factors that go into school finance.

One must keep in mind that examining the school in this manner is theoretical, but, as Walton points (1986), Deming's first concern revolves around the customer.

> Draw a flow diagram. Who's your customer? What comes in? What goes out? Do you know your customer? Do you know what he needs? Almost nobody does . . . (p. 27).

If the product that is being developed is too expensive for other school systems to adopt, is it a useful model? Let's assume that the costs are lower. The Gates Foundation has been experimenting with breaking up the schools into units, so perhaps the teacher expenses are lower, and the Foundation has made the finances attractive to regular schools. Eventually, they would want to transfer their results to existing schools, but this is also apparently a problem.

The Gates Foundation's primary focus has been to promote charter schools and smaller schools, therefore providing a laboratory to try out different styles of learning. In an outline of the Gates Foundations findings from 2000–06, they claim: (1) that change was difficult in older schools; (2) reform could take place more easily in new settings; (3) school district commitment to change is critical for success; and (4) policy sets the tone for school-level change. Their system, when perfected, will eventually have to go into the older schools that will largely have the old school districts and policies in place. Bill Gates, who has formulated software to meet the uncertain needs of the millions of users, knows something about meeting challenges.

The Gates Foundation has spent 1.9 billion to establish 1,124 new high schools and funded improvements for 761 currently in place. With the sheer volume of the effort, there will likely be success among the schools. The odds would be in favor of some of the schools being high performing. The problem is repeatability and sustainability. Can the small school process be repeated successfully in different schools?

The second question is sustainability. Does anyone believe the small schools will survive without Gates Foundation funding? A school district facing a budget glitch will either close a small school or expand it to take advantage of economies of scale.

The small schools are an experiment where a less-disordered environment occurs. They have more support, and therefore they have better learning environments. However, the Bill and Melinda Gates Foundation (2006) describes the problem with the system they're trying to fix:

> There are many factors that can undermine school reform efforts. These include the instability of school district leadership, regulatory complexity, and low high school standards that do not align with college requirements (p. 16).

Ironically, Gates (2008) recently gave a speech that essentially outlined the fact that we need a solid structure based on information that will take the education system forward:

> The education sector desperately needs an infrastructure for creating better instructional tools—always with measurement systems in place so we have

evidence that the new way works better than the old way. Without evidence, innovation is just another word for "fad."

We need to be able to determine which curricula, which software and other instructional aids are most effective in helping teachers teach and students learn (para 30–31).

One of the things that Gates said during his speech was that small schools funded by the Gates Foundation had actually underperformed district averages (para. 6), though positive results were found in the small schools in New York (para. 7).

It is consistent with a report by Leubchow (2007) who said that small schools funded by the Gates Foundation hadn't performed much better than their predecessors (para. 1). In an interview with Hammond and Lednicer (2008), Vicki Phillips, who directs the Gates Foundation's education initiatives said, "We have learned that small by itself is not enough. Good curriculum and instruction don't just show up. . ." (para. 26).

It is likely that the small schools were teaching the same lessons in a slightly different form. The results are similar to those found earlier with respect to the effects of class size reduction. Unless there's a change in the delivery and style of the curriculum, little change is likely to occur.

The *constancy of purpose* that the Gates Foundation tried to focus on was changing school size. Reducing school size does allow more attention to students, but is the necessary curriculum reaching the students who need it? It could be that schools with widely varying student populations (ability wise) would find it difficult to find appropriate class levels for each student.

Another problem that the Gates Foundation might suffer from is the ambitious standards of its founder. The Gates Foundation envisions that a college preparatory curriculum is within the reach of every child. However, many of the parents and students in schools merely wish to graduate without plans for further education. The Gates Foundation violates a premise of supply and demand by trying to supply a product (college prep academics) for which students have little appetite or demand.

One cannot fault the Gates Foundation for trying the small schools approach. The one problem with his system is its lack of focus on the core message–the lesson. The effort to examine school size mirrors classroom-reduction efforts. Anything the Gates Foundation can do to find better approaches to education is greatly appreciated. However, it might be best if their long-term model should be based on making decisions based on classroom results (Deming's methods) and to examine the question of education by examining the entropy (disorder) to determine whether change will be beneficial or not.

Since the Gates Foundation has a great deal of influence, there is a wish list of things they could work on. The first is a call for a common national educational goal for K-12 education. It makes planning a little easier. Perhaps partners could be induced to create school software reporting systems for expenses that can be easily used both for financial and student record-keeping purposes. Perhaps the foundation could champion a national test that could be developed to save the taxpayer money and accurately assess student progress in any school.

All of these suggestions would help lower the entropy of the education system and help the participants focus their energy on the student in the classroom. One last thing owed to Bill and Melinda Gates–a whole-hearted thank you.

6.B. CURRICULUM FRAMEWORKS

Each state has created a set of laws to dictate what students should learn to earn a diploma. Some state legislatures, including Colorado, North Dakota, Nebraska, Massachusetts, and Pennsylvania, allow local school boards to set graduation standards, but most set up rigid guidelines for state graduation requirements. The amount of time and energy spent by state legislators on matters relating to K-12 schools has been discussed previously. It is natural for legislators to try to influence education since education is a high priority to their constituents. Many legislators vote for tougher curriculum standards to try to help education.

The introduction of *tougher* standards to a process without actively changing the education process means little. Unless a standard is accompanied with a substantial change in the approach to classroom instruction, the new standard will probably mean little. What is important is creating substantial changes in the way things are done at the level of the classroom and the school. If implementing tougher standards was effective, there would be a positive relationship between strong curriculum standards and the education that a state provides. States with the strongest standards would have the highest achievement scores.

This was examined by looking at a survey for 2006–07 that determined the *Smartest States* using a variety of educational parameters (Quitno 2006-2007). The smartest states were Vermont, Massachusetts, Connecticut, New Jersey, Maine, Virginia, Montana, Wisconsin, Iowa, and Pennsylvania. Although it's difficult to judge the validity of school or state data (since districts and states vary in their methods), it was interesting to look at the relationship between *smart states* and educational standards.

The American Federation of Teachers (2008) ranked the states based on their education standards, with 0 percent weakest and a 100 percent maximal score. Seven states were reported as having 0 percent strong standards, and six states reported in the 1–24 percent range. It is ironic that in an era of attention to standards, six states rated as being *smartest:* Pennsylvania; Wisconsin, Iowa, New Jersey, Maine, and Vermont were identified as having *weak* state standards. One doesn't need to apply statistics to see that high standards were not a predictive barometer of academic performance. The data would seem to indicate a strong lack of correlation (if not a negative correlation) between strong standards and academic performance.

What it does suggest is that in the current form, the state standards do not mean very much. To the teachers working in the classroom, the current curriculum standards are guidelines that one tries to adhere to, but mean little on a day-to-day basis. As there's little direct contact between a state's curriculum and its application in the classroom, they mean little. As such, most state standards are merely violations of Deming's 10th and 11th points concerning management.

Deming's 10th point states that management must: "Eliminate slogans, exhortations, and targets asking for zero defects or new levels of productivity." It is a target that is non-descript, and there is nothing concrete being done to change the product delivered to students. The 11th point calls for management to focus on the process rather than an end product (numerical goals), rather than the delivery of the lessons themselves. The point is that education is like a factory. Merely setting a higher standard will not improve the means to meet the new standards that are put into place.

It is difficult to understand why states persist in setting higher educational standards when they aren't meeting the old standards. If you don't re-engineer how the product is built, you'll end up with the same product.

6.C. SERVICE, STANDARDS, AND GRADES

The previous section said that setting arbitrary standards doesn't do much good in school. However, the purpose of education is to set and enforce standards. In this section, one can see what happens when the free market meets academia.

It is easy to define education as a service enterprise. As businesses that compete for students, colleges are well aware of their role as a service provider. As a service enterprise, colleges have increasingly turned to student evaluations of faculty (SEF) members. According to Rosovsky and Hartley (2002), one of the problems with this practice is that the student is changed from a learner to a consumer (p. 13). The instructor's behavior can also be altered by student evaluations. One of the unintended side effects of SEFs is grade inflation that has become rampant on college campuses across America.

When a student enters a college class, the objective is to complete the class with a high grade. The students are not responsible for the content, nor the amount of material learned. That is the responsibility of the college instructor. In a free market where students can shop and where student surveys are used to evaluate their professors, is it possible for a school to uphold academic standards? Would students "shop" for easier ways to get their education and grades? One of the primary functions of any school is to set and enforce standards. What happens when the free market invades a school?

The standard for performance in a school setting is the letter grade, and in colleges, grade inflation has been reported to be a problem. A Carnegie Foundation article by Merrow (2006) called *Grade Inflation: It's Not Just an Issue for the Ivy League,"* reported that in 1950, 15 percent of Harvard University grades were B+ or better. In 2006, 55 percent of the grades at Harvard were A or A-, up from 22 percent in 1966. The article reported that 80 percent of grades at the University of Illinois were As or Bs. This inspite of the fact that the entering scores of college freshman measured by the Scholastic Aptitude Test (SAT) have declined (p. 1).

The article in question didn't mention the cause of the grade inflation, but one cause is related to market forces. In colleges, the student evaluation is having a critical effect on whether or not an instructor is retained. A faculty member who justifiably gives poor grades to students will be judged harshly by the students in a class on student evaluations. The faculty member who gets better student evaluations by posting better grades for his student has a better chance for maintaining employment. The market is calling for higher grades, and as faculty members respond, the result has been grade inflation.

If the elite colleges can have their standards bastardized by the free market, applying the practice to public schools would be a disaster. Imagine the situation in a high school. That tough teacher that didn't cut corners or accept excuses from students will be the one that disappears first. The first group of "C" grades from an instructor will tarnish his or her reputation. Students will not risk a bad grade by choosing a tough instructor. Teachers will not risk giving a bad grade since their performance would be tied to the customer's wishes. Grade inflation runs contrary to the entire premise of the education system.

Grade inflation is a common problem. If left to choose schools by performance, one could only imagine what people would choose for education if standards for learning are not enforced. Schools could become like junk food eateries that clog the minds of the citizens the way fast food clogs peoples' arteries. One might argue that food isn't a good analogy to use for the education process, and to that I'd agree because most people enjoy their food. For many students, education is an acquired taste, and given the choice, most would choose to learn "junk" rather than math, English, and history.

It is important for schools to maintain their standards since the basic function of a school is to present and evaluate the transfer of knowledge. What may be even more damaging to the education process is that instructors would offer a less competitive curriculum to avoid being harshly evaluated.

6.D. LET THE UNION FIX IT

How do teachers' unions contribute to disorder in the education process? The primary criticism leveled at unions is that they allow *poor* teachers to keep their jobs. The issue of tenure for teachers is often pointed to as a huge problem in the education system since it prevents management from getting rid of "bad" teachers. This idea is certainly alright since no one really wants their child to be taught by an incompetent or poor teacher, but it doesn't fundamentally change the "system" of education. The other question is what should a teacher's evaluation be based on?

Though it is convenient to blame unions, one must remember that management will always set the rules regarding employment practices. Neither the public or school management should blame the school system's employment problems on the union. The managers of schools have to negotiate agreements that promote the interests of their students and the community. If the administrators have allowed for contracts that seriously damage the product they produce, they should revise the contractual terms that are offered to teachers. It is management's duty to come up with terms and proper ways to evaluate teachers so that kids are protected.

On the other hand, the teachers' unions exist for the teachers, and their actions do not necessarily benefit the education system. This is demonstrated by the American Federation of Teachers (AFT), the largest teachers' union in the United States. It is a lobbying group that attempts to persuade lawmakers to support educational legislation. According to AFT (1999), by adhering to the following steps one can improve low-performing high schools:

I.   Conduct a self-study (audit) to identify the school's most pressing needs

II. Consider a research-based reform program

III. Establish entry-level standards for what first-year students need to know and be able to do—especially in reading

    IV. Establish an intensive intervention system for students who are strug-
         gling to meet the standards
    V. Establish a safe and orderly learning Environment
    VI. Establish high academic standards and provide *all* students with
         challenging coursework and the support they need to reach the standards
    VII. Work to ensure that teachers are fully certified in the subjects they teach
    VIII. Organize schools into personal Communities
    IX. Create incentives for students to study and achieve
         (AFT, 1999, p. 1–8).

You may have noticed that there isn't one measurable objective on this list that requires action by its members. However, the issue for the union is to represent dues-paying members, not students. Most of the items listed above all require an input of funds from the local education agency. As a teacher in a classroom, the use of the research-based reform program might be a good idea, but whose research is involved?

The influence of unions in the classroom is probably miniscule. One will disagree and say that unions give tenure to poor teachers. This isn't true. Administrators have given positive reviews to unqualified teachers that then gain tenure. The evaluation of teachers by administrators has been discussed in a previous chapter, but rest assured, teaching effectiveness is difficult to measure.

Since there isn't a "defined" guideline to the task of teaching, and teachers are allowed a lot of leeway in how they teach, some teachers aren't sure how they will be evaluated by a supervisor. The managers of education haven't found ways to consistently apply curriculum to students that will overcome the effects of income and parental education levels. Neither have the unions. Unions are found in both good and poor districts, and their influence on education is found in their ability to lobby for teacher's rights.

One of the items where unions definitely affect educationt is through political action committees that contribute to campaigns. They get legislators to promote educational bills in each state, and in doing so, add to the morass of rules and regulations that create a top-down environment. In essence, the unions work through the political process to add to the entropy or disorder of the system. Like politicians, and others who have an interest in controlling education, teachers' unions contribute to the creation of laws that turn education from children and toward administrative functions.

6.E. PAYING ATTENTION TO IMPORTANT DETAILS

While looking at data, there is one fact that is true about education. It is a very polarized institution, and people view the efforts of some from perspectives of political allegiance more than they do the facts. These pages have attempted to show that teaching in the classroom, and the quality of the lesson, matter. An argument has been presented for finding teachers who are presenting the best lessons in the country and making them available for teachers. That way, the brilliance of the classroom will be shared. However, there are some important things to consider.

Educational writer and consultant Dr. Mike Schmoker argues that one of the main problems in American schools is that teachers are asked to teach too much material. Creating the perfect lessons and putting them together will show the system what is possible in the confines of the current school. Schmoker and Marzano (1999) studied factors leading to school improvement and found that "Clear, common learning standards—manageable in number—promote better results" (p. 17).

The key word here is manageable in number. Writing too many standards will either cause the material to be passed over or taught poorly. This creates disorder in the learning process, thus learning suffers. One of the advantages of having master lessons that model teaching is that they would be a way to show what is possible in a "normal" classroom. Thus, having model lessons would not only give teachers the best metaphors and examples to base their own lessons on, but would guide them on what is possible in the classroom.

Another aspect that Schmoker (2003) covers is the lack of relevance of "strategic plans."

> School improvement planning, like its sister school "reform," merely distracts us from the hard work of improving teaching (para 2).

The plans are full of objectives for the school to strive for, but offer little in the way of day-to-day improvement. They offer little to the school and are really of value to district offices and accreditation agencies. The reports, which are a reflection of the top-down management, take a lot of effort to prepare, and distract personnel from working on improving classroom teaching.

The point is that schools often go off on tangents that take time and resources away from learning. There are reports that need to be made regarding school progress; however, the most important goal is to make sure that proper curriculum and instruction are being provided by teachers.

One of the effective methods that can be used in schools are learning communities which consist of teachers getting together to discuss ideas about teaching. Swapping lessons, sharing ideas, and trying to come up with better approaches to teaching is a good idea. People should use the best method of conveying information to the students they teach.

Wouldn't it be advantageous if teachers had the opportunity to access easily accessible *master* lessons created for all curriculum offered by schools? What if you could just access a Web site, call up some key words, and have modeled lessons available, along with the effectiveness of the lesson with particular demographic groups? A group of teachers could get together and say, "Hey, I like that idea. I'm going to use that." Perhaps they'd decide that their own lessons were better, but the fact that model lessons were available would help improve the lesson-planning process.

If you're a parent, wouldn't you want your child's teacher to use the best methods every day they walk into the classroom? Would you want their lessons modeled after inspiring lessons? You certainly would. Would you want a system that creates, evaluates, and makes curricular materials available to teachers and students at any time? Of course you would. Better yet, what if they were also available to you as well? If you home school your kid, you would get some value from your tax dollars, as a public school teacher could be called up to give your child an excellent lesson on practically any subject in a national curriculum.

6.F. FOLLOW THE SCRIPT

Most scripts are bad. I read a lot of them. (Joseph Gordon-Levitt, 2006).

The idea of a national curriculum is suggested in this document as a way to cut out the middleman. Cutting costs and improving classroom instruction is the goal. However, one of the ideas that is bandied about is an insulting concept to teachers. There are advocates who call for reading a scripted lesson in a classroom as the lesson plan.

The education community has termed the process Direct Instruction (DI; 2008). It is a teaching method in which a teacher reads scripted lessons to the class in patterns. Some of the examples viewed demonstrated a pattern of language similar to that a test administrator must use. The features of direct instruction are:

1. Explicit, systematic instruction based on scripted lesson plans.
2. Ability grouping. Students are grouped and re-grouped based on their rate of progress through the program.
3. Emphasis on pace and efficiency of instruction. DI programs are meant to accelerate the performance of students; therefore, lessons are designed to bring students to mastery as quickly as possible.
4. Frequent assessment (para. 3).

The last item includes careful monitoring of the program to insure "high fidelity of implementation." What one takes from this is that the teacher is reading the script correctly. If ever there was a program that would undermine the teacher, it is the implementation of a direct instruction program. If a person loves Thornton Wilder's play *Our Town,* and is excited to understand how the little things in life matter, just imagine how it would be to cover the play using a script. Rather than interjecting one's own understanding of the material to an audience, and interpreting what students in a classroom think, a scripted monolog is presented to a class. Proponents of direct instruction say that it ensures that content areas are covered "correctly."

The primary problem with the use of DI in classrooms is a loss of spontaneity. A second problem is the idea that every lesson is designed with the idea of being focused on the subject matter. They all involved large amounts of teacher modeling, and it is a very "teacher-centered" practice. One of the items that is discussed frequently in DI is the use of "advance organizers," or methods to help the students connect to the thing they are about to learn.

The idea for using DI as an instructional method is an anathema to the teaching process and the teaching profession. Reading from a script while sitting in front of a classroom takes away any personality, good or bad, that a teacher has. Worse, it doesn't give the students an example of how to use knowledge creatively. One of the things that teachers model when putting together lessons is the structure of thought.

Using other teachers' lessons to find good ideas for teaching may be a form of plagiarism; when the lesson is finally delivered, a person will take from it what they can. It will be a personal statement to the students.

TECHNOLOGY AND THE WORLD WIDE WEB IN EDUCATION

Over the years, new inventions have been introduced into society, and many of them have promised to change the education environment. Oppenheimer (1997) points out that motion picture, radio, and "teaching machines" with programmed instruction by B. F. Skinner have all preceded the computer. All of them have promised to change the education landscape (para. 1–2), and still students sit in classrooms while teachers lecture. The computer is the latest item that is supposed to revolutionize education; however, it won't do much unless decent software is developed.

According to Oppenheimer (2007), the Department of Education developed the What Works Clearinghouse (WWC). After spending four years and $23 million, the WWC evaluated 32 products. After criticism, the program sped up the evaluation process and by the end of 2006 had examined 51 products. A full 75 percent of the software products evaluated could not be verified as promoting education progress (para. 6).

Educational software sales to schools totaled $1.9 billion in 2006 (para. 13); however, software is unlike textbooks that a teacher can manipulate and supplement to meet the learning requirements. Once you get a software product, you are stuck with the content you receive. The software salespeople will show school district personnel information to support their products, but it is another area where the schools are gambling with kids' education. With educational resources so scarce, to buy into expensive software at the expense of other programs is very incompetent. Administrators gamble that unproven computer programs will work. It is another case where people are gambling with the education of American kids.

As one can see, the Department of Education needs to be the evaluator of not only lessons and curriculum that works in classroom, but also software. Where else can one get an unbiased research opinion? The states don't have the money to do the research, and doing research across the country will result in data that can be relied on.

During the last year, our district began to implement online courses. They gave teachers a crash course on how to implement a Web-based course, and then gave them laptops and tried out the program with some students. As one who participated in the program, I was both dismayed and heartened by the possibilities offered by the technology. The school worked with the University of California's online program, and one would think that the University of California would produce high-quality lessons that would be aligned with state educational standards. They did not. Why then, would the advent of online programs offer promise?

If the educational establishment gets wise, it is a perfect medium for developing high-quality lessons and a curriculum that everyone can use. It is the perfect medium that can be used to create high-quality interactive lessons that can work for students. It will require that specialists in both curriculum and media come together to develop lessons that can help students learn.

There are teachers that may be opposed to the idea of more control of the classroom by an "outside influence," but one would think that most teachers would welcome genuine help with the process of learning rather than getting

Online: Panacea or Problem

If there is any medium that shows the contempt that American society has for education, it is displayed in the software designed for education. What do I mean? Well, start by looking at the latest video game that has been offered to the market, with its multiple levels of interaction, layered and realistic graphics, and designed to engage the user at every turn. It is likely that the user will get the opportunity to blow up something or navigate to a new place, but overcome many obstacles on the way. The person who plays this game will want to learn the "tricks" to overcome obstacles and gain access to higher levels of action. If one examines software that is normally sold to teach K-12 kids, one notices that the material doesn't engage the learner at a level where they will truly want to come back and learn more.

For instance, the math programs available to remedial learners at our site were good at showing lessons. However, it did nothing with the medium to improve the experience for kids. The experience is rather flat and dead when compared with companies that have true graphical interaction with the user. Fantasy games that are invented by producers such as Sego, EA, PlayStation, and Microsoft are fun and challenging. Many of these games are interactive, laced with graphics that are realistic, and allow the player to have choices in the game. Kids spend a great deal of time learning how to overcome obstacles in these games.

Why couldn't a software company put together educational software that allows students to learn in an environment that would stimulate and challenge students? For instance, if a student who was being taught economics had to learn what the concept of supply and demand meant in order to get clues to solve a game, would they be more interested? If done right, they would. Why isn't this being done?

It is, but innovative software is generally reserved for businesses, the Department of Defense, or even sports. It is merely another area where the education system is substandard. Part of the problem could be the structure of schools themselves. With all the states creating their own standards for education, how much will a company devote toward developing programs that they could only sell to a few of them. Unified curricular standards would benefit the developers of educational software by creating larger potential markets.

It may be, as Roosevelt suggested, that we're prisoners in our own minds. In education, we're definitely prisoners of our own laws.

Chapter 7

Improving the System and Improving the Odds

This book has discussed several themes relating to the improvement of public education. It is important for students to receive a good education because failure to do so will compromise a person's ability to earn a decent living. When students are unsuccessful in school, their odds for success in life are limited. There are many factors that can be used to foresee the success and failure rates in public education. As shown in chapter 2, it is common knowledge that children educated in schools where parents make more money and have higher levels of education perform better. With knowledge of these factors and the right tools, the system of education can be improved.

A great deal of effort goes into trying to change schools where there are low-achievement levels. The data indicates that overall school quality is more determined by what is happening at home than at school. Thus, one can predict that schools having students with either high levels of poverty or low parental education levels will fail to properly prepare a large percentage of students it serves. The failure according to Bill Gates is in the education system itself. The premise of this book was to examine the education *system* to gain a better understanding of how it worked and to provide suggestions to make it work better.

There is great concern about the American education system, but it's probably a misnomer to call it a *system* at all. As defined in the American Heritage Dictionary (2000), a system is, "A group of interacting, interrelated, or interdependent elements forming a complex whole." What we have are over 14,000 school districts distributed in 50 states, and each district has different methods and levels of funding. School districts have the ability to integrate each others' students fairly effectively, schedule competitive events, and they follow similar rules. Although districts interact, for the most

217

part, they are independent entities. Many would argue that local control of education is a good thing—that is, when it works. What happens when a local district doesn't have the right system to deal effectively with the population of students it serves? What advantage does *independence* give the districts or the students served when local school systems do not have answers?

Why might local have difficulty addressing problems in education? In chapters 2 and 3 it is argued that school districts are called upon to fulfill state and federal requirements and forces school districts to have a staff of people to insure that state and federal laws are being met. District administrators usually reside in offices that are remote from the teaching process. Teachers often feel that local administrators are more concerned with fulfilling state and federal guidelines than providing guidance to schools. The local administrators provide leadership, the system requires their focus is on the mandates of government rather than kids served. Not that local school districts have much discretion with funds.

The costs associated with administrative expenses for a school district are surprisingly small at the local level. For instance, for San Diego Unified school district, School Data Direct (2005–06) only lists 7.5 percent of its budget for school administrative expenses and 0.3 percent for general administrative expense. The major expense in school district budgets is teachers, and in California, this is generally about 61 percent of a district's budget (Spending Distributions). Thus, the local school officials are primarily there to try to implement regulations and insure that districts meet legal requirements. Are they coming up with novel methods to improve education? Are their efforts going to maximize the education of children in the classrooms? Probably not; most of their efforts are devoted to fulfilling the requirements of a large bureaucracy.

As discussed in chapter 3, California's per student expenditures at the state level are reported to be over 20 percent above levels spent at the local level. Wouldn't it be a good thing if more of the funds actually served students at the local level? Couldn't administrative processes be streamlined to put more money toward classrooms? The problem is that all of the bureaucratic activity in the current education system takes money from the classroom and puts it into administration functions that often have little effect on student learning.

When writing this book, the goal was to examine Bill Gates' (2005) statement that the problem of public education was "the system" (para. 34). One of the system's obvious problems is with duplicative efforts that waste resources on administrative manners that have little, or even deleterious effects on the classroom. The system could save money by taking advantage of economies of scale if it accepts a philosophy of paring down the existing system into a simpler system.

The current education system has been built by legislators who have helped create a system that serves legislators rather than students. Ultimately, it will be legislators that will fix it. Lawmakers will have to find a way to dismantle the bureaucracies at the state and district levels by finding ways to put more educational value into the classroom. A central organization (such as the Department of Education) could work throughout the United States toward the goal of gaining continuous improvement. With such a system, one could determine what roles could be done centrally rather than being redone by each state and local educational agency. A consolidation of standards would save money and allow efforts to focus on the delivery of the lesson to students in the classroom.

To do this, the reader is asked to examine the education system as a factory system. The parallels of current schools with a factory are obvious. When students are "processed" through sequential learning processes and moved from one classroom to another, it's clear that schools were modeled after factories. What is unfortunate is that the system of education has not found a good way to optimize classroom and schools.

At a factory, the ultimate quality of the product depends on how well each step was done along the way. Education is no different. The education that a student receives will be determined by the quality of lessons received as a student. If one knew the best ways to teach a particular subject, wouldn't it improve the overall education? Unfortunately, the current education system creates mandates (test score requirements) that it hands down, but hasn't optimized how schools operate. Can one expect local districts with their pared down expenses to optimize education processes?

In chapter 4, the book examined the educational system using Edward Deming's 14 Points. Deming's guidelines were used to help management improve the performance of factories by infusing quality into each process in the factory. Deming's methods could be used to improve both lessons and the operation of the education system. It forces management to focus on what is important to improve the quality of the product. One thing that is certain is that improvements will come from the classroom, not from legislators or bills they write.

The only way to change the classroom is to improve the way that information is transferred from teacher to student. If a central system was implemented that could identify and share the best teaching methods ("not merely curriculum"), such methods could be shared across the country. With current technology, the best teaching methods could be on display (in digital form) giving teachers (and students) access to the best methods in the country. What is necessary according to Deming is to use the innovation of the members of a system to foster improvement.

Capturing the treasure that's right in front of you is an entrepreneur's dream. It needs to be done. There are brilliant lessons being taught by teachers every day. With a system that captures the best lessons, and with a system that optimizes continuous improvement, the best lessons could be available to put into classrooms. The education system must be examined from the perspective of the teaching and learning process. There are education methods that work well, and over time one could optimize methods that would insure continuous improvement of the education methods used in education.

It is not enough to merely have great lessons, but the lessons must also be employed under the proper conditions. Chapter 5 described the teacher as the "master of entropy" or disorder. Entropy is a measure of disorder in a closed system. For learning to occur, the entropy or disorder needs to be minimized in the learning environment to optimize the transfer of information. Since the goal of the teacher is to introduce new information or entropy into the classroom, the education system must supply conditions that support his or her efforts.

Where there is higher entropy, teachers and students have to compete with factors that interfere with the learning process. Thus, there will be less effective learning. Looking at an education system from the perspective of entropy is a good way to examine changes in a system. If a new idea can limit entropy in a school, district, grade level, or class to allow for a better teaching environment, it should be adopted.

The preceding chapter describes the difficulties that one will face trying to change the education system. The Bill and Melinda Gates Foundation have experienced difficulty overcoming bureaucratic obstacles as they try to present their agenda. The Gates Foundation is experiencing difficulty because it has encountered an entrenched system that doesn't want change. Unions, administrators, and teachers will all be reluctant to change because they worry about their own futures. However, education isn't really about serving the needs of its employees; it revolves around the kids. Right now, education for many doesn't work. The public education system needs to be altered for improvement to occur.

This book was called *Improving the Odds* because the school system does not work for many it serves. For the poor in America, the odds of getting a good education are low. This book argues that if you create a school system that presents better lessons, offers a better environment for teaching, and less bureaucracy, the public school system will improve.

References

Acaro, Jerome. (1995). *Quality in education: An implementation handbook.* Boca Raton, FL: St. Lucie Press.

Algebra Requirement. Calif. Educ. Code, Sec. §51224.5(a, b) (2001).

Alliance for Excellent Education. (2007). In need of improvement: NCLB and high schools. Policy Brief, June 2007. Accessed 10/30/2007, http://www.all4ed .org/files/archive/publications/NCLB_HighSchools.pdf.

Amato, P. R. (2005). The impact of family formation change on the cognitive, social, and emotional well being of the next generation. *Future of children,* 15(2). Fall. Washington DC: Brookings Press. http://www.futureofchildren.org/usr_doc/05 _FOC_15-2_fall05_Amato.pdf.

American Federation of Teachers. (1999). *Improving low performing schools.* Washington, DC: American Federation of Teachers.

American Federation of Teachers. (2008). Sizing up state standards 2008. Washington, DC: AP Courses and Exams on College Board for Students. Accessed 8/25/2008, http://www.collegeboard.com/student/testing/ap/subjects.html.

Arkansas School Board Association. (2006). Handbook of Arkansas school board members. Arkansas School Board Assoc., July 2006. http://www.arsba .org/Assests/PDFS/ASBA_Handbook.pdf.

Baier, S., Mulholland, S., Turner, C., and Tamura, R. (2004). *Income and education for the United States: 1840–2000.* Working Paper, Federal Reserve Bank of Atlanta. http://www.frbatlanta.org/filelegacydocs/wp0431.pdf#search='worker% 20output%20economics%20statistics.

Bakst, B. (2007). Levy requests widespread as schools struggle with budgets. *LaCrosse Tribune,* Nov 2, 2007. Accessed Oct. 20, 2008, http://www .lacrossetribune.com/articles/2007/11/02/mn/00lead.txt.

Barton, P. E., and Coley, R. J. (2007). The family: America's smallest school. Princeton, NJ: Educational Testing Services. Accessed 8/26/2008, http://www.ets.org/ Media/Education_Topics/pdf/5678_PERCReport_School.pdf.

Berliner, D. (2006). Fixing school isn't everything, *NEA Today,* Feb. 2006. http:// www.nea.org/neatoday/0602/berliner.html. *Burbs* refers to Gautreaux program that moved families from inner city neighborhoods to suburbs in the 1970s.

Bill and Melinda Gates Foundation. All students college ready: Findings from the foundations education work 2000–2006. Updated 10-20-06. *http://www.gatesfoundation.org/learning/Documents/EducationFindings 2000–2006.pdf.*

Bill and Melinda Gates Foundation. Making the case for small schools–The facts. Accessed 1/21/2009, http://www.windwardhigh.org/pdf/GatesFoundationFactsSS.pdf.

Blankinship, D. (May 1, 2007). Melinda Gates shares the lessons she's learned in 10 years of philanthropy. *The Seattle Times,* May 1, 2007. http://seattletimes.nwsource .com/html/localnews/2003687791_webmgates30.html?syndication=rss.

Boarding School Review. (2008). Yearly tuition: Day students. Accessed 10/13/2008, http://www.boardingschoolreview.com/.

Bork, R. H., and Troy, D. E. (2002). Locating the boundaries: The scope of congress's power to regulate commerce. *Harvard Journal Of Law And Public Policy.* Summer 2002, v. 25 i3 p. 849(45). http://www.constitution.org/lrev/bork-troy.htm#**.

Brady, R. C. (2003). Can failing schools be fixed? The Thomas P. Fordham Foundation. http://www.edexcellence.net/detail/news.cfm?news_id=2.

Braun, H., Jenkins, F., and Grigg, W. (2006). *A closer look at charter schools using hierarchical linear modeling.* U.S. Department of Education, National Center for Education Statistics, Institute of Educational Sciences. Washington, DC: U.S. Government Printing Office.

Braun, H., Jenkins, F., and Grigg, W. (2006). *Comparing private schools and public schools using hierarchical linear modeling* (NCES 2006–461). U.S. Department of Education, National Center for Education Statistics, Institute of Educational Sciences. Washington, DC: U.S. Government Printing Office.

Bridgeland, J. M., DiIulio Jr., J. J., and Morison, K. B. (2006). The silent epidemic: Perspectives of high-school dropouts. Civic Enterprises, LLC. http://www .gatesfoundation.org/nr/downloads/ed/TheSilentEpidemic3-06FINAL.pdf.

Brown et al. v. Board of Education of Topeka et al. Supreme Court of the United States 347 U.S. 483 (1954).

Brown, C., and Rocha, E. (2005). The case for national standards, accountability, and fiscal equity. Center For American Progress, November 2005. http://www .americanprogress.org/kf/standards-based_framework.pdf.

Bureau of Labor Statistics, U.S. Department of Labor, Occupational outlook handbook, 2008–09 Edition, Teachers—Preschool, kindergarten, elementary, middle, and secondary. Accessed August 11, 2008, http://www.bls.gov/oco/ocos069.htm.

California Constitution, Article IX, Section 1, Education.

California Constitution, Article IX, Section 9, Education.

California Department of Education. (2006 a). School report, base api ranks and targets, 2006 base academic performance index report for Corona Del Mar and Costa Mesa High schools in the Newport Mesa school district. Sacramento, CA: California Department of Education. http://www.cde.ca.gov/ta/ac/ap/apidatafiles.asp.

California Department of Education. (2006 b). 2004–2005 Growth API Academic Performance. Sacramento, CA: California Department of Education. http://www. cde.ca.gov/ta/ac/ap/apidatafiles.asp. The 2004–05 Growth API was downloaded, formatted, and graphed using Microsoft Excel.

California Department of Education, California High School Exit Examination (CAHSEE), CAHSEE Questions and Answers. Accessed 10/4/2007, http://www .cde.ca.gov/ta/tg/hs/info200506.asp.

California Education Code, § 305. English language education for immigrant children (Proposition 227) enacted by California voters in 1998.

California State Board of Education, Standards and Frameworks. Grades nine and ten, English and language arts content standards. Accessed 8/11/2008, http://www.cde .ca.gov/be/st/ss/enggrades9-10.asp.

Center for Education Reform. (2008). About CER, Center for Education Reform Web page, Accessed 10/10/2008, http://www.edreform.com/index.cfm?fuseAction= section&pSectionID=59.

Charter School Operations and Performance: Evidence from California. Rand Corporation, Santa Monica, California. http://www.rand.org/pubs/monograph _reports/MR1700/MR1700.ch3.pdf.

Chester, M. D. (2008). Welcome to the Massachusetts Department of Elementary and Secondary Education. Massachusetts Department of Elementary and Secondary Education. Accessed 12/8/2008, http://www.doe.mass.edu/mailings/welcome. html.

Child Nutrition Programs—Income Eligibility Guidelines. Federal Register Vol. 71, No. 50, Wednesday, March 15, 2006. Notices. http://www.fns.usda.gov/cnd/ Governance/notices/iegs/IEG06-07.pdf.

The Classroom Instruction and Accountability Act (Prop. 98). Calif. Education Code 41200–41207 (1988).

Cline, Malcomb A. (April 15, 2006). Educational epiphany of Bill Gates. *Accuracy in Media.* http://www.aim.org/guest-column/educational-epiphany-of-bill-gates/.

CNN/Money.com. (2008). Six figure zip codes. *Cable News Network.* A Time Warner Company. Accessed 10/10/2008. http://money.cnn.com/pf/features/lists/high _income_zips/.

Cole, M. (2000). Join the Discussion section. Frontline Web site. http://www.pbs. org/wgbh/pages/frontline/shows/vouchers/talk/.

Common Core of Data. (2006). Common core of data public school district data for the 2005–2006 school year. National Center for Education Statistics, Department of Education. http://nces.ed.gov/ccd/districtsearch/. Searches for numbers of districts in each state were made using search engine on site.

Cronin, J., Dahlin, M. Adkins, D., and Kingsbury, G. Gage. (2007). The proficiency illusion. Thomas B. Fordham Institute, Washington, DC. Accessed 10/30/07, http:// www.edexcellence.net/doc/The_Proficiency_Illusion.pdf.

Cunningham, Cindy. (2007). *Fact book 2007: Handbook of education information.* California Department of Education. Sacramento, CA: CDE Press.

Curriculum Standard adopted by California Department of Education.

Darling Hammond, L. (2000). Teacher quality and student achievement: a review of state policy evidence. *The Educational Policy Archives*, Vol. 8., No. 1, Jan. 1, 2000.

Dataquest. (2007). API scores from 2006, taken from California Department of Education. http://dq.cde.ca.gov/dataquest/.

Davey, Lynn. (1992). The case for a national testing system. Practical assessment, research & evaluation, 3(1). Accessed September 13, 2006, http://PAREonline. net/getvn.asp?v=3&n=1.

Deming. W. E. (1993). *The new economics: For industry, government, education.* Cambridge, MA: Massachusetts Institute of Technology Center for Advanced Engineering Study.

Deming, W.E. (2000). *Out of the crisis.* Cambridge, MA: MIT Press. Orignially published by New York: Dodd, Mead & Company (1982a).

Deming, E.W. (1982). *Quality, productivity, and competitive position.* Cambridge, MA: MIT Press.

Department of Labor. (2008). Occupational outlook handbook. 2007–08 edition. Educational administrators; nature of the work. U.S. Bureau of Labor Statistics. Accessed 10/23/2007, http://stats.bls.gov/oco/ocos007.htm.

John Dewey: American pragmatist. A wing of the pragmatism cybrary. International Pragmatism Society, maintained by John Shook. http://dewey .pragmatism.org/.

Dewey, J. (1916). *Democracy and education.* New York:The MacMillen Company. http://www.ilt.columbia.edu/publications/dewey.html.

Digest of Education Statistics 2006. (July 2007). What is direct instruction. National Center for Education Statistics Direct Instruction. Accessed 3/6/2008, http:// directinstruction.org/what-direct-instruction.

Drucker, P. F. (1993). *Concept of the corporation. Transaction publishers.* New Brunswick.

Earnings and education in the fourth quarter of 2006 (2006). U.S. Department of Labor, Bureau of Labor Statistics. Originally published Jan 29, 2006, *http://www .bls.gov/opub/ted/2007/jan/wk5/art01.htm.*

Edsource Online. (2005). Fifteen California high schools that beat the odds. *Edsource Online.* California Department of Education Web site, June, 2005. http://www .edsource.org/sch_hig_beatodds.cfm.

EducationPolicy.org. Education Policy Institute, Virginia Beach, VA. http://www .educationpolicy.org/.

Elementary school teachers, except special education: occupational wages and statistics, 25-2021 (2005). U.S. Department of Labor, Bureau of Labor Statistics. Washington, DC. http://www.bls.gov/oes/current/oes252021.htm#nat.

English language arts content standards for California public schools: Kindergarten through grade twelve. California Department of Education, Dec. 1997. http://www .cde.ca.gov/be/st/ss/enggrades9-10.asp.

Equal Education Opportunities Act. (1974). 20 U.S.C. § 1703, *Equal Educational Opportunities Act of 1974.*

Esquith, R. (2007). *Teach like your hair's on fire.* New York: Penguin Group USA (Viking).

Facilities, California School Finance, California School Finance, California Department of Education, hosted by *Ed Source*. Accessed 10/2/2007, http://californiaschool-finance.org/FinanceSystem/FacilitiesFunding/tabid/88/Default.aspx.

Farkas, S., Johnson, J., and Foleno, T. (2000). A sense of calling: Who teaches and why. New York: Public Agenda. http://www.publicagenda.org/files/pdf/sense_of_calling.pdf.

Fiecke, S. (October 30, 2005). Why do the Winona Schools need to pass a referendum? *Winona Daily News*. http://www.winonadailynews.com/articles/2005/10/30/news/00lead.txt.

Fiecke, S. (2006). Enrollment dropping for WAPS. *Winona Daily News,* April 2, 2006. http://www.winonadailynews.com/articles/2006/04/02/news/01waps02.txt.

———. (2001). Ford embraces six-sigma quality goals. Society of Manufacturing Engineers, posted 6/13/2001. http://www.sme.org/cgi-bin/get-press.pl?&&20012513&ND&&SME&.

Ford fuel fires, safety forum: Safety product news and resources. (July 27, 2000). Accessed 10/10/2008, http://www.safetyforum.com/fordfuelfires/.

Food Research Action Center. (2006). Income guidelines and reimbursement rates for the child nutrition programs. Effective July 1, 2005–June 30, 2006. http://www.frac.org/pdf/rates.PDF.

Forstmann, T. J. (1999). *A competitive vision for America's education.* Speech delivered in May 1999 at Hillsdale College's Shavano Institute for National Leadership Seminar: Education in America: Schools and strategies that work, Found at Radical Academy.com under Educational Resources on 9/21/2008. http://radicalacademy.com/forstmannessay.htm.

Frenette, Mark. (2007). Why are youth from lower-income families less likely to attend university? Evidence from academic abilities, parental influences, and financial restraints. statistics. Canada, Business and Labour Market Analysis. *Analytical Studies Branch Paper Series,* Vol. 2007, No. 295.

Talbot, S. (2000). Frontline Web site. In response to Talbot, S. The battle over school choice. S. Little in Join the discussion section. http://www.pbs.org/wgbh/pages/frontline/shows/vouchers/talk/.

Galbally, E. (2001) Winona schools face severe cutbacks, *Minnesota Public Radio,* November 1, 2001. http://news.minnesota.publicradio.org/features/200111/01_galballye_winonaref-m/.

Galindo-Rueda, F., and Vignoles, A. (2004). The heterogeneous effect of selection in secondary school: Understanding the changing role of ability. CEE Discussion Papers 0052, Centre for the Economics of Education, LSE.

Gates, W. III (2005). Prepared remarks to the National Education Summit on high schools. Washington, DC, Feb. 26, 2005. http://www.gatesfoundation.org/MediaCenter/Speeches/Co ChairSpeeches/BillgSpeeches/BGSpeechNGA-050226.htm.

Gates, W. III (2008). Prepared remarks at the Forum of Education. November 11, 2008. Accessed 2/16/2009, http://www.gatesfoundation.org/speeches-commentary/Pages/bill-gates-2008-education-forum-speech.aspx.

Gates, W. III (2009). How I'm trying to change the world now. *Technology, Entertainment, Design,* from Ted2009, February. Accessed 2/13/2009, http://www.ted.com/talks/bill_gates_unplugged.html.

Gitlow, H. S., and Gitlow, S. J. (1987). *The Deming guide to quality and competitive position.* Englewood Cliffs, NJ: Prentice-Hall.

Goldsman, A. (2002). *A beautiful mind: Screenplay and introduction.* New York: Newmarket Press.

Good, H. (2006). Believe and deceive: The strategic ambiguity of school slogans. *Education Week,* Vol. 25, Issue 43, p. 35.

Gordon-Leavitt, J. (March 31, 2006). BrainyQuote, from *Newsweek,* From silly to serious. March 31, 2006, URL: http://www.newsweek.com/id/47219. Accessed 10/21/2008, http://www.brainyquote.com/quotes/quotes/j/josephgord380882.htm.

Governor's Budget 2007–08. (Enacted budget detail) K-12 education. Accessed 10/2/2007, http://www.ebudget.ca.gov/Enacted/StateAgencyBudgets/6010/agency.html.

Governor's Budget 2008–9. K-12 education total spending per pupil: Proposed budget. California Department of Finance. Accessed 4/18/2009, http://www.dof.ca.gov/budget/historical/200809/governors/summary/documents/SK12.pdf.

Gravenese, R. (2007). *Freedom writers.* Paramount Pictures.

Greatschools.net. Test data. It is the Joseph Sears school (K-8) with 580 students. http://www.greatschools.net/cgi-bin/il/district_profile/582/.

Griffith, M. (2008). State funding programs for high-cost special education students. State Notes, Education Commission of the States. Accessed 9/3/2008, http://www.ecs.org/clearinghouse/78/10/7810.pdf.

Grow, Gerald O. (1996*).* Serving the strategic reader: Reader response theory and its implications for the teaching of writing, an expanded version of a paper presented to the Qualitative Division of the Association for Educators in Journalism and Mass Communication. Atlanta, August, 1994. http://www.longleaf.net/ggrow. Original paper available as Eric Documentation Reproduction Service No. ED 406 644.

Guternan, J. (April 2007). Where have all the principals gone?: The acute school leader shortage. *Edutopia Magazine.* Accessed 10/23/2007, http://www.edutopia.org/where-have-all-principals-gone.

Haahr, J. H., Neilson, T. K., Hansen, M. E., and Jacobsen, S. T. (2004). Explaining student performance: Evidence from the international PISA, TIMSS, and PIRLS surveys. Danish Technological Institute. http://ec.europa.eu/education/doc/reports/doc/basicskill.pdf.

Hammond, B., and Lednicer, L. G. (June 8, 2008). Oregon's small school experiment slow to see results. *The Oregonian.* Accessed Sept. 5, 2008, http://www.oregonlive.com/education/oregonian/index.ssf?/base/news/1212800118116920.xml&coll=7&thispage=1.

Harlow, C. W. (2003). Education and correctional populations. Department of Justice, Washington, DC., Bureau of Justice Statistics, Rpt. No. NCJ-195670. Accessed 10/11/2008, http://www.eric.ed.gov/ERICDocs/data/ericdocs2sql/content_storage_01/0000019b/80/1b/20/5a.pdf.

Hart, P. D., and Teeter, R. M. (2004). Equity and adequacy: Americans speak on public school funding. Educational Testing Services. www.ets.org.

Harvard University Gazette Online (June 7, 2007). Honorary degrees awarded at commencement's morning exercise. http://www.news.harvard.edu/gazette/2007/06.07/03-honorands.html.

The 2006 HHS Poverty Guidelines. (2006). *Federal register,* Vol. 71, No. 15, January 24, 2006, pp. 3848–49. United States Department of Health and Human Services. http://aspe.hhs.gov/poverty/06poverty.shtml.

Hill, P. T. (2006). Put learning first: A portfolio approach to public schools. Public Policy Institute, Policy Report, Feb. 2006. http://www.ppionline.org/documents/Portfolio_Districts021006.pdf.

Hoxby, C. M. (2000). The effects of class size on student achievement: New evidence from population variation. *The Quarterly Journal of Economics,* Vol. 115, NO. 4, pp. 1239–85.

Hussar. W.J. (2005). *Projections of education statistics to 2014* (NCES 2005-074). U.S. Department of Education, National Center for Education Statistics. Washington, DC: U.S. Government Printing Office.

Huxley, T. H. (1907). *Reflection #120, aphorisms and reflections, selected by Henrietta A. Huxley.* London: Macmillan.

Income Guidelines and Reimbursement Rates for the Child Nutrition Programs. Effective July 1, 2005–June 30, 2006. Food Research and Action Center, Washington, DC. Accessed 12/24/08, http://www.frac.org/pdf/rates.PDF.

Izumi, L. T., and Cox, M. (2003). California education report card; Index of leading education indicators, Third Edition. San Francisco: Pacific Research Institute. August 2003. http://liberty.pacificresearch.org/docLib/20070208_2003_Education_Report.pdf.

Johnson, B. (October 28, 2007a). 50 years of learning: Declining enrollment, diversity have changed Winona's schools. *Winona Daily News,* Oct. 28, 2007. Accessed 11/4/2007, http://www.winonadailynews.com/articles/2007/10/28/news/00lead.txt.

Johnson, B. (August 31, 2007b). Some area schools failing federal standards. *Winona Daily News,* Aug. 3, 2007. Accessed 11/1/2007, http://www.winonadailynews.com/articles/2007/08/31/news/00lead.txt.

Johnson, B. (December 31, 2006). Tension in the schools: Fear and teaching in Winona. *Winona Daily News,* Dec. 31, 2006. Accessed 10/31/2007, http://www.winonadailynews.com/articles/2006/12/31/news/00lead.txt.

Johnson, F. H. (2007). National public education financial survey, fiscal years 1990–2002. An historical overview of revenues and expenditures for public elementary and secondary education by state: Fiscal years 1990–2002. National Center for Education Statistics, Common Core of Data (CCD). Washington, DC: U.S. Department of Education.

Kattman, R., and Johnson, F.C. (2002). Successful applications of quality systems in K-12 schools by American society for quality education division. American Society for Quality.

Katzenbach v. McClung, 379 U.S. 294 (1964).

Kimmelman, P., Kroeze, D., Shmidt, W., van der Ploeg, A., McNeely, M., and Tan, A. (1999). A first look at what we can learn from high performing school districts: An analysis of TIMSS data from the first in the world consortium. U.S. Department of Education, National Institute of Student Achievement, Curriculum, and Assessment. Washington, DC: U.S. Government Printing Office.

Kimmelman, P. (2004). When more isn't better. Public Policy Institute, Front and Center, May 17, 2004. Accessed 2/22/2009, http://www.ideasprimary.com/ndol_ci .cfm?kaid=110&subid=136&contentid=252643.

Kirkpatrick, D. (July 17, 2007). How Microsoft conquered China. *Fortune Magazine,* July 17, 2007. Accessed 10/10/2008, ttp://money.cnn.com/magazines/fortune/ fortune_archive/2007/07/23/100134488/.

Kwoka, Jr., J. E. (2002). Governance alternatives and pricing in the U.S. electric power industry. *Journal of Law, Economics, and Organization,* Vol. 18, No. 1, pp. 278–294.

Kwoka, Jr., J. E. (2005). The comparative advantage of public ownership: Evidence from U.S. electric utilities. *Canadian Journal of Economics,* Vol. 38, No. 2, pp. 622–40, May.

Laney, M. (2005, March 21). Wilmette school board elections will show parents' power. *Chicago Sun-Times,* March 21, 2005.

Legislative Education Search (2007). Several states were chosen at random and searches for pending legislation regarding education were performed. Minnesota State Legislature, House Bill Information, accessed 10/5/2007, http://ros.leg.mn/ revisor/pages/search_status/status_search.php?body=House&search=topi. Arizona State Legislature, 48th Legislature, accessed 10/5/2007, http://www.azleg .gov/SearchResults.asp?SearchedFrom=%2FBills.asp&Scope=%2Flegtext% 2F48leg%2F1R&SearchPhrase=%22K-12%22+Education. *Missouri Revised Statutes,* accessed 10/5/2007, http://www.moga.mo.gov/statutesearch/Default. aspx. *The Vermont Legislative Bill Tracking System, 2007–2008 Legislative Session,* accessed 10/5/2007, http://www.leg.state.vt.us/database/search/ search.cfm?Session=2008. *North Carolina General Assembly, 2007–2008 Session, Full Text Bill Search Results,* accessed 10/5/2007, http://www .ncga.state.nc.us/gascripts/BillSearch/BillSearch.asp?typeToSearch=ALL&ch amberToSearch=&sessionToSearch=2007&searchCriteria=Education&sortBy =relevance. New York State Assembly, Bill Search, http://assembly.state.ny.us/ leg/?by=k&qs=education.

Leubchow, L. (June 18, 2008). How to handle bad news for small schools in Oregon. *The Ed Money Watch Blog.* New America Foundation. http://www.newamerica .net/blog/ed-money-watch/2008/how-handle-bad-news-small-schools-oregon- 4578, August 5, 2008.

Levin, H. M., and Belfield, C. R. (2007, Nov. 12). Investment in K-12 education in Minnesota: What works? Growth and Justice Conference, Nov. 12, 2007. Minneapolis. Accessed August 9, 2008, http://www.cbcse.org/media/download _gallery/GROWTH_JUSTICE_PAPER.pdf.

Levine, A. (2006). Educating school teachers. The Education Schools Project, Washington, DC. http://www.edschools.org/pdf/Educating_Teachers_Report.pdf.

Lewin, T., and Medina, J. (July 31, 2003). To cut failure rates, schools shed students. *New York Times,* July 31, 2003. Accessed 10/31/2007, http://query.nytimes.com/gst/fullpage.html?res=9501E0DA143EF932A05754C0A9659C8B63.

Lexile Framework for Reading. (2008). Book search: Title or author search and lexile range or keyword search. Durham, NC: Metametrics Inc. Accessed 10/14/2008, http://www.lexile.com/DesktopDefault.aspx?view=ed&tabindex=0&tabid=1&tab pageid=21.

Long, D. (2007). A message from the secretary of education, Dave Long. state of California, Department of Education, Office of Secretary of Education, Education, Initiatives. Accessed 10/11/2007, http://www.ose.ca.gov/yoer.html.

Lubienski, S. T., and Lubienski, C. (2005). A new look at public and private schools: Student background and mathematics achievement. *Phi Delta Kappan,* Vol. 86, No. 9. http://www.pdkintl.org/kappan/k_v86/k0505lub.htm/.

Mathews, J. (1988). *Escalante: The best teacher in America.* New York: Henry Holt & Company.

Mathis, W. J. (2005). The cost of implementing the federal No Child Left Behind Act: Different assumptions, different answers. *Peabody Journal of Education, 80*(2), 90–119.

Mathis, W. J. (2007). After five years: Revisiting the cost of the No Child Left Behind Act. In J. K. Rice and C. F. Roellke (eds), *The costs of accountability: Implications of high stakes education policies for resources and capacities.* Information Age Publishing.

Mayer, J., Mullens, J. E., Moore, M. T., and Ralph, J. (2000). *Monitoring school quality: An indicators report.* U.S. Department of Education Office of Educational Research and Improvement. NCES 2001-030.

McCluskey, N. (2006). Answer to NCLB failure is school choice. Washington, DC: The CATO Institute,. http://www.cato.org/pub_display.php?pub_id=6403.

McColl, A. (2005). Tough call: Is No Child Left Behind constitutional? *Phi Delta Kappan.* Accessed 10/9/2008, http://www.pdkintl.org/kappan/k_v86/k0504mcc.htm.

McLanahan, Sara, Donahue, Elisabeth, and Ron Haskins (eds.). (2005). Marriage and child wellbeing. *Future of Children,* 15 (2). Washington, DC. Brookings Press.

Meara, E., Richards, S., and Cutler, D. (2008). The gap gets bigger: Changes in mortality and life expectancy, by education, 1981–2000. *Health Affairs,* March/April 2008, Vol. 27, No. 2.

Merriam-Webster Online Dictionary. (2008). Accessed October 8, 2008, http://www.merriam-webster.com/dictionary/pony.

Merrow, J. (2006). *Grade inflation: It's not just an issue for the Ivy League.* The Carnegie Foundation for the Advancement of Teaching. http://www.carnegiefoundation.org/perspectives/sub.asp?key=245&subkey=576.

Metametrics, Inc. (2008). Lexiles: A system for measuring reader ability and text difficulty. A guide for educators. *Scholastic.* Accessed 10/14/2008, http://teacher.scholastic.com/products/sri/pdfs/139710_Schol_LR.pdf.

Minnesota Planning Perspectives. (July 2000). Implications of rural Minnesota changing demographics. http://www.gda.state.mn.us/pdf/2000/rural_01.pdf.

Miriam Webster Online Dictionary (2008). über- prefix that is derived from German. 1 : being a superlative example of its kind or class : SUPER-<*über*nerd> 2 : to an extreme or excessive degree : SUPER- <*über*cool>. http://www.m-w.com/cgi-bin/dictionary.

Mosteller, F. (1995). The Tennessee study of class size in the early school grades. *The future of children: Critical issues for children and youths,* 5 (2), pp. 113–27.

National Center for Children in Poverty. (2008). Quick facts. Columbia University, Mailman Center for Public Health. Accessed 10/10/2008, http://www.nccp.org/topics/childpoverty.html.

National Education Association (2007). Reading. Accessed 10/13/2008, http://www.nea.org/reading/index.html.

National Educational Association. (2007). Teacher salary lags behind inflation, Dec. 10, 2007. Accessed April 27, 2008, http://www.nea.org/newsreleases/2007/nr071210.html.

National Education Commission on Time and Learning. (2005). Prisoners of time [reprint of the 1994 report]. Denver, CO: Education Commission of the States. Accessed October 8, 2008, http://www.ecs.org/clearinghouse/64/52/6452.pdf.

NCSL Task Force on No Child Left Behind–Executive Summary. (2005). National Conference of State Legislators. http://www.ncsl.org/programs/press/2005/NCLB_exec_summary.htm/

N.Y. Educ. Law, § 3202 (1). Public schools free to resident pupils; tuition from non-resident pupils.

Occupational Employment (May 2005) and Wage (2006 1st Quarter Data). Employment Development Department, Calif. Gov., State of California. http://www.labormarketinfo.edd.ca.gov/cgi/career/?PageID=3&SubID=152.

Office of the Governor (2005). Governor makes major investment in vocational education with new law. Office of the Governor, Press Release, 9/27/2005. http://gov.ca.gov/index.php?/press-release/1393/.

Oppenheimer, T. (1997). The computer delusion. *The Atlantic Monthly,* Vol. 280, No. 1; pp. 45–62. http://www.theatlantic.com/issues/97jul/computer.htm.

Oppenheimer, T. (2007). Selling software: How vendors manipulate research and cheat students. *Education Next,* Vol. 7, No. 2. http://www.hoover.org/publications/ednext/6017486.html.

Parents United for Public Schools. St. Paul, MN. School district aid, property tax levy, and "grand total" revenue in inflation-adjusted dollars per pupil in FY 2003 and FY 2007. www.parentsunited.org. parentsunited.org/sites/ . . . /2003-2007_Grand_Total_Revenue-District.pdf.

Peres, S, Nobel Laureate. (2005). Op-ed. *The Boston Globe,* October 21, 2004, p. A-19. In M. McPherson, Developing human capacities in poor countries. Office of Education, Bureau for Economic Growth, Agriculture, and Trade United States Agency for International Development and Center for Business and Government, John F. Kennedy School of Government, Harvard University. Accessed 10/8/2008, http://qesdb.usaid.gov/ged/GEN&USEHumCapMFM.pdf.

Pinellas County Schools annual budget summary for the fiscal year beginning July 1, 2005 and ending June 30, 2006 (September 13, 2005). http://www.pinellas.k12.fl.us/budget/pdf/0506_abs.pdf.

Plessy v. Ferguson, 163 U.S. 537 (1896).

Poochigian, C. (2008). Algebra prepares students for the future. FresnoBee.com. Accessed 9/20/2008, http://www.fresnobee.com/opinion/wo/v-printerfriendly/story/758820.html.

Progressive Policy Institute (1998). About the progressive policy institute. Washington, DC: Progressive Policy Institute. The Third Way Foundation. http://www.ppionline.org/ppi_ci.cfm?knlgAreaID=87&subsecID=205&contentID=896.

Public Education Network (2003). Demanding quality public education in tough economic times: What voters want from elected leaders. Washington, DC: The Public Education Network. http://www.publiceducation.org/pdf/Publications/national_poll/2003_poll_report.pdf.

Public School District Finance Peer Search. In Education Finance Statistics Center, U.S. Department of Education online site. Analyzed financial indicators of schools within 10-mile radius of zip code in Riverside. Financial results were tabulated. http://nces.ed.gov/edfin/search/search_intro.asp. Riverside Unified School District is a K-12 district in Riverside, California that enrolls approximately 42,000 students.

Pugmire, T. (2005), Voters approve tax increases in many school districts. *Minnesota Public Radio* broadcast, November 9, 2005. http://news.minnesota.publicradio.org/features/2005/11/09_pugmiret_refrecap/.

Quitno, Morgan. (2006-2007). *Education State Rankings,* 2006–2007. Accessed 8/28/2008, http://www.morganquitno.com/edrank.htm.

Raffaele, M. (2005). Intelligent design dominates school board election. *USA Today,* 5/13/2005. http://www.usatoday.com/tech/science/2005-05-13-intelligent-design-dover-pa_x.htm.

Ramirez, E. (2007). Failing schools are hard to fix. *U.S. News & World Report,* November 2, 2007. Accessed 8/10/2008, http://www.usnews.com/articles/education/2007/11/02/failing-schools.html.

Reagan, R. (1964). *A time for choosing.* Speech for Barry Goldwater's campaign, Los Angeles, CA. Oct. 27, 1964. http://www.americanrhetoric.com/speeches/ronaldreaganatimeforchoosing.htm.

Reeder, S. (2005). Tenure frustrates drive for teacher accountability. Small Newspaper Group Springfield Bureau. http://thehiddencostsoftenure.com/stories/?press=display&id=266539.

Report of the National Reading Panel. (2000). *Teaching children to read.* D. Langenberg, chair. National Institute of Health. An evidence-based assessment of the scientific literature on reading and its implications for reading instruction. Reports of the Subgroups. Bethesda, MD: National Institute of Child Health and Human Development.

Research in the Education Department, Brown University. Accessed August 7, 2008, http://www.brown.edu/Departments/Education/research.php.

Romer, R. (2006). The mayor's bad deal. *Los Angeles Times,* June 25, 2006. Accessed 10/17/2008, http://articles.latimes.com/2006/jun/25/opinion/oe-romer25.

Roosevelt, F. D. (April 15, 1939). *Pan American Day Address.*

Rosovsky, H., and Hartley, M. (2002). Evaluation and the academy: Are we doing the right thing? Grade inflation and letters of recommendation. Cambridge, MA: The American Academy of Arts and Sciences. Accessed 9/4/2008, http://www.amacad.org/publications/monographs/Evaluation_and_the_ Academy.pdf.

Safety Forum. Safety Product News and Resources. http://www.safetyforum.com/fordfuelfires/.

Schmoker, M. (2003). Planning for failure? Or for school success? *Education Week,* Feb. 12, 2003.

Schmoker, M., and Marzano, R. (1999). Realizing the promise of standards based education. *Educational Leadership,* Vol. 56, No. 6, pp. 17–21.

Schmoker, M. J., and Wilson, R. B. (1993). *Total quality education: Profiles of schools that demonstrate the power of deming's management principles.* Quetia Media, Inc.

Schnur, J. (March 6, 2007). A clear powerful insight: Great schools are led by great principals, new leaders for new schools. Document prepared for U.S. Senate Help Committee Roundtable, March 6, 2007. http://help.senate.gov/Hearings/2007_03_06/Schnur.pdf.

School Data Direct. (2005–06). San Diego Unified School District, School Data Direct, Spending, Revenue, and Taxes. Spending distributions. State Education Data Center, funded by Bill and Melinda Gates Foundation. Accessed 10/19/2008, http://www.schooldatadirect.org/app/data/q/stid=5/llid=116/stllid=322/locid=1005837/catid=1020/secid=4530/compid=851/site=pes.

Schweizer, P. (1999). The dance of the lemons. *Hoover Digest,* No. 1. http://www.hoover.org/publications/digest/3506971.html.

Shanahan, T. (2006). *The National Reading Panel report: Advice for teachers.* Naperville, IL: Learning Point Associates. http://www.learningpt.org/pdfs/literacy/nationalreading.pdf.

Shannon, G. S., and Bylsma, P. (2004). Characteristics of improved school districts: Themes from research. Olympia, WA: Office of Superintendent of Public Instruction.

Singleton, K. (2004). Three candidates for top job talk up qualifications. *Winona Daily News,* Jan 7, 2004. http://www.winonadailynews.com/articles/2004/01/07/news/03lead.prt.

South Dakota v. Dole, 483 U.S. (1987), at 211.

Spelling, M. (2005). No Child Left Behind: A roadmap for state implementation. U.S. Department of Education. http://www.ed.gov/admins/lead/account/roadmap/roadmap.doc.

———. (2006). State Assembly approves Mayor Villaraigosa's school reform bill. *California Chronicle,* California Political Desk, August 30, 2006.

Stecher, B. M., McCaffrey, D. F., and Bugliari, D. (2003). The relationship between exposure to class size reduction and student achievement in California. *Education Policy Analysis Archives,* 11(40). http://epaa.asu.edu/epaa/v11n40/.

Stipek, D. (2002). *Our faculty. Stanford University School of Education.* Boston: Allyn and Bacon. http://ed.stanford.edu/suse/faculty/displayRecord.php?suid=stipek. Motivation to Learn: Integrating Theory and Practice.

Stuart, M. (2005). *The Hobart Shakespearians.* DVD. Stuart Productions Incorporated.

Talbot, S. (2000). The battle over school choice: Join the discussion section. *Frontline,* WGBH Educational Foundation. http://www.pbs.org/wgbh/pages/frontline/shows/vouchers/talk/.

The American Federation of Teachers. *Teacher quality.* Washington, DC. Accessed 11/6/2007, http://www.aft.org/topics/teacher-quality/index.htm.

The American Heritage® Dictionary of the English Language, Fourth Edition. (2000). Houghton Mifflin Company. http://education.yahoo.com/reference/dictionary/entry/perception.

The Center for the Future of Teaching and Learning. (August 2007). *Why do teachers leave?* http://www.cftl.org/centerviews/august07.html.

Thomas B. Fordham Institute. (2008). Who we are. Washington, DC: Thomas B. Fordham Institute: Advancing Educational Excellence. http://www.edexcellence.net/template/page.cfm?id=126.

Tobin, T. (2006). A pivotal school board election. *Saint Petersburg Times Online Edition,* January 29, 2006. http://www.sptimes.com/2006/01/29/Tampabay/A_pivotal_School_Boar.shtml.

Tortorella, M. J. (1995). The three careers of W. Edwards Deming. Siam News, July 16. W. Edwards Deming Institute. Accessed 7/16/07, http://deming.org/index.cfm?content=652.

Tzu, L. (1968). In E. Esar, *20,000 quips and quotes.* New York: Barnes and Noble Books.

U.S. Bureau of Labor Statistics. (March 2004). Postsecondary education opportunity. www.postsecondary.org.

U.S. Census Bureau. (1998a). *Educational attainment in the United States: March 1998.* Washington, DC: Author.

U.S. Census Bureau. (1998b). *Educational attainment in the United States: March 1997.* Washington, DC: Author.

U.S. Department of Education, National Center for Education Statistics, National Public Education financial survey, common core of data (CCD), fiscal years 1990–2002.

U.S. Department of Education, NCES, Schools and Staffing Survey (SASS), 1999–2000. (2004). Public School Survey and Public Charter School Survey. http://nces.ed.gov/programs/coe/2004/section4/table.asp?tableID=200.

United States Constitution. http://www.usconstitution.net/const.html.

United States Constitution. (1787). *Preamble.* Cornell Law School, Legal Information Institute. Accessed March 15, 1996, http://www.law.cornell.edu/constitution/constitution.preamble.html.

United States Constitution. Amendment X. Powers of the State and People. 12/15/1791.

United States Department of Education. (2007). Total expenditures for elementary and secondary education in the U.S., fiscal year 2007 budget summary. http://www .ed.gov/about/overview/budget/budget07/summary/edlite-appendix3.html.

U.S. Department of Labor. (2005). Elementary school teachers, except special education: Occupational wages and statistics, 25-2021. Washington, DC: U.S. Department of Labor, Bureau of Labor Statistics. http://www.bls.gov/oes/current/ oes252021.htm#nat.

United States v. Lopez, 514 U.S., 549 (1995).

Walker, K. (2007). School uniforms, research brief, the principals' partnership, Feb, 26, 2007. http://www.principalspartnership.com/. A Program of Union Pacific Foundation, http://www.principalspartnership.com/schooluniforms.pdf.

Walton, M. (1986). *The Deming management method* (p. 60). New York: Dodd, Mead & Company. From author's interview of Deming in 1985.

Warren, J., Gelb, A., Horowitz, J., and Riordan, J. (2008). One in 100: Behind bars in American in 2008. Pew Center on the States, The Public Safety Performance Project. Washington, DC. http://www.pewcenteronthestates.org/uploadedFiles/ 8015PCTS_Prison08_FINAL_2-1-1_FORWEB.pdf.

Waters, J. T., and Marzano, R. J. (2006). *The effects of superintendent leadership on student achievement* (A working paper, Sept 2006). Denver, CO: McREL. Accessed 11/11/2007,
http://www.cosa.k12.or.us/downloads/profdev/SuperintendentLeadership.pdf.

Webster, B. H., and Bishaw, A. (2006). Income, earnings, and poverty data from the 2005 American community survey. U. S. Census Bureau. Washington, DC: U.S. Govt. Printing Office. http://www.census.gov/prod/2006pubs/acs-02.pdf.

Weicker Jr., L. P., and Kahlenberg, R. D. (2002). The new educational divide. *Christian Science Monitor,* Oct 9, 2002. http://www.csmonitor.com/2002/1009/ p09s02-coop.html.

Wikipedia, The Free Encyclopedia (2008). The great man theory. Accessed October 18, 2008, http://en.wikipedia.org/wiki/Great_man_theory.

Wilde, Oscar. (2000). *An ideal husband.* Unabridged republication of the standard text (1895). New York: Dover Publications.

Willson, Meredith. (1957). *The music man.* Frank Music Corp. and Rinimer Corporation.

Winona Area Public School District. (2006). Student demographics, in classroom profile. School matters, a service of standards and poors. Accessed 9/27/2008, http://www .schoolmatters.com/schools.aspx/q/page=dl/did=2358/midx=StudentDemographics.

Zimmer, Ron W., Buddin, Richard, Chau, Derrick, Daley, Glenn A., Gill, Brian, Guarino, Cassandra, Hamilton, Laura S., Krop, Cathy, McCaffrey, Daniel F., Sandler, Melinda, and Dominic J. Brewer. (2003). Charter school operations and performance: Evidence from California. Santa Monica, CA: Rand Corporation. http://www.rand.org/pubs/monograph_reports/MR1700/MR1700.ch3.pdf.

About the Author

Rodney Larson lives in Riverside, California, where he has worked as an independent study teacher for ten years. His prior experience included land-use permitting and financing of waste-to-energy facilities, consulting, and working as a laboratory researcher

Breinigsville, PA USA
12 November 2010
249199BV00003B/57/P